JAMES AND JOHN

Possible Dreams: Personal History of the British Christian Socialists
Stafford Cripps: The First Modern Chancellor
Glenda Jackson: The Biography
Parliament: The Biography – Ancestral Voices (vol. 1)
Parliament: The Biography – Reform (vol. 2)
Entitled: A Critical History of the British Aristocracy
The Glamour Boys: The Secret Story of the Rebels Who Fought
for Britain to Defeat Hitler
Code of Conduct: Why We Need to Fix Parliament – and How to Do It

CHRIS BRYANT

JAMES —AND— JOHN

A TRUE STORY OF PREJUDICE AND MURDER

BLOOMSBURY PUBLISHING

LONDON · OXFORD · NEW YORK · NEW DELHI · SYDNEY

BLOOMSBURY PUBLISHING
Bloomsbury Publishing Plc
50 Bedford Square, London, WC1B 3DP, UK
29 Earlsfort Terrace, Dublin 2, Ireland

BLOOMSBURY, BLOOMSBURY PUBLISHING and the Diana logo are trademarks of
Bloomsbury Publishing Plc

First published in Great Britain 2024

A catalogue record for this book is available from the British Library

ISBN: HB: 978-1-5266-4497-8; EBOOK: 978-1-5266-4498-5; EPDF: 978-1-5266-7709-9

2 4 6 8 10 9 7 5 3 1

Typeset by Newgen KnowledgeWorks Pvt. Ltd., Chennai, India
Printed and bound in Great Britain by CPI Group (UK) Ltd, Croydon CR0 4YY

To find out more about our authors and books visit www.bloomsbury.com
and sign up for our newsletters

JACOB

Contents

Preface

Early on the morning of Saturday 26 September 1835, Henry Buckler left his home in Islington for work. It was just over two miles to the Old Bailey, where his desk, penknife, quills, inkstand, sand and blotting paper awaited him, but it might have been in a different world. Fields had once separated Islington from the City of London, but these were fast disappearing and many feared that 'the tumbling up of tumble down houses' was increasing so rapidly 'that in a year or two there will be scarcely a green spot for the resort of the inhabitants'.[1] However, the Old Bailey stood in the heart of the ancient City of London, with its crooked alleyways, its tenements, courtyards, rookeries and teeming masses, and the first case would be heard in the Old Court at nine o'clock.

Henry was thirty-nine, the father of four children, and he had already been the official shorthand writer at the Old Bailey for nineteen years. It was a skilled profession. People said it took three years to master the complex Gurney system of 'brachygraphy', named after one of Henry's predecessors at the Old Bailey, Thomas Gurney, but Henry could manage the required 140 words per minute by the time he was twenty and in the intervening years he had risen to respectability as a 'gentleman' entitled to vote in parliamentary elections and serve on the powerful Vestry Committee at Holy Trinity, Cloudesley Square.

Buckler knew one case that was set to be heard that day would be sensational. The recorder of London, Charles Ewan Law MP, had warned the court about it in the darkest of terms at the beginning of the week. Three men, James Pratt, John Smith and

William Bonell, were to be tried for 'an unnatural crime'. It was sensitive and potentially salacious. Women might be barred from the courtroom. There was a mawkish, prurient excitement about the case. The senior judge, Sir John Gurney, had been itching to get on to it and Law, who had not yet overseen a single hanging in his time as recorder, was intimating that James and John's offence might lead to the first hanging at Newgate for years – and a double one at that. It was difficult to avoid sensing that Law was pleased.

This presented Buckler with a dilemma. The Corporation of London, which governed the court, stipulated that the details of trials of 'remarkable indecency or for any unnatural crimes' should not be published unless they raised an important point of law and had sacked his predecessor for publishing salacious details of another case, so all he could include in the official *Proceedings of the Old Bailey* were the bare bones – the nature of the offence, the verdict and the sentence. Yet judges sometimes asked for Buckler's verbatim records to check what a witness had said and the Home Secretary often relied on his records when considering appeals for mercy, so he had to keep full details.

Buckler came up with a clever solution to his quandary. He stuck to the prescribed formula in the official record, but he published a much longer appendix alongside the *Proceedings*. It is the only appendix he ever printed and from it come the details of the events of 29 August, when James and John were caught having sex in William's rented room in Southwark and were arrested. Buckler clearly knew this case was special. His appendix means it is possible to reconstruct James and John's trial. Without it, they would be just another statistic, another notch on the gallows post. And without it we would not be aware of one of the great injustices of British legal history – the judicial murder of two men for adult consensual sex.

CENTRAL CRIMINAL COURT, OLD BAILEY—M'NAUGHTEN'S TRIAL.

A trial in 1843 at the Central Criminal Court at the Old Bailey, with Henry Buckler taking shorthand notes in the bottom left-hand corner.

Introduction

On 27 March 2010 Jared Cranney and I held hands, exchanged vows and rings and formed our civil partnership in the Members' Dining Room in Parliament. Two hundred friends attended that first same-sex union to be celebrated in the Palace of Westminster, but so many old portraits grace the Dining Room walls that it felt as if previous generations were also present, and I wondered what the men whose portraits looked down upon us would think of it. Each was a heroic champion of freedom. William Wilberforce, the great anti-slavery campaigner; Richard Brinsley Sheridan, the Irish dramatist who was said to be the greatest public speaker of his time; his great friend and ally Charles James Fox, who supported the revolution in France; John Wilkes, supposedly the ugliest man in England, who was repeatedly thrown out of Parliament for exposing the tyranny of ministers; Edmund Burke, who advocated for the American colonists. Each argued passionately for freedom. Yet they shared England at least briefly with the subjects of this book and supported a system that saw men like James and John hang. How could they not see the hypocrisy of campaigning for emancipation for some and not for all? How could they allow the thread of life to dangle so precariously? Why did they permit reform to be so slow and limited?

That is why I wrote this book – to expose the hypocrisy of an era that was full of calls for supposedly universal liberty, to try and understand what happened to James and John and others like them, and to point out that the freedoms we enjoy today carry no guarantee of permanence. Complacency is no protection against the forces of reaction. You only have to look around the world. Homosexuality remains a criminal offence in thirty-four out of fifty-four countries in the Commonwealth, in large measure thanks to Britain exporting its strict laws across its Empire. Homosexual acts still carry the death penalty in Iran, Brunei, Mauritania, Nigeria, Qatar, Saudi Arabia, Afghanistan, Somalia and Sudan. Mehrdad Karimpour and Farid Mohammadi were hanged in a prison in the north-western city of Maragheh in Iran in January 2022 after spending six years on death row. And even in the United States of America, the 'land of the free', Pastor Dillon Awes of Stedfast Baptist Church in Texas believes homosexuals 'should be sentenced with death. They should be lined up against the wall and shot in the back of the head.'[1]

I particularly wanted to explore why England has had the most shameful record in Europe. The new French penal code of 1791 did not even mention sodomy, nor did Napoleon's code of 1804, which rapidly spread around the globe. Yet we did not achieve that for nearly two centuries. Most other nations never executed people for homosexuality, and those that did abolished the practice long before the nineteenth century. Germany's last case was in 1537, Spain's in 1647, Switzerland's in 1662, Italy's in 1668 and France's in 1750. Only the Netherlands executed a man for sodomy during the period covered by this book, when Jillis Bruggeman was hanged in 1803. Yet between 1806 and 1835, 404 men were sentenced to death for sodomy in England, of whom 56 were hanged.* Many more were imprisoned or transported. It was the harshest period in our history and we should never forget it.

What inspired that cruelty? Religion played a part. The Church of England was all-powerful. It preached conformity and the law enforced it. For much of this period only practising members of the Church of England could hold public office and candidates for a wide range of posts had to swear an oath that denied transubstantiation, the Catholic tenet that the bread and the wine

---

*This number includes cases involving children, women and animals. I have attached, in the appendix (p. 241), a comprehensive list of the executions for adult homosexual practices from 1800 to 1835.

were transformed into the body and blood of Christ in the mass. Bishops were princes in their dioceses and magnates in the House of Lords. The parish was the only local administrative body. The vicar and churchwardens ran the village school, employed the constable, elected the gravedigger, charged the rates, fixed the sewers, ran the workhouse and doled out relief to the poor, to widows and to orphans. The church separated the deserving from the undeserving poor. It ruled your life from baptism to burial. It offered hope after life and threatened damnation for the impenitent sinner. It enforced obeisance and deference to authority.

By the 1830s this conformity was fraying at the edges. Methodism and other brands of non-conformism had made inroads, and Catholics were allowed to take public office in 1829. But successive waves of religious revival preached that all sexual activity outside marriage was to be abhorred and, panicked by a supposed rising tide of immorality, William Wilberforce and Bishop Beilby Porteus persuaded the king to issue a *Proclamation for the Discouragement of Vice* in 1787, which had to be read out in every church in the land four times a year and at the start of assizes. It demanded that the authorities be 'very vigilant and strict in the discovery and the effectual prosecution and punishment of all persons, who were guilty of excessive drinking, blasphemy, profane swearing and cursing, lewdness and profanation of the Lord's Day, or other dissolute, immoral, or disorderly practices'.[2] Wilberforce launched a society to ensure adherence to the Proclamation and in 1802 its successor, the newly formed Society for the Suppression of Vice, pronounced it 'a truth too evident to be denied … that vice has of late advanced upon us with almost unexampled rapidity' and was 'stalking abroad in open day, both in defiance of shame, and of the correction of the laws'.[3] Others joined the chorus, railing against 'libertinism', 'the rage of pleasure' and the 'vices and licentiousness of mankind'.[4]

Top of the list of vices was *the* unmentionable sin of 'sodomy' or 'buggery'. Both words were drenched in bigotry. Sodomy was the more biblical term, as it referred to the sin of the city of Sodom, whose men had supposedly tried to engage in 'unnatural' sexual relations. The fact that Genesis chapter 19 could be interpreted as referring to Sodom's failure to show due hospitality to foreigners, rather than any sexual deviancy, or that the intended victims were angels and no sexual relations actually transpired, was immaterial. As far as the Society was concerned, sodomy was 'an abomination'. As for the virtually interchangeable term 'buggery', most people thought its origins lay in xenophobic religious hostility to a group of Bulgarian heretics, the Bogomils, and their thirteenth-century French counterparts, the Albigensians, who condemned matrimony and were referred to as '*bougres*'.[5] Buggery was also a crime, as Henry VIII had made 'the detestable & abominable vice of buggeri committed with mankind or beest' a felony punishable by death and dispossession under the Buggery Act of 1533. It was a specific offence. Lawyers argued about what proof was necessary, but it involved anal intercourse, it required penetration and it implied corruption, degeneracy and unnatural deviancy. Even attempting to commit buggery was a crime.

Yet for all the denunciations, there was a bizarre and hypocritical determination never to mention the subject. There were plenty of terms of abuse for homosexuals, including ingle, pathic, chicken hawk, Ganymede, molly, he-she thing, jemmy, catamite, macaroni, margery, madge and poof. Other terms included 'backgammon player', 'indorser' (from boxing slang for beating a man over the back with a stick) and 'windward passage' (for those who navigate the windward passage).[6] But politicians, lawyers, judges, clerks and writers jumped through all manner of hoops to avoid anything explicit. The law was crystal clear about this. Seventeenth-century chief justice Sir Edward Coke was scathing on the subject, including it in his analysis of the laws on treason. 'Buggery is a detestable, and abominable sin', he wrote, as it is 'committed by carnal knowledge against the ordinance of the Creator and order of nature'. He ludicrously claimed, without any evidence, that 'the sodomites came to this abomination ... by pride, excess of diet, idleness, and contempt of the poor', but most importantly, he insisted that it was an offence 'amongst Christians not to be named'.[7] The jurist William Blackstone reiterated the point just over a century later when he noted that 'the delicacy of

English laws ... treats [sodomy], in its very indictments, as a crime not to be named'.[8] Formal court indictments universally used the same formula: 'the detestable and abominable crime, *among Christians not to be named*, called buggery'. This was illogical and hypocritical. How could you be charged with a crime that could not be named? Yet everyone in the criminal justice system adopted the same nonsensical primness. Judges were especially coy. When, for instance, Sir William Garrow presided over the Assizes at Chester in 1814, just after the reading of the *Proclamation* he drew the jury's attention to a case they would be trying later in the week. 'It is for an offence,' he said, 'in the noticing of which I shall follow the delicacy of the law, by not calling it by name. It is one of that depravity – that unnatural description – and will come before you attended with evidence of so offensive a nature, as will render the execution of your duty disagreeable and disgusting.'[9] When the case came up, he excluded women and children from the court and told the press to refrain from making it public. Warders at Newgate, officials in the Home Office, clerks at the Old Bailey and shorthand writers at the Old Bailey followed suit, refusing even to write out the whole word and inscribing 'b-gg-ry' or 's-d-y' instead. This meant that in many sodomy cases all that was recorded of the trial was the name of the criminal, the nameless offence, the verdict, the sentence, the jury and the judge. Thus, the only court record of the trial of David Robertson, the keeper of the Jerusalem Hotel in Charles Street in Covent Garden, reads as follows: 'was indicted for an unnatural crime. GUILTY, Death. Second Middlesex Jury, before Mr. Baron Graham.'[10] Robertson was hanged on Monday 18 August 1806.

Politicians were equally coy. When Sir Robert Peel introduced the Offences Against the Person Bill in the Commons in 1828, which included a clause aimed at making it easier to obtain sodomy convictions, he did not even say the phrase 'the crime amongst Christians not to be named', but rendered it in Latin instead. There is one example of a politician defending men convicted of sodomy. Edmund Burke was so incensed by the treatment meted out to Theodosius Reade and William Smith (a plasterer and a hackney coachman) when they were sent to the pillory for 'sodomitical practices at the Magdalen Coffee-House'[11] that he publicly demanded an end to the pillory. Yet even Burke felt the need to say, 'the crime for which the poor wretches had been condemned was such as could scarcely be mentioned, much less defended or extenuated. The commission of sodomitical practices! a crime of all others the most detestable, because it tended to vitiate the morals of the whole community, and to defeat the first and chief end of society.'[12] The *Morning Post* and the *Daily Advertiser* nevertheless robustly accused Burke of being 'unmanly' for seeking 'mercy for sodomites' and ranted that the men's crime had been 'shocking to nature', that the state had been too lenient and that 'every man applauds the spirit of the spectators [who killed Smith outright], and every woman thinks their conduct right'.[13]

Some newspapers provided a few details of court cases, but many more made a virtue of drawing a veil over proceedings, claiming that such unspeakable acts could never be detailed. The *Public Ledger* claimed 'we cannot particularize the evidence', when it reported that Richard Oakden was capitally convicted of an unnatural crime at the Old Bailey in 1809.[14] The *Leeds Mercury* said it did not even wish to repeat the name of the crime when reporting a similar trial in 1822 and the *Bury and Norwich Post* said that a pamphlet vendor called James Watling had attempted to commit an unnatural crime 'in a way not to be named'.[15] Some newspapers expressly criticised others for relating details of such debauchery, complaining that instead of 'merely noticing the misdemeanour, which would have been the course most consonant not only with public decency, but also with public justice, they gloat on it as a kind of godsend in newsmongery and recur to it with most damnable iteration'.[16] This was patently absurd. The uninitiated reader's interest would have been piqued, but they must have wondered what precisely had happened, while only the more worldly (or 'depraved') reader would have understood the coded references.

It had not always been like this. Trial records in the eighteenth century are much more detailed. We know all about Mother Clap's molly-house because when it was raided in 1726 the court records were replete with information. Newspaper reports were also fuller. The particularly scandalous case of Captain Robert Jones in 1772, for instance, had seen the intimate details rehearsed in several periodicals amid claims that the country was 'over-run with Catamites', because the 'spindle-shanked Gentry' had only made the Grand Tour 'to bring home the vices of our Neighbours' and had therefore imported sodomy from Italy.[17] When Samuel Drybutter, a wealthy jeweller and toymaker with a house in Pall Mall, indicated in a coffee house that he sympathised with the convicted sodomite, a barmaid poured hot chocolate down his breeches, a waiter threw him out and a crowd chucked him in the horse-pond. A few days later a pint was thrown in his face, he was basted in front of a fire and rolled in sawdust. Drybutter was remarkably aware of how he was viewed. When some wags presented his name for the post of petty constable of St Margaret's Westminster in 1771, he told Sir John Fielding, 'Sir, I think I am not eligible; but supposing I was, I am a very improper man; you know I am the detestation of all mankind.'[18] He suffered for such boldness, though. When a soldier denounced him for attempting to pick him up in St James's Park in 1777, a crowd smashed up his house and beat him so severely that it was said (erroneously) that he died of his injuries.[19] Drybutter was unusually open about his preferences, but the point is that although homosexuals were equally violently detested in the eighteenth century, newspapers recounted these stories.

However, something changed around the turn of the century. Moral panic meant that sodomy was dealt with harshly and almost entirely in secret. That strict *omerta* means that today's history books make it look as if homosexuality completely evaporated between the molly-houses of the early eighteenth century and the trial of Oscar Wilde, and early nineteenth-century Britain seems a virtually homosexual-free zone. This is infuriatingly ironic. After all, the prosecuting counsel Charles Gill famously asked Oscar Wilde, who was in the dock of the Old Court at the Old Bailey charged with sodomy and gross indecency in 1895, 'What is the "love that dare not speak its name"?' It was a reference to a line in a poem by Wilde's lover Lord Alfred Douglas, but Wilde had used the phrase in a supposedly incriminating letter and he claimed it for his own now, stating, 'It is beautiful, it is fine, it is the noblest form of affection ... There is nothing unnatural about it ... That it should be so, the world does not understand. The world mocks at it, and sometimes puts one in the pillory for it.'[20] His words convicted him and by the end of the year Wilde was in Reading Gaol serving the maximum sentence, two years with hard labour.

It is therefore hideously paradoxical that in the period covered by this book, buggery was the crime that dared not speak its name.

To the casual eye, the story of James and John is no different from any of the other thirty-eight hangings for consensual homosexual sex from 1800 onwards. They were just two more victims of an era of spectacularly cruel and bloodthirsty prejudice. Yet their story stands out as one of the great injustices of the English justice system on three counts.

The first is laid bare by the contents of a large, battered, tan-coloured book in the National Archives in Kew. For twenty years between February 1817 and July 1837, prison clerks at Newgate Gaol painstakingly dipped their quills in black ink and inscribed in it the names of every inmate sentenced to death at the Old Bailey. Each page has five columns, in which are noted the year, the month, the name of the inmate and his or her age. In the last column the clerks noted each criminal's date of execution – or the date when they were reprieved and their sentence was commuted to transportation or imprisonment. Each double-page spread has forty-eight names and forty-eight sentences of death.

One thing sticks out when you get to page 58. Every single prisoner was reprieved. It is the same on page 59 – and on page 60. So common was a reprieve that the clerks took to writing 'ditto' in the final column. So, it comes as a shock to find at the bottom of page 61 the word 'Executed', underscored with a thick black line, opposite the entry for James Pratt, followed by another 'Executed' for John Smith, and the date, 27 November 1835. Seventy-three other prisoners had been sentenced to death at the Old Bailey that year, but every single one of them was reprieved. The same was true of 1834. The last Newgate execution before that of James and John was that of George Comey, aged twenty-two, who was executed for housebreaking on 23 April 1833, thirty-one months earlier, and the Privy Council had not ordered an execution for sodomy at Newgate since 1823. So why them?

The second injustice might just be seen as poor timing. This story starts in the reign of George III and continues through the Regency years of 1811 to 1820 and the reign of George IV from 1820 to 1830, but its main events occur in the reign of William IV. It was an in-between time. Regency frippery was over, but the Victorian era of high moral seriousness had not yet begun. Jane Austen was dead but Charles Dickens was still a shorthand writer and journalist and his first novel, *The Pickwick Papers*, would not appear until 1836. Many careers were coming to an end. Rossini's opera *William Tell* was first performed in London in 1830, but it was his last. John Constable and J. M. W. Turner had already completed their greatest works. The Welsh tragedienne Sarah Siddons delivered her final sleepwalking scene as Lady Macbeth – and cried for ten minutes afterwards – in 1812 and died in 1831, and her brother John Philip Kemble bowed out as Coriolanus in 1817 and died in 1823. Kemble's rival and heir, the diminutive Shakespearean actor Edmund Kean, collapsed in his son's arms giving his last Othello at Covent Garden in 1833. Keats, Shelley, Byron and Blake died in the 1820s and Britain's most successful poet and novelist, Sir Walter Scott, died in 1834.

The word 'scientist' would not be coined until 1840, but it was a time of rapid invention. 'Tarmac' was spreading across the nation. As gas lighting was installed on London's major thoroughfares including Westminster Bridge, Pall Mall and the Strand from 1816, lamplighters became a feature of city life. Robert Stephenson's steam engine started travelling the twenty-five miles of the Stockton to Darlington railway in 1825, and from 1821 a steamship could take you from London to Edinburgh in sixty hours, thus beating the mail coach with the 'full advantage of sleep and stretching of limbs'.[21] Farmers were using mechanical threshing machines for the first time. The first patented concrete, Portland cement, was appearing in residential buildings. Public houses were using soda fountains and smokers were lighting their pipes with 'lucifers'. A Brighton stationer called S. K. Brewer sold the first British wraparound envelopes in 1820.[22] Louis Daguerre and Charles Marie Bouton opened their diorama at Regent's Park to the public for the first time in 1823. George Shillibeer's horse-drawn 'omnibus' picked up its first passengers between Paddington and Bank in London in July 1829. Harvey Nichols opened its doors in 1831 and Harrods moved from Southwark to Knightsbridge in 1839.

It was a time of spasmodic revolution, when everyone dreamed of change. The public would only get to read Wordsworth's *The Prelude* in 1850, but the words he wrote at the turn of the century epitomised the radicalism of a revolutionary era: 'Bliss was it in that dawn to be alive, but to be young was very heaven'. The old political parties – the Whigs and Tories – were straining at the seams. The earl of Liverpool lasted nearly fifteen years as prime minister from 1812 to 1827, but by the time he died, his party, the Tories, were tearing themselves apart. In 1830 his successor, the duke of Wellington, the famed victor of the battle of Waterloo, resigned and handed over the reins to Earl Grey, whose Whig administration was sustained by radicals, liberals and reformers. They had behemoths to slay and temples to pull down. Sometimes it was difficult to know which political cudgel to take up first. Slavery, rotten boroughs, child labour, bribery and corruption in elections, stamp duty on newspapers, the exclusion from office of non-conformists, Catholics and Jews, the ban on trade unions and on civil marriage, the system of tithing, the 'bloody code' that treated 200 property crimes as capital offences, the appalling state of Britain's prisons – they all had to be reformed, however hard the old guard fought to conserve its decrepit system. Each of these was a hard-fought battle. The Manchester Yeomanry attacked peaceful demonstrators for parliamentary reform in the Peterloo massacre of 1819, and the Reform Act had to go through three versions before it became law in 1832. The slave trade was abolished in 1807, but emancipation only came in 1833 when millions of pounds of compensation was promised, not to the enslaved, but to their 'owners'.

Each delayed reform had victims, but none more obviously than the delay in changing the 'bloody code' and repealing the death penalty. Herein lies the terrible tragedy and injustice of this story. If James and John had been caught a year or two later, they would have been reprieved and transported. But their fate was not just a fluke of timing. It took a whole kingdom to hang a man. Parliament drew up the laws; police officers, magistrates and judges enforced them. Private individuals acted as prosecutors, the king and privy council sanctioned each execution, the home secretary heard or ignored pleas for mercy, and the public gathered in their thousands to applaud the execution. The revulsion and cruelty could be visceral. When the married tradesman David Myers was convicted of an 'abominable crime' with the apprentice tailor Thomas Crow at Peterborough in 1812, the press said the court was crowded and 'there never was a verdict recorded in it that gave more universal satisfaction'.[23] So why did England abominate homosexuality? And more specifically, why did England want James and John to hang? Some spoke up for them. A number of James's friends stood character witness for him in court, and after his conviction his wife Elizabeth persuaded dozens of neighbours to sign her petition for a conditional pardon. Hensleigh Wedgwood, the magistrate who committed the men for trial, begged the home secretary for mercy, as did John's former employer Thomas Phillips. Even the lead prosecutors and witnesses, John and Jane Berkshire, asked for the sentence to be commuted. In virtually every other contemporary case, such a list of petitioners was successful – but not in this. Why? In the absence of answers, it is difficult not to conclude that James and John were judicially murdered by the system.

The petitions landed on the desk of the home secretary and leader in the Commons, Lord John Russell. Why did he do nothing to save the men? After all, he was known to favour repeal of capital punishment except for murder and he must have known that his cousin Gertrude, the daughter of Lord William Russell, had been living in exile by Lake Como with her husband, the former radical Whig MP Henry Grey Bennet, ever since Bennet had been threatened with prosecution for propositioning a male servant in Spa in 1825. Russell must also have known that Bennet had been romantically linked with another MP, Richard Heber, as all three had been members of the Commons at the same time. Moreover, tales of an affair between Heber and Charles Henry Hartshorne had ended up in the magazine *John Bull* and then in the courts. Russell may have turned a blind eye to his cousin's predicament, but he must have been aware of Heber's fate. As one obituary of Heber put it in 1833: 'he returned to England, but not into the society he had left; for rumours had been in circulation degrading to his moral character. With the exception of his visits to the auction-rooms, and booksellers' shops, he lived entirely secluded among his books.'[24]

So, it is galling that Russell did not intervene, either at the meeting of the Grand (or 'Hanging') Cabinet, which considered all capital cases from the Central Criminal Court, or on his own initiative, as he was legally entitled to do. It is irritating to see him in a boastful painting by Sir George Hayter of the first session of the new House of Commons in 1833, which hangs in the National Portrait Gallery. All the other leading Whigs are there, including Melbourne, Palmerston, Lansdowne and Spring Rice, looking superbly proud of their 'Great' Reform Act. Yet two years later, as members of the 'Hanging Cabinet', these five proud reformers sent James and John to the gallows. Perhaps they feared the wrath of the mob or the ardent sanctimony of moralists like the magistrate Sir Richard Birnie, who ran a determined campaign against gay pubs, and the pitiless judge Sir John Gurney, who presided over James and John's trial and denounced the 'sins of Sodom and Gomorrah' in a similar case. Perhaps they were swayed by another shadowy figure, the recorder of London and newly elected evangelical Tory MP, Charles Ewan Law, who sentenced James and John to death at the Old Bailey with evident relish and omitted the most important extenuating facts from his recorder's report at the fatal meeting. It is perplexing too that although the law was not changed until 1861 and the penalty remained death by hanging, each and every subsequent case was reprieved. It is difficult not to conclude that the bloodthirsty English justice system wanted a hanging, that James and John were in the wrong place at just the wrong time and that Russell could neither be bothered to save them, nor dared to court public opprobrium by changing the law.

The third injustice stemmed from the fact that they were from poor, labouring, working-class families. They had moved to the sprawling metropolis to evade rural poverty, but they lived a hand-to-mouth existence as domestic servants, their finances always bumping along just above the poverty line. All three were 'out of place' at the time of their arrest and even a brief period of unemployment would have rapidly eaten up the meagre savings a servant might be able to set aside. They could afford neither the privacy that would have protected them from prosecution, nor a lawyer to defend them. By contrast, wealthy homosexuals had to be careful, but they could normally rely on the discretion of their peers and if they were ever charged with an 'unnatural offence' they would expect any court to acquit them on the basis of the 'quality' of their character witnesses. If it came to the worst and prosecution seemed imminent, a young aristocrat could flee into exile on the continent. None of this was available to James and John, whose crime was committed daily with impunity by their 'betters'.

Although only James and John were hanged, this is the story of three men. They came from different parts of England. William Bonell was born in the newly industrialised town of Bilston in the underskirts of Wolverhampton. John Smith came from the ancient cathedral city of Worcester. And James Pratt was born and baptised in Great Burstead, a rural hamlet in Essex. Much of their life is hidden from view. But by reconstructing the world in which they lived and by detailing the many people who had an impact on their fate, I hope to reveal them at least in silhouette, to give them back their lives and most importantly to expose the injustice they suffered.

Their story has a wider importance. Human beings have many instincts, including self-preservation, self-expression, an urge to have children, tribal loyalty, greed, jealousy and the desire to form lasting relationships. But there is another universal human instinct that is often overlooked: a natural abhorrence of injustice. It's what makes the outraged toddler scream 'that's not fair' and makes humanity rail against tyranny. It inspires freedom-fighters. It drives campaigners to battle against human rights abuses and miscarriages of justice. It motivates a desire for a fairer distribution of power and of the world's resources. It compels us to protect the weak, the vulnerable, the marginalised and the dispossessed. In short, it impels us towards building a better, fairer world.

James and John's execution was a manifest injustice. It falls on us to take up arms against a sea of modern troubles and never to take justice, liberty and freedom for granted. Wilberforce and Burke would have condemned same-sex relationships, including my own, as unnatural, but, as Thomas Cannon put it in 1749 in *Ancient and Modern Pederasty Investigated and Exemplified*, 'unnatural desire is a contradiction in terms; downright nonsense. Desire is an amatory impulse of the inmost human parts.'[25] Cannon's book was banned, as were same-sex relations, on pain of death. We can only strive to ensure we never return to that dark place by recalling those historic injustices.

PART I

Shapen in Iniquity

Baptism in the name of the Father, the Son and the Holy Ghost was far more than a naming ceremony. It was a celebration of a child's safe entry into the world, it claimed a child for Christ and without it there could be no Christian burial, no salvation, no eternal life, because as the psalm put it, 'Behold, I was shapen in iniquity; and in sin did my mother conceive me.'[1] It was also the first legal record of a child's existence. So, we start with three baptisms.

The first was on Saturday 23 September 1769, when Robert Bonell, aged thirty-one, and his slightly older wife Ann stood round the font in St Leonard's Chapel in the township of Bilston near Wolverhampton in Staffordshire. With them were their seven-year-old daughter Elizabeth, their son Robert, who had turned two that spring, and three godparents, two women and one man, as tradition and the Church of England demanded for the baptism of their young boy. Neither Robert nor Ann was originally from Bilston. Robert's father John was from Longdon, 'a long straggling village on the Rugeley Road'[2] about three and a half miles north-west of the cathedral city of Lichfield, his mother Ann was from the neighbouring village of Colton, and his parents had moved to the tiny hamlet of barely 150 souls called Farewell, lying on the eastern side of Cannock Chase. Here Robert had been born, the fourth of eight sons. His wife Ann Ironmonger came from the more populous and affluent market town of Penkridge, which was twelve miles west of Farewell, and when they married at St Peter's Church in Wolverhampton on

12 October 1761 Ann was already pregnant with their first child, Elizabeth, who was baptised at St James the Great, the beautiful twelfth-century church on the top of the hill in Longdon, on 21 June the following year. But by the time Elizabeth was joined by a baby brother in December 1764, Robert and Ann had made their family home in Bilston. Then came a common tragedy. They had christened this young boy 'William' at St Leonard's on St Stephen's Day, 26 December 1764, but had buried him before his fourth birthday. So now they wanted their third son also to be baptised as 'William'. It was not to be their only sadness. Four weeks later, the fragility of life was yet again drummed into them, when Elizabeth died, and the Reverend Edward Best intoned the words of the committal over her tiny grave on 27 October. 'In the midst of life we are in death ... deliver us not into the bitter pains of eternal death.' The Bonells were not alone in their grief. That same Friday, Best buried two other Elizabeths, neither of whom had reached their second birthday.

John and Anna Pratt suffered a similar fate thirty-four years later, when they appeared at the font of St Mary Magdalene, the parish church in Great Burstead, on Easter Sunday, 10 April 1803, carrying a baby son to be baptised as James. Neither John nor Anna was originally from Great Burstead, but they were both born and bred in Essex, as John had been baptised in 1766 in the chapel of St Edward the Confessor in the market town of Romford, which lay about twelve miles north-east of London, and Anna had been baptised in Bradwell-on-Sea as Anna Maria Aylett in 1761. However, when the Reverend Peter D'Aranda published their banns of marriage in Great Burstead and married them on Saturday 3 July 1784, he described them as bachelor and spinster 'of this parish'.

Easter Sunday in 1803 was extra special for the Pratt family, as not many infants were baptised during Morning Prayer on the holiest day of the year. Neither John nor Anna could read or write – they signed the register on their wedding day with their 'mark' – yet they knew the significance of the day's events. Lent was over, the gloom of Good Friday was past and this was a day for celebrating the triumph of the risen Christ. Yet John and Anna also knew that a child's grasp on life was tenuous. This was the seventh time they had brought a child to the font at Great Burstead, but at least two and possibly four of their children had died young. Sarah, born in 1785, died in 1799; Maria, born in 1789, died before her sixth birthday; and although Hannah and Lydia were baptised in 1798 and 1800, they left no trace thereafter. This left only John and Anna's eldest son John, born in 1788, and another daughter named Maria, born in 1795. This was no more unusual in Great Burstead than in Bilston – D'Aranda buried eleven infants in 1803 alone – but it meant the excitement of the baptism was always tinged with memories of infant siblings who had not survived.

As for the baptism of our third protagonist, the evidence is hard to find, as it is not easy to track down a man named John Smith, let alone one born before the statutory registration of births. The few clues we have lead to a historical cul-de-sac. The records of his trial, the accompanying newspaper reports and the burial register disagree about his age, suggesting that he was thirty-four, forty or forty-two in 1835. That would indicate that he was born between 1793 and 1801. The 'ordinary', or chaplain, of Newgate also recorded that he was from Worcester. It is possible that this should read 'Worcestershire', where at least sixty-seven John Smiths were baptised between 1793 and 1801, but the registers list only three John Smiths baptised in the city in that period. One was baptised at St John in Bedwardine on 7 March 1795, but he was buried there two weeks later. Another was brought to be baptised by his unmarried mother Mary at St Martin's on 3 June 1796, but he may either be the John Smith who was buried there just under a year later on 30 May 1797 or another John Smith buried there on 10 January 1802 (although neither of these is recorded as an infant). A third John Smith, the son of Edward and Mary, was baptised on 17 April 1797 at St John in Bedwardine, but he may be the John Smith who was buried there on 10 April 1800 (whose burial was also not recorded as that of an infant). It is possible, although it would be unusual, that our John Smith was never baptised, or that his baptismal records are lost. A letter, which formed part of his appeal for mercy in 1835, also suggests that he had 'relatives', but we have no idea who these were.[3] So, all we know with any certainty is that he hailed from Worcester or Worcestershire and that he was close to his mother, who was living alone in 1835.

The communities the three men were born into could not have been more different.

Bilston was the epitome of the industrial revolution. It was brimming with opportunity. Three industries predominated, as for decades, Bilston had made the metal chapes that fixed buckles made in neighbouring Wolverhampton to belts and shoes; it had become famous in recent years for intricate, decorative japanned and enamelled tinware; and since a Cumbrian industrialist called John 'Iron Mad' Wilkinson had launched the most lucrative and innovative of his many Black Country ironworks there in 1766, it was claimed that more iron was produced in Bilston 'than in the whole kingdom of Sweden'.[4] The town was a magnet for those in search of work and its numbers grew rapidly. In 1736 it had just over 350 households, by 1771 there were 775, but in 1801 it had 6,914 inhabitants. Because it was not allowed to hold its own fair and was therefore not considered a town, it acquired the reputation of being 'the largest village in England'.[5] One other thing distinguished it from rural Staffordshire – it was generally held that 'the inhabitants [of Bilston] are composed chiefly and almost entirely of the Labouring Classes'.[6]

It was not to everyone's taste. As one commentator put it, 'the hissing of the blast furnaces, the clanking of forge hammers, the dusty appearance of the workmen, and the various operations upon unwieldy masses of red-hot iron, combined to excite an idea of terror in those who are unaccustomed to such noisy scenes'.[7] Another was equally critical: 'For miles around Bilston it is one vast workshop and mine and the busy hum of industry sounds like the dull roar of the tempestuous ocean.'[8] Dr Richard Wilkes, the self-taught physician of neighbouring Willenhall, also complained that 'for want of some liberal person to govern it, [Bilston] is very irregular and many robberies and some murders have been committed by persons belonging to it.'[9]

*William Bonell was born in Bilston near Wolverhampton, the epitome
of the industrial revolution, where the hissing of blast furnaces and the
clanking of forge hammers filled the air.*

But with industry came work – with work came income – and
with income came commercial opportunities. So Bilston had
everything: booksellers, cabinet makers, druggists, confectioners,
hosiers, milliners, straw hat makers, as well as five dozen inns and
taverns and so many beer houses that the *Gazetteer* in 1834 added
three exclamation marks after the number, '53!!!'.[10]

Worcester, by contrast, was an ancient cathedral city with
'the reputation of being one of the cleanest and finest old cities
in the kingdom'.[11] The streets were broad and spacious. It had
'generally a brisk current of air'.[12] Its plan and construction was
'as perfect as any city in the kingdom'.[13] If you had travelled
there from Malvern, paid the toll and stood in the middle of the
bridge crossing the River Severn before entering the city, you
would have set eyes on one of the finest views in eighteenth-
century England. Its shops were plentiful and well stocked, the
streets were well paved and had 'no projecting signs' and since

1790 the city had a subscription library with 5,000 volumes. As one publisher put it, 'the general appearance of the whole City does credit to its inhabitants, and indicates at the same time both taste and opulence.'[14] The fishing in the Severn was not as good as it had once been, but Worcester had a thriving market every Wednesday, Friday and Saturday, five cattle fairs and five other annual fairs, including its famed annual hop and cheese fair on 19 September.

Like most cathedral cities, Worcester had a mix of established trades. The hop market was one of the busiest in the land; the distillery was a large concern, paying roughly £700 a week in duty; and there was also a carpet factory. The owners of the Royal China Manufactory, Messrs Barr, Flight and Barr, boasted that their china far exceeded every other in fineness and whiteness and was 'much harder and more durable than the body of any other porcelain whatever'.[15] The chemists John Wheeley Lea and William Henry Perrins did not start fermenting their anchovy sauce in Worcester until 1837, but Cowell, Crane and Kilpin had been producing British wine in Worcester since the 1760s and there was a large rectifying house and a distillery by the riverside. However, the main industry had long been glove-making. A whole street was devoted to glove makers in the fourteenth century and there had been a Glovers' Guild since 1497. Half of Britain's glove makers were based in and around the city, and by 1790 Bedwardine alone was home to dozens of manufacturers producing coarse leather work gloves, intricately decorated ladies' gloves and kid leather gloves so delicate they could be rolled up inside a walnut. The *Penny Magazine* described a common family set-up: 'The sewing of a pair of gloves requires so little preparation or arrangement, that an humble cottager can carry on the occupation in her own poor dwelling; while her husband and perhaps her children, are at work in the fields or the farm-yard.'[16] This would not make the family wealthy. Agricultural labourers worked for a pittance and had to rely on spreading the higher income that might come with a good harvest across the leaner months and years. The glove company owners were also extremely jealous of their trade, which was strictly licensed. When Susannah Banks of Ledbury was caught selling the gloves that she had been contracted to make up in 1790, her employer had her arrested, charged as a 'notorious offender' and whipped in the local marketplace; and the glove manufacturers combined to caution the public not to buy gloves from anyone other than authorised dealers under threat of a £40 fine.[17]

Where Worcester differed most from Bilston was in its social make-up. *Pigot's Directory* of 1828 listed 156 'nobility, gentry and clergy' in the city. It had a lord bishop, Richard Hurd, who held the see from 1781 until his death in 1808, and was so popular a figure at court, where he was clerk of the closet, that he was offered Canterbury in 1783, but turned it down. Unmarried and precious, he was nicknamed 'the Beauty of Holiness' in reference to the line 'O worship the Lord in the beauty of holiness' in the psalms, and Dr Johnson claimed that he was 'a man whose acquaintance is a valuable acquisition'.[18] In addition, one dean of the cathedral was nephew to the speaker of the House of Commons, his successor was nephew to the prime minister and both sitting MPs were wealthy directors of the East India Company.

As for Great Burstead, it was a tiny rural village, consisting of a single street and a few scattered farmhouses. Its trade, primarily in corn, was 'inconsiderable', and some said its only distinction was that it housed the parish church of nearby Billericay, where most of the 1,500 parishioners lived and where 'a considerable market' was held every Tuesday.[19] The church, which was dedicated to St Mary Magdalene, was similarly dismissed by the well-travelled. It was 'a neat building', they said, but it contained 'nothing to compensate the inquirer for his time in viewing the interior'.[20] The vicar, the Reverend Peter D'Aranda, might have disagreed. He came from exiled Huguenot stock and liked exploring historical antecedents. Now in his seventies, he had been in post since 1767, and he knew every inch of the place, the old Norman window with its odd heraldic lion, the fourteenth-century carvings of a king and queen, the Annunciation over the north porch, the medieval sundials scratched in the stonework in the south porch, the sixteenth-century Tyrell family chapel with its 'very handsome monuments', the memorial to Ursula

Cooke who had died in 1705 'of that mercyless distemper the
Small Pox' and the massy chest, where the parish registers of
baptisms, marriages and burials were kept.[21] He could have
shown a casual visitor the view, as everyone admitted that from
both Great Burstead and Billericay 'on a clear day the coast of
Kent is discernible by the naked eye', including the downstream
limit of the Port of London, the Nore Sand, which was 'plainly
distinguishable'.[22]

   Great Burstead typified the struggle facing rural England. Rural
life was tough. The Reverend David Davies, the vicar of Barkham,
computed the average annual income of a typical agricultural
labourer and his wife in 1795 at £22 2s, and the cost of food as £23
4s 9d, before factoring in fuel, rent and clothes. A similar instance
in 1787 reckoned that the total family income stood at £39 17s 4d,
with expenditure of £39 14s 4d. That left a financial leeway of just
three shillings a year. A bad harvest, an injury or an illness could
swiftly ruin a family – and that was without considering keeping
a child in school beyond their rudimentary education. What was
even worse was that many landlords denied tenants the small
sliver of land that they had formerly cultivated. This had reduced
many thousands of 'small farmers into day labourers, and a great
body of day labourers into beggars', while larger farmers felt able
to 'tyrannise over their inferiors ... [and] vie with the landlords in
dissipation and expense'.[23] The philanthropic social researcher Sir
Frederick Eden claimed that 'a benevolent attention to the wants
of the Poor, is a necessary part of a virtuous character'.[24] But the
experience of many agricultural families was that destitution,
malnutrition and starvation were their lot.

   The parish records in Great Burstead repeatedly hint at a
community bumping along the poverty line. Just one page of the
burial register records Edith Thrift, pauper, buried 11 January
1793; Nathaniel Atheridge, soldier, pauper, buried 18 January
1793; Mary Clarke, pauper, buried 23 January 1793; Judith Hervey,
a widow, pauper, buried 6 June 1793; Mary Martin, widow, aged
70, pauper, buried 25 September 1794.

Despite these differences, two things were constant across the realm – the Poor Law and the Church of England.

Politicians had amended the Poor Law many times since it was introduced by Queen Elizabeth, but there were two key aspects: indoor relief, which meant being confined in the workhouse and working for your keep; and outdoor relief, which the parish overseers paid to supplement family incomes of widows, orphans, invalids and the indigent. There were problems with both. Sir Frederick Eden claimed that the local authorities in Worcester had not skimped in their creation of the new Worcester House of Industry on Tallow Hill, which replaced five separate parochial workhouses in November 1794. 'The increased comforts of the Poor, who are taken into the house,' he wrote, 'are not less evident to every visitor: they have excellent dinners, chiefly of animal food; with good malt liquor.'[25] Likewise, the Great Burstead workhouse was said to be 'well-conducted' by the longstanding governor, William Brown.[26] Yet most people would do anything to avoid the workhouse, which was often made deliberately degrading. Inmates in Essex, for instance, were required to wear a badge on their right shoulder with the letters 'BP' or 'RP' for 'Billericay Poor' or 'Romford Poor'. As one account put it, 'Pride, tho' it does ill become poor Folks, won't suffer some to wear the Badge; others cannot brook Confinement; and a third sort deem the Workhouse to be a mere State of Slavery.'[27] They had a point. One parish clergyman described a typical workhouse 'whose walls of mud scarce bear the broken door', as full of 'putrid vapours', with children who know no parents' care, forsaken wives, dejected widows and 'moping idiot[s]'.[28] The diet was meagre – sheep's head broth and pease pudding – the work was menial, repetitive and mostly nugatory, endlessly turning a treadwheel or picking oakum. The Bilston workhouse was built for sixty inmates, but was so overcrowded that there were not enough beds for all the occupants 'but an equal number of them retire to rest in rotation'.[29] Yet sometimes there was little choice. Confinement brought warmth, safety, food and medical treatment and at another Essex workhouse 'bread and beer are allow'd to all without Limitation'.[30] Often it was the best place to retire to die.

Outdoor relief was rarely generous enough to stave off poverty, either, as one notorious incident brought home in 1769 when James Eaves, his wife and two of their children were found naked lying on straw on the dirt floor of their cottage in Datchworth in Hertfordshire, having starved to death. Their eleven-year-old son survived, but their outdoor relief for three weeks had amounted to just 2s 6d, barely the equivalent of two days' wages.

The Church of England was part and parcel of the Poor Law, as the 'new' Poor Law of 1786 charged the churchwardens and overseers of the poor in every parish to draw up the Poor rates, run the workhouse, make outdoor payments to the poor and if necessary apply for removal orders for paupers from other parishes to lighten the burden on local ratepayers. Invariably this meant making judgements about who constituted the deserving and the undeserving poor.

The Church's message on sex, sexuality, motherhood and the nature of humanity was relentlessly negative. No new mother could appear in public until she had been 'churched' in a ceremony of thanksgiving which started with the words laid down in the *Book of Common Prayer*: 'Forasmuch as it hath pleased Almighty God of his goodness to give you safe deliverance, and hath preserved you in the great danger of child-birth; You shall therefore give hearty thanks unto God.' The vicar would remind the woman in the words of the psalm that 'the snares of death' had compassed her round about in childbirth. He would lead the congregation in the Lord's Prayer, and they would listen carefully to hear her alone say the words 'and deliver us from evil'. It was a ritual act of purification. She had been unclean. She had been physically purged of 'noxious and venomous impurities'[31] and now she had to be spiritually cleansed of sin and shame. If her new baby had not required an emergency baptism, she could join her husband for the christening.

The baptism service proclaimed the same message. The vicar reminded the 'dearly beloved' parents and godparents who gathered at the font that 'all men are conceived and born in sin' and asked them to renounce 'the devil and all his works, the vain pomp and glory of the world, with all covetous desires of the same, and the carnal desires of the flesh'. They had to pray that 'all carnal affections may die' in their infant child, before the vicar took each of the infants in his arms in turn and asked the godparents to name it before 'discreetly and warily' dipping it three times in the water. After the congregation mumbled 'Amen' and intoned the Lord's Prayer (and hoped the baby would cry, to show that the devil had been cast out), the vicar reminded the parents and godparents to make the child listen to sermons, so that it might lead a 'godly and a Christian life', thereby 'continually mortifying all our evil and corrupt affections'.[32]

If William Bonell's parents followed this advice, the young boy would have heard the sermons of the Reverend Edward Best, who had a clerical pedigree that stretched back centuries to John Best, bishop of Carlisle under Elizabeth I. Edward was a traditionalist, who voted for the two Tory candidates in the rumbustious election for the knights of the shire for Staffordshire in 1747. He kept notebooks in Latin and preached sermons on texts like 'Be angry and sin not', 'He that committeth sin is of the Devil' and 'How shall they preach except they be sent?'[33] In one oft-repeated sermon on 'the horrid nature and evil of sin', he denounced those who 'assemble themselves together in rioting and drunkenness, in chambering and wantonness' because 'a course or habit in any sin obstinately persisted in ... is a rebellion against God'.[34] His personal favourite, which he delivered seventeen times, included a denunciation of damnation 'when we suffer our passions to dethrone our reason, and hinder the free use and exercise of our understandings, when they drive us on headlong, and (as it has been well expressed) the Beast rides the Man'.[35] It is difficult to avoid the impression that sex was the obsessively forbidden fruit. It was a mortifying message and led many into a life of hypocrisy, shame and fear.

What do we know about the early lives of our three men?

William Bonell had two further brothers – Matthew, baptised in April 1772 and Edward, in July 1775 – and their father Robert Bonell was renting a cottage and a small slip of land from William

Shaw in 1781, for which he was charged 9d a year in land tax. Like all his brothers, William could read and write, so he most probably attended the parish school next door to St Leonard's church where ten poor children were educated for free every year. The education would have been rudimentary. He would have learnt some things by rote, including the Lord's Prayer and the creeds. Arithmetic involved little more than addition, subtraction, division and multiplication. This was hardly the classical education that contemporaries would have received at Wolverhampton Grammar School, but while there was no need for young men destined for the iron furnaces of Bilston to learn Latin, life in an industrial town increasingly required some degree of literacy. You had to be able to read a sign, find an address, add up a bill or pay the rent correctly. Besides, more and more people preferred to read the Bible for themselves or frame their own opinions by picking up one of the many newspapers that were available in coffee houses and taverns. Here they could find out the price of grain and the names of bankrupts, read about the colonists' war in America and proceedings in the 'Imperial Parliament', or look for jobs.

We know a few other things about William. In old age he was five feet five inches tall (the national average), he had a high forehead, brown eyes, a long nose, a wide mouth and a large chin.[36] Newgate's records say that he had hazel eyes. He lost his mother when he was fourteen and since he claimed in 1835 that he had been a gentleman's servant for forty-six years of his life, it seems he entered service sometime before 1788. Given the dearth of gentry in Bilston, it seems likely that this was also when he moved to London.

There is one other intriguing fact. According to Tasmanian convict records, William was a widower and had at least one child by the time he arrived in Hobart.[37] Parish registers record more than two dozen William Bonells (or similar) marrying between 1791 and 1833 in England, and it is possible that our William married Elizabeth Harling at St Martin in the Fields in London on 23 October 1805, when he was thirty-six. If so, they brought their daughter Elizabeth to be christened at the same church three months later and in 1809 a brother, Joseph, followed her. By then William's father Robert had been buried at St Leonard's in Bilston, and his brothers Robert, Matthew and Edward had moved respectively to Birmingham, Shropshire and Yorkshire, where they married and launched families of their own. By the time William enters our story in 1835, he cuts a lonely figure.

We know nothing of John Smith's early life. It is possible he relied on the kindness of Worcester's charities. Bishop Lloyd's school educated three children of parents who were unable to provide for their education from St Martin's. Moore's Hospital provided free schooling for ten poor boys aged between four and twelve from the parish of St Martin's; it also gave ten poor children dinner on Christmas Day and handed out a shilling each to fifty poor people every New Year's Day. But John Smith never learned to read and write, which puts him in the less-educated 40 per cent of the population. Worcester offered few opportunities to an illiterate young man, so perhaps he applied to one of the local gentry for a post in service, or else to the china works, the rectifying house or one of the tanneries that prepared the leather for gloves. Perhaps he drew a blank there. Or perhaps he felt the need to leave the tight confines of the cathedral city in search of greater anonymity in the fast-growing metropolis of London. All we know for certain about his appearance comes from the records of Newgate Gaol, where a turnkey noted that he was five feet three inches tall, stoutish, with light brown hair, green eyes and a fair complexion.

We can glean more about James Pratt from the parish records. On 31 March 1804 the Great Burstead overseers of the Poor Law paid two shillings 'for 2 Pair Stockings for Prat's Children'; and not long after his twelfth birthday, when he was officially no longer a child, James appears in the overseers' cashbook in his own name, when the overseers described him as a 'poor boy' and in 'distress', and gave him 1s 6d on 13 May 1815.[38] We do not know what prompted James's application for outdoor relief. The tithe records show a John Pratt with a smallholding measuring two roods (roughly four tennis courts) between 1805 and 1809[39] and the overseers charged a John Pratt a two-shilling poor rate

between 1811 and 1813, but James's parents' fortunes seem to
have collapsed. By 1814 there is no John Pratt in Great Burstead
and James was orphaned in the autumn of 1817. His mother Ann
died first, in the century-old but much expanded West Ham
workhouse, which housed up to 155 inmates, on 26 October
and his father John died days later, aged fifty, in the Romford
workhouse that had been built in 1787 to house 250 inmates
on a field called Joy's Mead.[40] He was buried on 3 November
at the church where he was baptised and married, St Edward
the Confessor. Reduced to paltry handouts from the Poor Law
guardians at the age of twelve, James was an orphan by the time
he was fifteen. Essex held nothing for him and like thousands of
others, including William and John, he made his way to London
to seek his fortune or at least to scrape a living.

2

Know His Business

It felt as if everyone converged on London in the first quarter of the nineteenth century. The imperial beehive hummed and buzzed. Trade was brisk and competition fierce. Fishwives, orange-women, chimney sweeps, broom-men, muffin-men, all cried for custom. Costard-mongers trundled their donkey-carts as itinerant shopkeepers, selling artichokes, cucumbers, white St Thomas's onions, ripe young beans and baking pears. By 1818 the days were long past when Finsbury and Clerkenwell had cattle pasturing in pleasant groves and St Martin's church was 'literally in the fields'.[1] But by eight o'clock every morning milkmaids were shouting 'milk below' throughout the metropolis and selling fresh butter and cheese. The place was so busy that the crowds felt like a mob as they sauntered or trudged along the pavements. The city's own professions careered along the Strand or up Ludgate Hill. Veterans from the Napoleonic wars begged or hustled. Apprentices opened shutters on a shopkeeping nation. Ladies in crinoline were driven along in broughams with lapdogs at their side. Omnibuses disgorged clerks at Somerset House or the Bank of England. Swift, grimy little steamboats darted along the 'Silent Highway' of the Thames, competing with police hulks and lighters laden with bricks and ashes. Barristers drove across the 'crazy arches' of Westminster Bridge in small phaetons and their wives rustled in shiny silks.[2] In the city's rookeries, tenements and slums, down-on-their-luck families mixed with thieves and cut-throats and hustled to avoid the debtors' prisons at the Fleet or the Marshalsea.

The metropolis had long encompassed two ancient cities –
London and Westminster – but it was rapidly extending its tentacles
as the population grew by a fifth every decade. People had been
complaining since the 1780s that 'the contagion of the building
influenza' had extended its virulence 'with unabating violence'
and that as street was added to street and square to square, the
metropolis was 'manifestly the centre of the disease'.[3] By 1800
it had started to encroach on country villages in the counties of
Middlesex, Surrey, Essex and Kent and as the new century got
into its stride dozens of speculative developers filled in the green
spaces with row upon row of profitable properties.

By 1818 this, the greatest city in the world, the swarming
capital of a mighty empire, was home to James Pratt, John
Smith and William Bonell. A primary source of work for young
country lads was domestic service, and despite their different
backgrounds, ages and abilities, all three worked as domestic
servants. Service had its attractions. Instead of slaving away for a
pittance in the filth of the London streets or as an unskilled daily
labourer on a building site, you would be working and living in
a well-appointed house. You would be fed, housed and clothed.
There was the prospect of promotion. If you showed deference
and worked hard in a large establishment you could rise from the
post of groom to valet or butler. William spent several decades
in service, which would have enabled him to set a little aside for
his retirement. Larger households were a better guarantee of job
security, too, although there was always the danger that the family
would dismiss some of its staff when they went on a foreign trip
or retired to their country home.

The three men had four ways of finding a position. They could
have answered one of the advertisements which appeared on the
front pages of the Tory-supporting *Morning Post*, or the Whig-
supporting *Morning Chronicle* and *The Times* every day; or placed
an advertisement in the 'Want Places' columns, which were often
on the back page. These specified the qualities families sought in a
footman. He should be tall, respectable, young and, in a frequently
used phrase which implied all-round competence, compliance and
discretion, he should 'know his business'. All the adverts reflected

this. A gentleman's family sought 'a young man as footman', who 'must be tall and highly respectable in appearance'.[4] Another family in Blackheath wanted 'an experienced Servant, not under 25 years of age' and stipulated that his 'height must exceed five feet eight inches'.[5] As if in response, one candidate advertised that he was 'a tall, single man, 37 years of age, who perfectly understands his business as an Indoor Servant'.[6] Another billed himself as 'a tall, genteel, active young Man, aged 23; stands five feet nine inches high'.[7] A twenty-three-year-old claimed he was 'a sober, steady, active young man' who could be 'well recommended from his last place'.[8] Another, who was 'desirous of living in a Nobleman's house', claimed to be a 'tall, strait, active Young Man, 20 years of age, stands five feet ten inches'.[9] In one advert for a footman, two young gentlemen stated 'a man of colour, if a thorough good servant, will not be objected to; but no aged man, nor anyone accustomed to live in large families, will suit'.[10]

Even more important was attitude. Many London employers preferred servants straight from the country, presuming that they would not be so cocky or conniving as a city servant. Hence one lad advertised himself as 'a tall respectable Youth from the country, fifteen years of age, and of obliging disposition'.[11] A family of seven adults and two children living near Regent's Park advertised in the *Saint James's Chronicle* – in between notices for Mr John Clark's dental cement and Mr Cockle's Anti-bilious Pills – for a footman to join a below-stairs complement of cook, housemaid, upper maid and nursery maid. The successful candidate, they made clear, must 'thoroughly understand his business and be of a ready and good disposition'.[12] Another advertisement placed by a gentleman seeking a footman 'where only one is kept' insisted that he must be 'a respectable person, and have a good character: must understand his business, without being above it, and be active and willing to make himself generally useful'.[13] A 'quiet regular family' in Hampstead warned 'no one need apply who has lived in a fashionable family at the west end of town'.[14] And another large family near town sought an upper footman out of livery and an under footman in livery, the latter of whom 'must understand gardening and waiting at table'.[15]

One final thing recommended a candidate. He should preferably be single and if he were married, he should have no 'incumbrances'. One advertiser in *Saunders's News-Letter* was typical. He described himself as 'a young man from the country, who understands his business perfectly well and can attend inside if required, and make himself generally useful'. He added that he had 'no incumbrancers or followers whatever'.[16] This was such a prerequisite in many households that one contemporary footman, William Taylor, hid from his employer the fact that he was married and only visited his wife and family on his day off.

The third route was the employment agency. 'Families in want of really good servants, of every description, both Male and Female', claimed an advertisement in the *Morning Chronicle*, 'will decidedly find their interest better consulted, and their object much sooner attained, by a visit to the DOMESTIC BAZAAR, No. 134 Oxford-street, near Holles-street ... than through the adoption of any other method whatsoever.'[17] There were similar agencies across the city. Mrs Milward ran an agency in Blackheath which traded on her husband's connections as former coachman to George IV when he was regent. Some people warned that these agencies, or 'Intelligence Offices', were a swindle. 'Country people', wrote Richard King in 1795, 'have often been made a prey by these voracious animals, after dancing attendance on them every day for several months together, making a thousand applications in vain, and being fooled out of some pounds.'[18]

Finally, probably the most common way to find a new position was through personal recommendation. Sometimes a family would do their best to help a faithful servant if they had to let him go. One family who were compelled to part with their coachman 'in consequence of a reduction in their establishment' advertised on his behalf in the *Morning Post*, guaranteeing his 'undeniable character'.[19] Young men hung out in one of the taverns frequented by footmen, including the Running Footman in Charles Street in Mayfair, in the hope of picking up news of an opening and a recommendation from a well-regarded incumbent.

Others exploited every connection they had, or went door to door, knocking at the servants' entrance and hoping for a warm reception.

THE

YOUNG GROOM'S GUIDE,

AND

VALET'S DIRECTORY.

By JEREMIAH WEAL.

•

LONDON:
SAMPSON LOW, 42, LAMB'S CONDUIT STREET.

MDCCCXXXIII.

There was plenty of advice on offer for young servants like James, who could read and write, including this popular volume, which started by recommending that a groom start at six o'clock, 'for if you expect to get your work done in proper time, you must begin early'.

James Pratt had several things going for him when he arrived in the metropolis, aged fifteen. He could read and write. He was single. He was willing. And at some point in 1818 he found a position as a groom for William Scott Preston, who was twenty, fresh out of Trinity College Cambridge and had recently been admitted to Lincoln's Inn as a trainee barrister. Preston was following in his father Richard's footsteps, as Richard had made a substantial fortune as a lawyer, first as an attorney in his home county of Devon and subsequently as a barrister, conveyancer and member of the Inner Temple. So lucrative was Richard's business that he was able to purchase large estates in Devon. Richard later boasted in his will that the 'ample estate I have acquired has not been obtained without a devotion to my profession which has been rarely surpassed',[20] but he also devoted six years of his life to politics, as he sat as MP for Ashburton in Devon from 1812 to 1818. For three decades he also rented a house in Grove Crescent in Camberwell, which was where James Pratt started his working life as William's groom.

James must have felt at home in Camberwell, which was still a farming village. Camberwell Green had a working farm and nearby Myatt's farm was famed for its strawberries. There was such a plague of caterpillars in 1782 that the overseers of the poor paid £10 to have them 'apprehended' and for much of the nineteenth century the parish overseers offered rewards of 4d for a dead hedgehog and a shilling for a polecat. The terrace of eight houses that formed Grove Crescent was newly built in the latest fashion, with tall plain sash windows, broad front doors and basements protected by decorated wrought-iron railings. The Prestons were not the only family to take advantage of speculative builders' steady and profitable encroachment south of the river, as although Camberwell's population stood at just 7,059 in 1801, 'with the dawn of the century, [it] suddenly broke through the trammels which had been imposed upon suburban buildings'.[21]

There were two additional qualities that may have recommended James to William Scott Preston. Many advertisements from young men seeking posts as either groom or footman emphasised in addition to being steady, sober and young that they were, like the twenty-seven-year-old who advertised in the *Morning Post* in January 1818, men 'of light weight who thoroughly understands the management of horses'.[22] James was just five feet one inch tall – and the management of horses would have been part of his daily life in Essex.

It would have been a lively household. William's elder sister Elizabeth was already married, but his five sisters and two brothers were still at home and the youngest, Catherine, was still an infant. James's primary duty was to look after his master's horses. He may have started as little more than a stable boy, but his tasks remained the same. The day started very early: 'not later than six o'clock', recommended one contemporary manual.[23] He had to feed and groom the horses and muck out the stables so that everything was ready for whatever the family required. Mucking out was hard work. Clean straw had to be set aside, soiled straw had to be pitch-forked into a muck sack or onto the dunghill, dung had to be carted away, the floor had to be swept dry and the right amount of fresh straw had to be laid to allow the horse to 'stale', and to protect it from draughts or injury. Grooming was equally physical. William Preston would have complained if his mount had been dusty or dirty or if there had been a single twist of straw in his mane or tail. So, James would have had to apply himself vigorously to rubbing the horses down, switching between a currycomb, a wisp, a whalebone brush, a sponge, a stable rubber and a cloth. He would build up a sweat. He would brush up and down, backwards and forwards, three or four times and then clean the brush by drawing it through the currycomb, before starting again. Several times a day he would have to pick out the horses' hoofs lest a stray stone made the horse go lame. Once the horse was ready, it had to be dressed, which could take between thirty minutes and two hours. Whether the family went out in the carriage or William Preston rode into town alone, the horses would need rubbing down, walking off, feeding, watering and grooming again on their return. At the end of the day the horses would be 'set fair'. If his horse or carriage was not taken out by the family, James would have to exercise the horse for a couple of hours. Then there was the tack, the saddles, bridles, stirrups, straps and harnesses, which had to be brushed, sponged, oiled, cleaned and kept in good repair, with special attention to the seams and stitches. If his master dined at home, James would smarten up in the basement so as to wait at table, but if William decided to go out in the evening, James had to repeat the preparation of the horses and stay up until he returned or signalled that he was done for the day. There was plenty of advice on how to manage this relationship. 'Be steady, sober, merry and wise', wrote Jeremiah Weal in a handbook for young servants in 1833, but above all 'a gentleman's servant must be alert when wanted'.[24]

There were downsides. James had to be constantly at his master's beck and call. He was a hired hand, an extension of his master. His time was his master's. He enjoyed no privacy. Virtually the only security a servant had was the strongbox or trunk in which he kept anything of financial or personal value. When the 'poor honest sodomite'[25] John Atwood Eglerton was convicted and hanged for 'an unnatural crime' in 1816, the main evidence came from a series of letters he had sent to a groom, which the lad had stored in his strongbox, supposing them safe. The coachman and butler 'conceived strong suspicions that all was not right'; they broke open the box, found the letters, took the lad to task and 'so the whole of this detestable story came out'.[26] Likewise, the common practice in the duke of Newcastle's household was for all letters to his servants to be addressed on the envelope care of him with nothing more than the name of the sender. It was thus by accident that he opened a letter 'from Henry Hackett' which was intended for his valet, Benjamin Candler, and began with the words 'my beloved Benjamin'. Hackett, a draper's apprentice from Grantham, was prevailed upon to give evidence against Candler and two others, a gentleman called William Arden and a cabinet maker, John Doughty, all three of whom were hanged at Lincoln Castle in March 1823.

Many hated being in service. Some were appalled by London. A young countrywoman called Mary Ballard wrote to her sweetheart Billy back in the country that the people she had settled with 'have treated me with civility; nor can I say that they exact more from me, than I am able to perform'. Yet she worried for her health because she was used to getting up every day at six and going to bed at ten, 'but, alas! What a change has taken place? Here we breakfast at noon, dine at seven in the afternoon; then our gentry go out to spend the evening, and seldom return 'till three in the morning.'[27] A male servant – also from the country – likewise complained that his family had twice dragged him before a Justice of the Peace and accused him of stealing a spoon, before finding it. 'Here', he wrote, 'is nothing in our family but drunkenness and rioting; the conversation at table would make you tremble; and every night there is a different woman brought home.'[28]

Servants had little time that they could call their own. Jeremiah Weal also advised a young groom, 'never think of going out in the evening on your own account'. Yet James might have been tempted by the entertainments on offer in Camberwell. The three-day fair on Camberwell Green every August was reckoned to be 'one of the most amusing and orderly occurring near the metropolis'.[29] Everyone went – masters and servants alike – to visit the many booths selling corn-crakes and gingerbread, to catch one of the shows at Richardson's theatre, to laugh at the clowns or the comic ballads, to ogle the outlandish exhibits (including 'the lately-caught, and highly-accomplished young Mermaid'), or to carouse at Alger's Crown and Anchor tavern which was fitted with chandeliers, variegated lamps, flags and banners, which presented 'a very splendid effect'.[30] They could also enjoy some stand-up comedy:

Q: Which of the taxes does the month of March remind us of?
A: The windy tax.
Q: What religious book is a sheriff like?
A: The Companion to the halter.[31]

The fair was also renowned for its pickpockets. The year James started work, a Mr Cary was robbed of his pocket-book containing £197 and Mr Tobin of Croydon, Mr Hall of Tooley Street and Mrs Wade of Camberwell were robbed of their watches at the fair, at which fourteen thieves were apprehended.[32]

Taking on a groom when William Scott Preston was still little more than a student was an ostentatious display of his wealth, as male servants were an especial luxury at this time. Male and female servants had always been treated differently. Females were rarely if ever seen in public. Their role was to relieve their mistress of all the household drudgery. They cooked, cleaned, washed, scrubbed, sewed and mended. Their male counterparts – the butlers, footmen, valets and grooms – also had onerous duties, but they were a conspicuous sign of their master or mistress's prestige. So, in order to fund the war with the American colonists, the prime minister Lord North decided to tax luxuries in 1777, including hair powder, carriages, horses and male (but not female) servants. This servants tax was increased and extended to include female servants between 1785 and 1792, and when the Napoleonic wars needed financing the male servants tax was increased in 1812. This meant that when James Pratt started as a groom, a household incurred an 'assessed tax' of £2 8s for a single male servant and £3 2s for each additional male servant. Considering James's salary was likely to be £20 to £25 a year, this was a substantial additional consideration. A large aristocratic household might have a full set of butlers, footmen, valets, grooms, coachmen, gardeners, gamekeepers and masters-of-the-horse – all of whom were men – but from 1812 a household with eleven male servants was charged £9 11s for each one. Most families evaded the tax by only employing female servants, including Richard Preston, who employed seven servants at Leigh House in Devon, all of them women. Fortunately for James, though, there was a tax exemption for the male servants of bachelors, so while William Scott Preston remained unmarried he could take James on tax-free.

John Smith also entered service in London at about this time, although he seems to have worked longer as a labourer and may occasionally have returned to Worcester to look after his mother. His employer, Thomas Phillips, was more established than William Preston. He was a wealthy man of many parts. He had been born in London in 1760, the son of an officer in the excise revenue department, but he had been brought up in Radnorshire in rural mid-Wales, schooled in Bedfordshire and apprenticed to an apothecary in Hay-on-Wye on the Welsh border. From pharmacy to medicine was a small step and after a pupillage under the Jermyn Street surgeon John Hunter, he entered the medical service of the Royal Navy and the East India Company, serving in Canada, Calcutta and Botany Bay. A two-year stay back in England led to his marriage to Althea Edwards in 1800, at the late age of forty, but soon the couple sailed to India where he became superintending surgeon of the Bengal Medical Board – a post he held until 1817 when he returned to London and set up a household. The couple had no children, but they spent considerable time and energy on a range of philanthropic ventures, including creating a library of more than 50,000 books with the sole intention of passing it on to colleges in Lampeter and Llandovery in Wales. He was wealthy. His annual pension of £1,500 alone was enough to fund a luxurious lifestyle. But he also had significant investments across the globe. Most notably he purchased the Camden Park Estate on St Vincent – and in 1834 he claimed £4,737 8s 6d in compensation for the freedom granted to its 167 enslaved Africans.

The Phillips family lived at 5 Brunswick Square. We can guess at the size of their household from the census in 1841. In addition to Thomas and Althea and a friend Amelia Bayley, there were five servants, William Davies, Ann Green, Harriet Graves, Sarah Slade and Matilda Hale, who was just fifteen. The contents of another house in Brunswick Square were listed when its owner, a timber merchant called William Smith, died in 1819. They included a pianoforte, 'handsome window-curtains', carpets, sideboards, dining tables, card tables, Pembroke tables and dressing-tables, pier and swing glasses, mahogany and painted chairs, wardrobes, chests of drawers, bookcases, night-tables, wash-stands, bedsteads and furniture, 'prime feather beds, blankets, sheets, table linens &c.'.[33] No. 5 would have been no different, except that we know from Phillips's many bequests that in addition to books he had a large quantity of artefacts from around the world.

As for Brunswick Square, it would never be included in the list of the most important streets in London in the *Footman's Directory*, but it was elegant, in a restrained way, and relatively new. It was the brainchild of Samuel Pepys Cockerell, the chief architect and surveyor of Thomas Coram's Foundling Hospital, whose governors resolved in 1790 to lease out several acres of their land for the speculative development of new townhouses, under Cockerell's overall supervision. There was plenty of local opposition to the plan from wealthy residents of Queen Square and Great Ormond Street who had thus far benefited from

uninterrupted countryside views, but in 1792 the governors
granted a lease to the ambitious twenty-nine-year-old property
developer James Burton for the construction of ten townhouses
on the south side of the square 'on a handsome scale'.[34] Such was
Burton's 'unwearied industry'[35] that by 1802 he had completed
586 houses, creating two imposing three-sided squares, Brunswick
and Mecklenburgh, flanking the hospital gardens on the west and
east, and rebuilding Guilford Street. As one writer put it, Burton's
houses were 'built to popular taste, and at popular prices'.[36] The
style was neoclassical and each terrace of near-identical houses
in light ochre brick was built to impress, with a larger central
property and two end properties projecting into the street so
as to frame the range. But the ironwork for the balconies was
simple and mass-produced, the staircases had identical narrow
mahogany handrails, the dados, skirtings, coving and cornices
were barely ornamented and the only external ornamentations
were the fanlights above the doors and red-painted window
heads. Cockerell and Burton knew their market well, though.
After all, this was not central London. Brunswick Square was not
even in the parish of St George the Martyr, but was consigned to
St Pancras, and 'the wealthy type of resident who spent extravagant
sums on ornamental plaster decoration and painted ceilings
simply did not come to St Pancras'.[37] Yet these four-storey houses
over basements, with slate roofs, high first-floor ceilings and a
moulded stucco cornice made Burton 'gratifyingly rich'.[38] And
Thomas Phillips lived in the grandest house in the run, with a
three-storey bay into the square. It had been the home of Peter
Mellish, the governor of the Foundling Hospital, until 1818 and
other occupants in the square included solicitors, barristers and
a Royal Navy captain. It even got a mention in Jane Austen's
Emma, when Isabella Knightley boasts 'Our part of London is
so very superior to most others', adding, 'You must not confound
us with London in general, my dear sir. The neighbourhood of
Brunswick Square is very different from all the rest.'

This was where John Smith lived and worked for at least two
years after 1818. He would have slept in the attic or the basement
and his days would have been long, but it was probably the

smartest house he would ever live in and he would have been surrounded by elegant furnishings and books he could not read. The square was paved and lit with gas. The house had running water and drains. It also brought John close to the heart of one of the largest cities in the world. Privacy would have been hard to come by, but the sheer mass of people in the metropolis granted anonymity, which was itself a form of privacy.

Employment as a servant was precarious, as it depended on the whim and personal circumstances of the employer. James Pratt found this out on Wednesday 22 May 1822, when 'William Scott Preston, bachelor of the parish of St Giles Camberwell, barrister at law', took the hand of Margaret Grace Gordon Lawrie at St Alphege's church in Greenwich. Margaret's father Peter did not give her away, as he had been buried in the same church two years earlier, but her mother Anne and William's father Richard acted as the two witnesses. It was an advantageous marriage for both of them. Margaret's father Peter Lawrie had been born in Penninghame in Wigtownshire in Scotland and had inherited Ernespie, a minor castle in red sandstone near Castle Douglas, from his father Alexander, but he had married Anne in London and made his fortune as a London merchant based in Blackheath. Since Peter and Ann's only son had died at the age of twelve, Ernespie and 11 Blackheath Hill came to Margaret and her elder sister Anne on their father's death; and since Anne was already married, the Prestons took up residence in Blackheath.

We do not know whether it was the loss of the male servant tax exemption for bachelors that made Preston let James go. It is possible that James moved into Blackheath Hill for a while along with his master. But by 1824 they had parted on good terms and James was living just over a mile from Blackheath in Deptford.

3

Its Excellent Docks

The royal shipyards at Deptford echoed with the noise of chopping, hammering and sawing. Men wielded adzes to trim the bark off tree trunks and shape them into masts, they split logs with heavy axes and carved them into blocks, they sawed through hundred-year-old oak trees in pairs astride a sawpit to fashion sturdy beams, they hammered wooden trenails into boards with steel mauls, they drilled, they filed and they rasped. Always working with the grain, they carved vast timbers into elegant curved boards that would lock together to form a watertight seal for the hull or the keel. Mostly they would lean into the long slender handle of their two-handed chisel, or 'slick', and let the tool do the work, but sometimes they would use a mallet and chisel. Some were tapping oakum into the wedge-shaped space between the boards with their caulking mallet and iron. Others were scraping off the pitch and raking out old oakum as part of the regular servicing these wooden ships required. It was hard physical work, and shipbuilding required an army of specialist craftsmen. You had to have an eye for the limb of the tree that had grown at the right angle to form the joint between the keel and the sternpost. You had to have a feel for the wood. You had to know when to get the new mast out of its seawater bath. You had to be strong and work as part of a team.

Deptford was a place of intermittent industry. Henry VIII had spotted its potential four miles from central London on the north-east corner of Kent, affording easy access to the Thames and the Channel, and the Royal Navy had built and repaired its

ships in its royal dockyard for more than two and a half centuries.
The East India Company had added an adjacent dockyard for its
larger (500 ton and more) merchant ships and the Evelyn family
had constructed 'Deadman's Dock', where 74-gun men-of-war
were built.[1] Henry VIII had also added a great storehouse, from
whose vast stores came the provisions for much of the Royal Navy.

The air was full of the smells of other industries: glue factories,
gas works, tar distilleries, breweries and manufacturers of
artificial manure. There was a large chemical manufactory, where
a predominantly French forty-strong workforce produced
sulphuric, nitric and oxalic acid in fifteen large furnaces. Passenger
ships arrived from Rotterdam, St Petersburg and Hamburg,
members of the royal family regularly disembarked here before
completing their journey into London by carriage, and convict
ships like the *Royal Sovereign*, the *Hive* and the enormous
320-convict *John Barry* picked up troops and set sail for New
South Wales or Van Diemen's Land. There were fishermen, too,
as the best part of 400 fishing boats worked the Thames between
Deptford and Richmond.[2] The numbers of fishermen had fallen
recently – and there were no salmon in the Thames any more –
but although Deptford never had a market, it was as populous
and busy as a small city and it was difficult to avoid the fact that,
as one gazetteer later wrote, 'the main support and consequence
of Deptford arose from its excellent docks'.[3]

This was where James's brother John, who was fifteen years
older than him, had moved after leaving Great Burstead and
marrying Margaret Brown in Berwick-upon-Tweed in 1811.
By the time John and Margaret's first son Joseph was born
the following spring, the couple were living in Giffin Street in
Deptford and John was working as a shipwright in the royal
dockyards. Giffin Street was also where Elizabeth Moreland had
been born and brought up, the daughter of another shipwright,
James Moreland. She had been baptised at St Paul's in 1895, but
her father died in 1807, when she was just twelve. Somehow, she
and James met and hit it off; and on Monday 2 June 1823 the
vicar of St Edward the Confessor in Romford pronounced them
husband and wife. It is unclear why they chose Romford. The

law required them to marry in the parish where they resided unless they were using a special licence. That would have meant St Alphege's, Greenwich, or St Paul's, Deptford. The family connection with Romford was through James's father, who had already been dead for five years, but James's elder sister Lydia lived there briefly in the early 1820s with her grocer husband Joseph Ramsden and their two sons John and Joseph, which may explain why the vicar, the Reverend William Everett, described James and Elizabeth as bachelor and spinster 'of this parish' in the register, which they both confidently signed, although neither Lydia nor Joseph acted as witnesses. They were both well over the legal marriageable age (of fourteen and twelve respectively for men and women), but James had not yet reached twenty-one and had no parents to vouch for him and neither of Elizabeth's seem to have been alive. Perhaps James turned to Everett as the priest who had conducted his father's funeral.

Or perhaps both of them had visited Essex in search of work. After all, they would have known that getting married would require James to find a new position, especially if they intended to have children. Few employers kept a groom on when he married. However, James was in luck again – and found employment closer to home. Eight years after Waterloo, the government slashed the rate on a single male servant to £1 4s, which was four shillings less than the duty on keeping a horse.* Many more families could now afford a male servant and new opportunities opened up in relatively modest households. Even a merchant or a tradesman might now have a footman or groom in addition to a maid-at-all-work. And according to the *Ambulator*, Deptford had 'many good houses, and an extensive population'.[4] What with senior managers of the dockyards, the victualling-house and other maritime businesses, the town had a significant number of gentlemen who had the money and the status to employ servants, including Charles Augustin Ferguson of Slade's Place, Deptford, who took James on as footman sometime in 1823 or 1824, on a salary of about £40 a year.

---

* By way of comparison, the window tax came in at £1 8s for ten windows.

*James Pratt married Elizabeth Moreland on 2 June 1823 in the parish
church of Romford in Essex, where they were both listed as resident,
although they met and lived in Deptford. Both signed their own name.*

Ferguson's father Gilbert had lived, worked and made his
fortune in the parish of St Nicholas, Deptford for upwards of
forty years as 'head surveyor of shipping to the Honourable
East India Company'.[5] He had married Mary Warrington,
the daughter of another Deptford shipwright, in 1754 and it
was here that Charles was baptised in 1757, followed by eight
siblings. Gilbert Ferguson's success as a shipwright had enabled
him to purchase one of the impressive townhouses on Butt Lane
known as Slade's Place, which went up in the late 1770s. These
had a colourful history, as they were built by an extraordinarily
independent shipwright and carpenter, Mary Lacy, who had
served on board ship, disguised as a man, in the Royal Navy in the
Seven Years' War and subsequently retired, with a navy pension,
to Deptford, where she married another shipwright, Josias Slade.
Quite exceptionally for a woman, she designed, constructed and
decorated ten substantial three-storey brick-built houses on land
formerly belonging to the Church with a 200-foot frontage on
Butt Lane. Mary and Josias took for themselves the largest of the
houses, which had a thirty-foot double front, a central pathway
lined with trees and a double-storeyed bay at the rear overlooking
a 250-yard-long garden that opened out into a 120-foot square.
When Mary died in 1801, Gilbert Ferguson moved in – and when

Gilbert died aged seventy-nine in 1811, he left his fortune and the house to Charles.

Charles was a leading figure in shipbuilding. He had married Elizabeth Stevenson of St George's Middlesex at St Paul's Deptford in 1784 and a few months later their first and only child was born and christened Catherine Todd Ferguson. The house was not vast (although it was rated at £60 a year in rent). Nor was it a lively household, as Charles was already in his sixties and Catherine Todd Ferguson had married and left home in 1806. But Ferguson also owned the 'garden field' behind the house and a tenement in next-door Effingham Place, which ran parallel to Giffin Street. Since the upper floor in Slade's Place had just two bedrooms and there was no attic for servants to sleep in, it was convenient that unlike most domestic or 'menial' servants (who by definition lived within the home or *moenia*), James and Elizabeth could live round the corner in the Ferguson tenement as a married couple.

James would have been the only male servant in the Ferguson household. His duties included carrying coals up to rooms, cleaning boots, trimming and cleaning lamps, caring for the silverware and glasses, preparing his master's clothes, laying the table for meals, serving at table, answering the front door, announcing visitors' names and locking up at night. Plenty of advice was available, from other servants and from manuals. A footman should 'keep himself clean and well dressed', but not spend so much time on his appearance that he forgot his duties. He should steer clear of either a 'slovenly habit, or a foppish and extravagant one'. He would need a watch. He should always address his master as 'sir' and should only ever speak when spoken to. He should never sit down in front of his master or mistress and avoid talking loudly, 'singing, bawling and whistling'. He should memorise the numbering of the major streets of London so as to save time on a visit and master the order of precedence for a seating plan so that he didn't seat an army officer ahead of a naval officer. The first requisite, though, was 'early rising', which would allow the dutiful footman to complete the dirtiest part of his work without interruption. That meant rising before the sun.[6] After all, wrote one solicitous father, 'consider what you was [sic] sent into this world for. It was not to sleep away your time in a lazy, indolent manner; not to become pests of society, but to improve your rational faculties in the stations in which Providence has placed you.'[7] If he were admonished for a supposed fault, he should 'take it patiently and never reply in passion', even if he had done nothing wrong. One dutiful servant took this especially to heart, telling his father back in the country, 'my master is very good-natured: if I do wrong, he tells me of it without anger; and I shall deserve to be reminded if I do it again, after such warning.' Yet he admitted, 'I have a great deal of time upon my hands, but I shall be careful not to misapply it. I am making myself perfect in writing.'[8]

Despite their free lodging, setting up home in Effingham Place cannot have been easy for James and Elizabeth. Their room would have come with something on which to sit and sleep, and at which to cook and eat. There might be curtains at the window and blankets on the bed, but they would provide their own sheets. Reports suggested that families rarely washed them. The brick-built terraced houses or 'tenements' were virtually identical – three storeys with six unadorned rooms. The sanitation in these rented properties varied between rudimentary and non-existent. The Kent Water Works supplied water from the River Ravensbourne to the surrounding parishes 'by a powerful steam engine'[9] but many landlords refused to provide plumbing, for fear that the lead pipes 'would be there in the evening and gone in the morning',[10] and the only water supply consisted of a water butt in the courtyard at the back, which would often have a filthy film on the surface. Families would carry water back to their rooms to cook and drink – but there too it would soon be covered with black scum. There were no drains to speak of, either. As one physician complained in 1844, dirty household water flowed in a similar area in nearby Rotherhithe 'through gully-holes into the kennels in the street, where it frequently remains stationary, producing in warm weather the most offensive exhalations'.[11] As late as 1855 the medical officer complained that several Deptford streets had not a single gutter for refuse water, 'the whole of which is thrown over the streets, and there allowed to evaporate'. Nearby Creek Street was twelve inches deep in mud and filth and consisted of an open ditch, 'the receptacle of the privies and drains'. Inevitably, he concluded, 'the inhabitants themselves are of the most dirty and filthy character, pale-looking and constantly inhaling the effluvia of their own filth'.[12]

Deptford was rough, too. The numerous bands of footpads who 'infested the town and neighbourhood'[13] had led to the formation of a separate bench of local magistrates in 1813. The taverns down by the docks often saw violent fights, the Red Cow still held one of Deptford's cockpits and according to the *Standard*, 'the most severe dog fights very frequently took place in Deptford at what was called the Deptford dog-pit, where vagabonds, well dressed and ill dressed, crowded to see and bet upon the sports'.[14]

Pigot's Directory in 1823 also reckoned that since the withdrawal of new naval shipbuilding Deptford had 'sunk from prosperity to a state of poverty and distress'.[15] Row upon row of houses lay untenanted, and many others were let at a very reduced rental, 'to prevent them getting into a state of complete dilapidation'.[16] There was an air of decay and abandonment, especially down near the river. This posed a challenge for the St Paul's overseers of the poor. The parish rates book is full of properties listed as 'empty' or 'poor', but empty properties meant fewer people paying rates and more 'poor' meant fewer people to charge and more people requiring assistance. When this was considered at a vestry meeting in 1824, a committee reported that 'those whose property consisted mainly in personal and mental labour, sensible of its precariousness, appeared foremost in their anxiety to succour those amongst whom the fickleness of fortune might one day possibly place themselves'.[17]

The shipwrights were consequently in a rebellious mood. Competition between the shipyard owners had driven down wages and at the end of 1822 not a single ship was being built on the Thames. Other industries around the country had started disputes over pay and conditions, including carvers and gilders, rope makers, tin-plate workers, carpenters, cabinet makers and ladies' shoemakers[18] – and the shipwrights joined their calls for the repeal of the Combination Acts of 1799 and 1800, which banned strike action and collective bargaining. Parliament agreed the repeal without a vote or a word of debate in June 1824, and within weeks the shipwrights launched the Thames Shipwrights' Provident Union with John Gast as their secretary. Gast was an engaging, passionate man. Originally from Bristol, he had moved to Deptford, where he practised as a dissenting preacher. He was briefly and unsuccessfully the landlord of the King of Prussia in Union Street, and for twenty-eight years he worked as a 'leading hand' shipwright in charge of a team of sixteen at Deadman's yard, building 'not less than twenty or thirty sail of men-of-war' and countless merchant ships.[19] The campaign gathered momentum throughout 1824. Nearly three-quarters of all London's shipwrights soon joined the union. Most worked in the merchant shipyards, but a few of the royal dockyards' men joined, too, including James's brother John, who was one of 212 shipwrights to sign a petition to the Navy Board in December 1824 complaining about the recent 20 per cent cut in salaries which meant they were no longer 'able to support their wives and families, many of them being numerous, with decency and credit'.[20] They also suspected the royal dockyards had deliberately discharged men and taken on apprentices with a view to 'break up the Union'.[21] One speaker, Mr Phillips, launched into a long angry metaphor. 'The masters', he said, 'had all turned husbandmen, and had planted a tree, the root of which was oppression; they had grafted it with deceit, injustice, heavy work and at the very top, they had grafted the means of discord among them.'[22] The Thames shipwrights went on strike for the first seven months of 1825, but this 'mischievous spirit of combination' so infuriated William Huskisson MP, the Tory president of the Board of Trade and treasurer of the navy, that he issued a thinly veiled threat that if such excesses continued, the House would be compelled 'to resort again to the former laws'.[23] When the shipwrights refused to back down, the government followed through on the threat. A new Combination of Workmen Bill was on the statute books in July 1825. Collective bargaining was again illegal.

In the midst of this industrial ferment (in which James's brother and master, who voted Tory, took opposing sides), James and Elizabeth started a family. James's sister-in-law Margaret had been constantly in labour throughout the last decade. By the time James and Elizabeth married Margaret had given birth to two boys and three girls and was heavily pregnant again. And at the end of August 1824, Elizabeth Pratt also fell pregnant.

Giving birth was a dangerous business in London. A poor diet, short on fruit, left many women with rickets and pelvic deformities. Roughly one in 200 English pregnancies ended with the death of the mother, but some London parishes saw the numbers rise to between two and eight in a hundred deliveries. Even the royal family knew this. George IV's only daughter Charlotte had died six hours after the stillbirth of her first child in 1817 at the age of twenty-one. George was without an heir, the succession passed to his younger brother and Charlotte's obstetrician took his own life. Things were even more problematic in Giffin Street and Effingham Place. Hot water and clean towels were the preserve of a very few, and disinfectant was yet to be discovered. Puerperal fever was endemic.

The quadrant of streets incorporating Giffin Street, Effingham Place and Cross Street (which connected the two) was also severely overcrowded, with 1,023 souls living in the 128 properties in the three streets, 117 of them infants under the age of four. Few houses were occupied by a single family. Most listed eight or nine names, often from several families, each occupying a single room in which they cooked, ate, drank, washed and slept. One house was home to five Callaghans, seven Roaches, three Newingtons, three Roberts and William and Jessie Say, twenty names in all. Dozens of residents of the three streets were listed as 'labourer', 'I.S.' for 'In Service' or just 'Poor', although a few trades were represented. The two neighbours Daniel Richardson and James Shaw were in business together as fishmongers, William Roberts at no. 14 Giffin Street was a retired shipwright, there were two bricklayers, a blacksmith, a butcher, two caulkers, a bookbinder, a tailor, a shoemaker, a carpenter and a cordwainer. A few of the women worked as well. Elizabeth Doddridge was a nurse,

Mary Hansford sold barley, Elizabeth Morgan took in laundry, Elizabeth Guthrie was a charwoman (at the age of seventy-two) and Elizabeth Bason did needlework. Perhaps the most impressive figure of all was Mary Minikin at no. 17, a widowed coal dealer. One local physician claimed that overcrowding led to people being 'emaciated, pale and thin' and complaining of 'sinking, depression of the strength, of spirits, loss of appetite, accompanied by pains in different parts of the body, with disturbed sleep'.[24]

All of which meant it was difficult to lead a healthy life if you were poor in Deptford. A major outbreak of typhus at the St Paul's workhouse in 1817 killed several inmates and only ended when the workhouse was quarantined for several weeks. As one philanthropist put it, 'Afflicted with disease, perhaps borne down with the weight of a numerous family, how are the honest poor to retrieve themselves? Toil they cannot without health, and that wanting, where may they find the means to regain it?'[25] The danger was that people resorted to quack remedies 'or the predacious ravage of daring Empirics'. So, in 1783 the Kent Dispensary was set up in a house on the Broadway. Its aim was to provide free healthcare to the poor in Deptford, Greenwich, Lewisham and Lee. It would have a resident apothecary – furnished with £60 per annum, 'proper apartments, coals, and candles'[26] – surgeons and medical assistants, all free and paid for by subscriptions from wealthier residents. The intention was simple: 'to give assistance not only to the lowest class of the people, but to poor housekeepers, and others whose income will not enable them to pay for it'.[27]

The Kent Dispensary was a godsend when it came to Elizabeth's lying-in or 'accouchement' in April 1825, as she was able to call on the services of the dispensary's surgeon, Robert Hatfull, for free. Midwives had traditionally been women and male medical practitioners were only called in when the labour was endangered, but the trend since the middle of the eighteenth century had been towards man-midwives, physicians who incorporated the delivery of both straightforward and complex births into their normal medical practice. By the time the Kent Dispensary was founded such man-midwives had almost swept aside their female counterparts, claiming that they brought a rational, anatomical and medical approach to childbirth and demonstrating new techniques such as the use of forceps (although chloroform would not come until 1847 and antiseptic not until 1870). In fact, their presence often brought greater danger to the expectant mother, as they carried disease from one patient to another, often without even washing their hands between visits. Alexander Gordon, a Scottish naval surgeon and accoucheur, had an epiphany following an epidemic of puerperal fever in Aberdeen and wrote in 1795: 'It is a disagreeable declaration for me to mention, that I myself was the means of carrying infection to a great number of women.'[28] But his was a lone voice.

Yet Elizabeth was delivered of a healthy baby girl at home in Effingham Place on 25 April 1825 and after four weeks of lying-in she was churched before she and James brought their newborn baby to St Paul's for baptism. It was a fine church, which had been commissioned under the New Churches in London and Westminster Act 1710 in an attempt to keep a growing population of skilled tradesfolk within the fold of the Church of England. Built in Portland stone by the gentleman architect Thomas Archer just over a hundred years earlier, it was the most elegant in the area – 'a beautiful and commodious structure' was how one gazetteer described its external Tuscan columns, its internal white Corinthian pillars, its plasterwork, its parquet flooring and its clear windows.[29] It had recently gained an enamelled east window depicting St Paul by the artist William Collins[30] and in the twentieth century Nikolaus Pevsner proclaimed himself an ardent admirer, describing St Paul's as 'one of the most moving eighteenth century churches in London: large sombre and virile'.[31] However, it may have been intimidating for James and Elizabeth, who would not have been allowed to sit wherever they chose, as the Dutch oak box pews were numbered, paid for and reserved. The bombe-shaped pulpit was a triple-decker, so sermons could be delivered with added conviction from on high. St Paul's was the physical embodiment of the established order, yet the Church of England did not have a complete stranglehold on Deptford. Some shipwrights took their political dissent to a theological conclusion in one of the Methodist, Baptist or independent dissenting congregations. John and Margaret Pratt, for instance, took their first son Joseph for a non-conformist baptism in the Butt Lane Independent Chapel. But they dutifully brought the rest of their children to the marble font at St Paul's, as did James and Elizabeth on Wednesday 22 May 1825, when their newborn was christened Elizabeth after her mother. Two years later Robert Hatfull was in attendance again and Elizabeth gave thanks for the safe deliverance, on 21 July 1827, of a baby boy, who was baptised William Samuel at St Paul's on Saturday 12 August 1827.

In work, solvent, and with a wife and two children, James Pratt was the epitome of the respectable industrious working class.

Deptford owed its living to its docks, but it was struggling when James came to live here in 1823. Many houses were left untenanted and the prison hulks lowered over the town.

4

Margeries and Poofs

As far as his friends and neighbours were concerned, James Pratt was happily married, but from his youth he knew that he was sexually attracted to men. His move to London must have seemed a godsend, as the metropolis offered sexual opportunity in abundance. It teemed with available men. Tens of thousands of army veterans had been discharged at the end of the Napoleonic wars and many of them had fought in lands where homosexuality was not so harshly condemned as in England. The Royal Navy had also discharged thousands of seamen after years cooped up in the sole company of other men. Rural poverty and the enclosure of swathes of common grazing land had forced many men to abandon the villages of England in search of work in the city. There were bored and impecunious infantrymen and guardsmen living in single-sex barracks; gentlemen and aristocrats, who had been taught at Eton, Harrow or Winchester; draymen and colliers, muscled from carrying heavy beer casks or hauling coals; 'out of place' labourers and servants with time on their hands; young country lads far from their families; errand boys, porters, waiters and deliverymen. It was not just agricultural poverty that had led to this mass migration. Life in Bilston, Worcester or Great Burstead must have been stifling for men like James, John and William. Everyone lived cheek by jowl and knew each other's business. But London was so large and its population was so constantly expanding that it cast a generous cloak of anonymity over its huddled migrant masses.

The best way to take advantage of that anonymity was to hang out in one of the many spaces where the public gathered in large numbers and where you could loiter without suspicion. Some called this cruising 'caterwauling', when men went out 'in the night in search of intrigues, like a cat in the gutters'.[1] But most gay men preferred to call it 'picking up trade', 'making a bargain' or 'biting a blow'. It only took a glance that lingered slightly too long to spot a potential pick up. If you fancied him, you could follow him until his interest was piqued or the trail ran cold. If you both paused on a street corner or in front of a shop window, you might catch each other's eye and strike up a conversation. Perhaps you might ask the time, or seek directions. Or, as one writer, who loathed 'pooffs', put it, 'when they see what they imagine to be a chance, they place their fingers in a peculiar manner underneath the tails of their coats, and wag them about – their method of giving the office'.[2] If that worked, you might go to a friendly tavern, or find a niche or a recess where you could feel each other's 'yards'. One successful liaison might embolden you to try the same place again and soon you could spot likely partners in the constant flow of humanity.

This was Thomas Rix's experience. He was a forty-seven-year-old chair-upholsterer when he was arrested with others in a raid on a house near Warrington in 1806, but he admitted to the chaplain at Lancaster Gaol that his favourite pick-up place when he first moved from Salford to Manchester was the old Exchange building in the centre of the city, which had been built in 1729 to house the cotton exchange, but had 'long afforded a lounging place for idleness and petty criminals, and a nest for diseases'.[3] Rix detailed how things worked. Men would stand in a corner at night as if they were 'making water' and if another man stood close enough and 'put their hands behind them', they would 'put their yards into their hands'. He claimed that similar encounters occurred on a nightly basis in Rope Walk and Dale Street in Liverpool.[4]

London also had a Royal Exchange, 'where fashionable ladies went to shop, and sometimes to meet their lovers'.[5] Ned Ward claimed he had been jostled there in 1699 'in amongst a Parcel of swarthy Buggerantoes, preternatural Fornicators, as my Friend call'd them, who would ogle a handsome young Man with as much Lust, as a true-bred English Whore-master would gaze upon a beautiful Virgin'.[6] One popular song that did the rounds in the eighteenth century included the verse:

When Sodomites were so impudent
To ply on the Exchange;
And by Day-light the Piazzas
Of Covent Garden to Range.[7]

The 'piazzas' or porticoes and empty niches provided recesses where men might sidle up to one another after dark. As the *London Journal* put it, this was one of the 'markets' where sodomites 'make their execrable bargains, and then withdraw into some dark corners to perpetrate their odious wickedness'.[8] The surrounding area was also a popular cruising site. In 1772 the *London Evening Post* claimed that 'the set of detestable villains who nightly infest the piazzas' had moved westward to engage in their 'diabolical practices'. The paper was scandalised that 'their amours are carried on in the open street; but to prevent any surprise, a watchman, or more, is placed at the avenues'.[9] Nearby Pope's Head Alley was another favourite meeting place; 'breeches-clad bawds' gathered in the adjoining Sweeting's Alley; Wolfe Lyon and John Barlowe were spotted having sex in nearby Lombard Street and Lyon was captured in St Paul's Churchyard.

It was the same in Covent Garden, where, according to police constable Joseph Sadler Thomas, his colleagues were daily 'thronged with every description of nuisances', especially from 'a number of the worst characters, which scarcely deserve the name of men', whom he had every reason to believe 'were of the most infamous description'.[10] William Beckford, one of the wealthiest men in England, who spent several years in continental exile to escape prosecution, enjoyed cruising the nearby area round Seven Dials, which he called the 'Holy Land' where he loved to 'kiss the relics'. One anonymous 'advocate for police reform' wrote to Sir Robert Peel in 1829 to complain about a 'notorious evil' afflicting

Drury Lane and Covent Garden, namely that 'swarms of lads
who carry on the infamous portion of <u>Catamites,</u> infest the streets
at night'.[11] The *Yokel's Preceptor* claimed that there had been an
increase 'of these monsters in the shape of men, commonly called
Margeries, Pooffs, &c., in recent years' and that the Quadrant,
Fleet Street, Holborn and the Strand were 'thronged with them'.
The author was writing (anonymously) in 1855, but it was also true
in the 1820s, and he complained that gay men were so numerous
in the vicinity of Charing Cross that publicans had posted bills in
their windows saying 'Beware of Sods'.[12]

London's parks and open spaces offered similar opportunities.
Writing in 1781, the soldier, itinerant actor and writer George
Parker deplored men 'who signal to each other in St James's Park,
and then retire to satisfy a passion too horrible for description',[13]
and in 1810 John Brady admitted that he liked to walk up and
down Birdcage Walk in St James's Park reading a novel to cover
his amorous intentions. The Ordinary of Newgate also claimed
that because Drummer Rowley Hanson was 'young, and a youth
of a comely aspect', he was daily taken notice of by 'one or
other of those vile miscreants, called Sodomites' as he walked in
St James's. They would apparently take him 'into bye walks, or
sometimes to taverns, or alehouses proper for the purpose; 'till
at length he became as common as the night'.[14] Likewise, Hyde
Park was said to be a place of 'nocturnal rendezvous for *male
prostitutes*, who were commonly private soldiers';[15] Orange Street
behind the newly completed National Gallery was meant to be a
safe trysting place; Thomas Brewer 'took liberties' with a young
man in Kensington Gardens in 1826; and Ambrose Crofton was
apprehended in the fields in Somers-town in 'an unequivocal
situation' with William Clarke, a private in the 1st Grenadier
Guards, in 1823. Crofton's defence – 'The soldier was inebriated,
and I, like a good Christian, was kneeling by his side to administer
comfort' – did not impress the magistrates, who sent the two men
to Clerkenwell prison 'guarded by a strong escort of officers to
protect them from the multitude'.[16]

Public toilets, 'bog-houses' or 'offices of convenience' also
provided a place for men to meet. When Charles Gibson took a

shine to a nineteen-year-old in the Red Lion in Moorfields, they went out the back together to make water and after they had admired each other's yards, they went to the bog-house, where they had sex. Likewise, for Samuel Taylor and John Berry the bog-house on the Strand was their final resort after a desperate search 'from one part of the Town to another, to find a convenient Place'.[17]

Thanks to the twin innovations of bow-fronted glass shopfront windows and boxwood prints, print-shop windows were a favourite place to loiter, as it was easy to hang around in the crowd examining the latest prints and caricatures without anyone noticing. As one commentator put it, 'pooffs ... generally congregate around the picture shops and are to be known by their effeminate air, their fashionable dress &c.'.[18]

Many taverns, inns, coffee houses and public houses had also gained a reputation over the decades, including the Bell Tavern in Westminster, the Royal Oak in Pall-Mall, the Harlequin in Drury Lane, the Red Lion in Moorfields, the Talbot Inn and the Rummer Tavern. The White Lion, the Rose and Crown in St Martin's Lane and the Bull and the Barley Mow in the Strand were said to be good places to find a guardsman for hire. Although the term 'molly-house' rarely appeared in print in the nineteenth century, several of these taverns effectively acted as such, providing a safe place for gay men to gather, fondle, kiss, dance, have sex and entertain one another. The *London Journal* had claimed a hundred years earlier that there were at least twenty of these 'sodomitical Clubs'. A smaller number was listed by Robert Holloway in his scabrous book, *Phoenix of Sodom; or The Vere Street Coterie* in 1813. He meant to attack those who attended four male brothels in the Strand, in Blackman Street in the Borough, near the obelisk at St George's Circus and in Bishopsgate, calling them 'these reptiles' and 'this lump of excremental filth', but his account is more intriguing than frightening. One was run by the Countess of Camomile, and the list of characters included Kitty Cambric, a coal merchant; Miss Selina, a runner at a police office; Black-eyed Leonora, a drummer; Pretty Harriet, a butcher; Lady Godina, a waiter; the Duchess of Gloucester, a gentleman's servant; the Duchess of Devonshire, a blacksmith; and Miss Sweet Lips, a country grocer.[19]

THE

Trials and Behaviour

OF

GEORGE CROPPER, and WILLIAM ALLEN,

WHO WERE

EXECUTED

This Morning, December 26, 1833,

In Front of the New Sessions House, Maidstone, Kent.

IT is happily now an event of very rare occurrence, that three culprits should be ordered for execution at one time ; but no person will be surprised, if they peruse the Kent Goal Calendar of the last assizes, and they will be convinced of the necessity of making such a public and melancholy example—the perusal of the various heinous and dreadful crimes there enumerated, makes the heart sicken at the depravity of human nature. If females are not to be protected from the unbridled passions of man, the sooner society is broken up, the better. Where is Woman to look for succour and protection, if she find it not in Man? whose bounden duty it is to cherish and to guard her from every ill, and not by taking advantage of her unprotected state, worse than murder her, merely to gratify his devilish and damnable lust !

The crimes of which the above wretched men were found guilty, being of such a disgusting and frightful nature, we are precluded from entering into the details of their respective trials, being unwilling to insert anything that should not meet the public eye. It must therefore suffice to say, that the following are the names and the crimes of those who were ordered for execution.

George Cropper,

A soldier, aged 27, was charged, together with Charles Pike, another soldier, aged 18, with having feloniously committed an abominable offence at Deptford, and found guilty. Pike was acquitted.

William Allen,

Labourer, aged 25, was found guilty of having committed a rape upon Ruth Roffe Austen, wife of Jeremiah Austen, at Lydd.

Thomas Turner,

Labourer, aged 18, was found guilty of a capital assault on the body of Emma Carrot, a girl of 11 years of age.

It appeared, that the child had been desired by her mother, on the 13th of November last, to go in the fields to gather acorns, and she accordingly proceeded to a place called Laurence's Field, near Tunbridge, and not finding many, began to pick up wood : the prisoner, who was working in a different part of the field, then came up, and said, " there is a nice bough in the wood," and endeavoured to entice her into it, but she would not go. Prisoner proceeded into the wood, and brought the bough, he then caught hold of her by the head and heels, and threw her down (she then detailed the circumstances of the assault) when he got up, prisoner told her, if she acquainted her mother, she would be beaten, and he, the prisoner, would beat her too. When she got home, she was unable to speak for half an hour, through fear and agitation, but afterwards told her mother about it, upon which the mother went for a doctor, who, when called proved the completion of the capital part of the charge.

At the conclusion of the assizes, Mr. Justice Gaselee, in the most impressive but firm manner, pronounced the awful sentence of the law. Allen was in a most pitiable state of grief. He was obliged to be supported by two persons, and uttered the most heart-rending cries for mercy. While the learned Judge was passing sentence, one gentleman fell down in a fit, and was carried out, struggling violently, and every one present was considerably affected.

William Allen while under sentence of death, and awaiting his awful doom, suffered under a severe hysterical affection, which, it was thought could not allow him to live out the time allotted him.

A Respite during His Majesty's pleasure, arrived at the Goal on Sunday morning last, for THOMAS TURNER.

Cropper was executed at 10 o'clock in the morning : he acknowledged his guilt, and seemed penitent. Allen not before 1 o'clock: he seemed a very powerful man, and left a family of two children and a wife in confinement. There were from 6 to 7000 persons present to witness the sad scene, the majority of them being women.

COPY OF VERSES.

OUR thoughts on awful subjects roll,
  Damnation and the dead ;
What horrors seize the guilty soul,
  Upon a dying bed !
Ling'ring about these mortal shores,
  She makes a long delay,
Till, like a flood, with rapid force,
  Death sweeps the wretch away.
Then swift and dreadful he descends,
  Down to the fiery coast,
Among abominable fiends,
  Himself a frightful ghost.
There endless crowds of sinners lie,
  And darkness makes their chains ;
Tortur'd with keen despair they cry,
  Yet wait for fiercer pains.

Men were regularly hanged for the 'nameless offence' of buggery and publishers rushed to sell broadsides with the details, as here following the execution of George Cropper (27) who was hanged for sodomy in Maidstone on Boxing Day 1833.

The trouble was, this was fiercely forbidden fruit. England's abhorrence of homosexuality was remarkable and at its peak. It shocked visitors like the Prussian Professor Johann von Archenholz almost as much as it does us today. He wrote after a visit in the 1780s that the English 'hold a *certain unnatural crime* [his italics] in the utmost abhorrence. They speak in no part of the world with so much horror of this infamous passion, as in England.' When someone stood accused of it, he noted, 'the fury of the populace is unbounded, and even the better sort of people have no compassion for the culprit'.[20] So acute had this revulsion become that although Englishmen had normally greeted one another with a kiss in the seventeenth century, another foreign visitor, Johann Bornemann, noted that everything had changed by 1819, when 'the kiss of friendship between men is strictly avoided as inclining towards the sin regarded in England as more abominable than any other'.[21] Henceforth Englishmen merely shook hands and left kissing to women. We still haven't got over it.

That sense of irrational antipathy permeated everything. As we saw in the introduction, every part of society cast a pall of unknowing over any reference to homosexuality. The press focused on the execution of an offender rather than the nature of the offence, which was simply described as 'unnatural' or 'unmentionable'. Some newspapers, including *Bell's Weekly Messenger* and William Cobbett's *Weekly Register*, refused to report arrests or convictions and accused newspapers that did so of promoting immorality. The *Morning Chronicle* claimed in 1825 that it was 'always with the greatest reluctance that we break silence with regard to those unnatural offences and disgusting practices which now, unfortunately, engross so much of the public attention'.[22] Those that reported criminal proceedings larded their reports with abhorrence. Homosexual acts of any kind were 'wicked', 'diabolical', 'disgusting', 'detestable', 'horrible', 'abominable' and 'against the order of nature'. Offenders were 'beasts', 'nasty fellows' and 'shockingly depraved'. Respectable dictionaries and lexicons omitted any definition of sodomy, buggery, catamite or pederast and classical historians purged all references to male couples. Patroclus became a platonic admirer of Achilles, the ancient Theban band of 150 same-sex warrior couples gained lady friends and Rome's historian Edward Gibbon decried the 'odious vice, of which modesty rejects the name, and nature abominates the idea'.[23]

The church fulminated. The views of the anonymous Church of England clergyman who authored *The Sodomite's Shame and Doom* in 1702 were still standard: sodomites were 'as stables of unclean beasts, defiled, deformed, destroyed by the most execrable abominations', and their minds were 'polluted by the filthiest imaginations'.[24] William Wilberforce worried that the multiplication of great cities and frequenting of 'a splendid and luxurious metropolis powerfully tend to accelerate the discontinuance of the religious habits of a purer age, and to accomplish the substitution of a more relaxed morality'.[25] Inspired by ferocious antipathy, self-appointed moral guardians demanded action from the authorities and brought their own prosecutions. Hence a string of trials at the Guildhall and the Old Bailey in 1798 initiated by gentlemen living in and around Finsbury Square near Moorgate. The Society for the Suppression of Vice, which promoted George III's *Proclamation for the Discouragement of Vice*, was as interested in blasphemy and observance of the Lord's Day as it was in obscene publications and 'disorderly houses', but they trawled the city for miscreants and prided themselves on the prosecutions they brought.[26] Some, who feared a new plague of sodomites, blamed it all on the 'unnecessary war' with France, which had seen British troops sent 'to associate with foreigners'.[27] Another writer bemoaned the absence of 'some mode of restraining this vice, either by castration, or some other cogent preventative, without waiting for the completion of the offence, which enacts the penalty of death'.[28]

This peculiar and illogical British obsession led Parliament constantly to tighten the ratchet. The Vagrancy Act of 1824 termed men who loitered or begged 'rogues and vagabonds' and repeat offenders 'incorrigible'. When Sir Robert Peel introduced his Offences Against the Person Bill in 1828, he said that in his six years as home secretary he had found that 'public justice was often thwarted by [the] unnecessary difficulty'[29] of proving in sodomy cases that there had been ejaculation as well as penetration. According to *Hansard* there was then 'a long and desultory conversation', but the *Morning Post* reported that when Peel suggested that he had already gone into sufficient detail, Members shouted 'hear, hear'.[30] So, with remarkably little ado, it became law that it would no longer be necessary in buggery or rape cases 'to prove the actual emission of seed in order to constitute a carnal knowledge, but that the carnal knowledge shall be deemed complete, upon proof of penetration only'.[31] From then on, as the eminent lawyer Sir William Oldnall Russell explained, 'the crime is complete on proof of penetration, and even if emission be expressly negatived'.[32] Even if sodomy with or without emission had not taken place, or could not be proved, Parliament ensured men could be convicted of a misdemeanour such as an assault with 'sodomitical intent'. During James and John's time in London, prosecutions were brought against men for 'meeting in a certain privy' for the purpose of committing 'divers filthy, wicked, nasty, lewd and beastly unnatural and sodomitical acts and practices';[33] laying hands on another man in the street and meeting in the street for the purposes of committing 'sodomitical acts and practices';[34] permitting another man to handle his 'private parts naked'; and 'unlawfully receiving the naked private parts of the person in his mouth'.[35]

Although veiled public declarations of moral outrage were commonplace, not everyone felt the same. One writer caustically denounced the Society for the Suppression of Vice for its 'imaginary evils' and its 'excess of goodness, whose zeal assumes a right to persecute and annoy those, who may not have attained to the same degree of perfection'.[36] Moreover, the recently discovered diary entry of a Yorkshire farmer called Matthew Tomlinson hints at what may have been a more common private view. Writing in January 1810, Tomlinson commented on the case of Nehemiah Taylor, a surgeon on the 26-gun HMS *Jamaica*, who had been court martialled and hanged on the yardarm for 'an abominable crime' in December. Several newspapers reported that Taylor had 'seen the act committed' in France and the Mediterranean where 'it was not considered a crime' and consequently claimed that 'he had a right to do with himself as he pleased'.[37] Tomlinson sympathised with Taylor's bold belief that his propensity was innate. 'It appears a paradox to me,' wrote Tomlinson, 'how men, who are men, shou'd possess such a passion; and more particularly so, if it is their nature from childhood (as I am informed it is) – If they feel such an inclination, and propensity, at that certain time of life when youth genders into manhood; it must then be considered as natural otherwise, as a defect in nature – and if natural, or a defect in nature; it seems cruel to punish that defect with death.' Above all, Tomlinson thought it 'strange indeed that God Almighty should make a being with such a nature, or such a defect in nature; and at the same time make a decree that if that being whom he had formed, should at any time follow the dictates of that Nature, with which he was formed, he should be punished with death'.[38] Tomlinson's enlightened thoughts were never intended for publication – and it is likely that he kept them to himself – yet he still thought homosexuality a crime that should be punished by castration, not hanging.[39]

The utilitarian philosopher Jeremy Bentham went further in a thesis he wrote in 1785. 'I have been tormenting myself for years,' he wrote, 'to find if possible a sufficient ground for treating [homosexual acts] with the severity with which they are treated at this time of day … but upon the principle of utility I can find none.'[40] He saw things rationally. Since homosexuality between willing participants caused pleasure, not pain, he could see no reason for punishing it at all, 'much less for punishing it with the degree of severity with which it has been commonly punished'.[41] He derided the view that if it were decriminalised men would abandon their wives. 'If … the case really were that if all men were left perfectly free to choose, as many men would make choice of their own sex as of the opposite one, I see not what reason there would be for applying the word natural to the one rather than to the other.'[42] Sadly, Bentham's views were so far ahead of his time that he never published them.

Likewise, despite Lord Byron's many affairs with men, his fragmentary poem 'Dives' gives a fleeting glimpse of what it felt like to be ostracised for 'deeds accurs'd', but it too was only published posthumously in France in 1833:

Unhappy Dives! in an evil hour
'Gainst Nature's voice seduced to deeds accurst! ...
How wondrous bright thy blooming morn arose!
But thou went smitten with th' unhallow'd thirst
Of crime un-named, and thy sad noon must close
In scorn, and solitude unsought, the worst of woes.[43]

James and John must have been sharply aware of this visceral public repugnance – and the concomitant legal peril. Memories of the treatment of the 'Vere Street Coterie' would still have been vivid, even though the events happened in July 1810. It had all started with 'representations' to the magistrates at the Bow Street police office concerning the Sunday night activities of 'a number of persons of a most detestable description' at the White Swan in Vere Street by Clare Market, which was run by James Cooke. Plainclothes police officers visited twice before officer Samuel Taunton sought a magistrates' warrant, raided the pub and arrested twenty-three men, most of them 'flashy dressed fellows … all hale robust fellows, the oldest not above 33'.[44] A large, angry crowd gathered for their appearance before the magistrates. Nine men, including Cooke, were remanded for trial, but those who were discharged 'were very roughly handled; several of them were hunted about the neighbourhood, and with great difficulty escaped with their lives'.[45] When the crowd refused to disperse, the remanded prisoners had to climb over a wall at the back of the court to be taken safely to prison. One of the released men was walking up Tavistock Street later that day when a complete stranger, Thomas Haylett, launched a ferocious attack on him. Another stranger intervened, but lost three teeth when Haylett presumed that he too had been at the Swan.[46]

The trial came in September when seven men were charged with conspiring together to commit a detestable offence. All were found guilty. One, with a previous conviction, was sentenced to three years in prison. Five received two-year sentences. These six were also to stand in the pillory in the Haymarket. A seventh received a single year's prison sentence. Yet again, as the defendants left court, the crowd 'assailed them with fists, sticks,

and stones' and the men had to run as fast as they could to the
Cold Bath Fields prison. The pillory came later in September,
when, as the *Star* put it, 'the disgust felt by all ranks in society
at the detestable conduct of these wretches occasioned many
thousands to become spectators of their punishment'.[47] Some
even sat on the rooftops. Once the men had been placed in the
stocks, fifty women 'vigorously expressed their abhorrence of the
miscreants, by a perpetual shower of mud, eggs, offal, and every
kind of filth with which they had plentifully supplied themselves
in baskets and buckets'.[48] This included dead cats, rotten eggs,
potatoes and buckets filled with blood, offal and dung. Eventually
the men were taken down and placed in a van to take them back to
Newgate, but still the missiles continued until 'the caravan was so
filled with mud and ordure as completely to cover them'.[49] Several
of the men were already bleeding profusely from being hit on the
head with brickbats, but as a final *coup de grâce*, a coachman took
aim from the top of his box as they passed by on the Strand and
gave Cooke, who was by this stage virtually senseless, five or six
cuts of his whip across the face.

The message was simple. Rage, hatred, violence and humiliation
were all a gay man could expect from the public. A reminder came
in 1825, when the autocratic and ambitious Bow Street magistrate,
Sir Richard Birnie, determined to crack down on homosexual
impropriety in the taverns around the Strand. He became
convinced in July of that year 'that there was strong reason to
believe that a gang of fellows were in the habit of meeting at the
Barley Mow public-house, in the Strand, for the purposes that
cannot be named in a public journal', so he ordered two police
officers to visit the upstairs club-room, under cover, eight times.
Constable George Thissleton found that there were regular 'free-
and-easy' meetings on a Sunday and Monday, when 'scenes of the
most horrible kind took place' and claimed that a man had touched
his knee and squeezed his thigh and that he had seen men taking
liberties with one another. Most of the men had dressed smartly,
but Thissleton was not impressed. 'Broken-down dandies' was
how he described them.[50] Birnie ordered that the Barley Mow be
raided. Several men tried to escape, but twenty-five were arrested.

Birnie was keen to deal with them before crowds gathered, but when he committed eight of them to trial, there were terrific 'hootings, hisses and groanings' and the crowd pelted the inmates 'with whatever missiles they could find'.[51] The seven-and-a-half-hour trial at the Middlesex Sessions in September saw all bar the landlord convicted and sentenced to twelve months in the House of Correction. The public fury was even more intense this time. The *Observer* reported: 'all the avenues leading to the Court were crowded by a mob of men, women and children vowing vengeance against the wretches inside; and, in the absence of their victims, they flung, with indiscriminate aim, amongst the crowd, all the dead cats, rotten eggs, and other implements of destruction, they had collected'.[52] In a curious twist, some of the female inhabitants of Whitechapel subsequently complained that a man had been hawking around 'an abominable picture, purporting to be a faithful representation of the recent disgusting transaction at the Barley Mow, and of the orgies of its diabolical frequenters'.[53] This too led to a three-month spell in the House of Correction for the pamphleteer for perverting morality.

Birnie was still not satisfied, as he also had his eye on the Rose and Crown in St Martin's Lane where a private in the 60th Rifle Corps claimed two men had made 'an infamous proposal to him', and subsequently offered to buy his secrecy when he confronted them. This 'disgusting case' was dismissed at Bow Street, 'there being no other evidence against them than the unsupported testimony of the soldier', but Birnie was not impressed by the landlord, Mr Brown, who denied that soldiers used to resort to the back parlour for nefarious purposes. Birnie said that he had heard 'very bad stories about your house', referred darkly to 'rumours that are now floating in my mind' and said he would ensure that the Rose and Crown was 'well watched'. He even admitted, 'I myself have paid it a visit before now, and perhaps I may do so again before long.'[54]

Whatever James and John felt about their attraction to men, however they dealt with feelings of shame and guilt and whatever tender hopes of love they entertained, they must always have lived in fear. If they misread the brush of a hand, a throwaway look or a wink, they could find themselves beaten to a pulp, ostracised or hauled up before a moralistic, self-righteous magistrate. A single misstep could lead to terrible recriminations.

This exaggerated national moral panic led to a preposterous double bind. Homosexuals were so terrified of exposure that blackmail was a constant threat but, as Mr Justice Ashurt ruled in a 1796 case, threatening to accuse a man of committing unnatural acts effectively constituted robbery because 'to most men the idea of losing their fame and reputation is equally, if not more terrific than the dread of personal injury'.[55] When Percy Jocelyn, the aristocratic bishop of Clogher, was caught having sex with a guardsman, John Moverley, in the back room of the White Lion in St Alban's Place in 1822 and Peel's colleague, the foreign secretary, Robert Stewart, Viscount Castlereagh, slit his throat after telling the king that he was being threatened with exposure for the same crime, the government took action. Three new laws laid down that any threat of accusing a man of committing a capital felony or 'infamous crime' was akin to the felony itself, including alleging an *attempt* to commit a felony.[56] Theoretically, the truth or otherwise of the threatened allegations was not a matter for the court and was impermissible evidence – but the danger was that the defendant would claim that the allegations were true. Many such prosecutions followed – especially where a servant had dared to accuse a gentleman of assault 'with sodomitical intent'. Yet again, the law was far from impartial. The wealthy and well-connected could defy the system. They might be scared witless, but they knew that they could front it out, that they could rely on the discretion of a jury of their peers to acquit them and denounce a servant or labourer who dared to accuse them. The hypocrisy was astounding, but then the criminal code was designed to reinforce the social order and the rights of the propertied classes, not disturb the equilibrium.

A SKETCH OF OUR WORTHY MAGISTRATE SIR RICHBIRNIE.

The Scotsman Sir Richard Birnie was a magistrate at Bow Street Police Office and was determined to crack down on homosexual impropriety in the taverns around the Strand.

5

Reform!

James's employer, Charles Augustin Ferguson, who was now in his seventies, started dismantling his business interests in 1829, leaving the mast-making business in Millwall to his cousin Charles Augustus and preparing his will. On 21 March 1830 he died, leaving most of his estate to his only surviving younger brother Robert. A year later Charles's widow Elizabeth also died, and a marble tablet was erected to the couple in the chancel at St Paul's, Deptford. It still bears Charles's coat of arms. But by the time it was carved, others were living in Slade's Place and James Pratt was 'out of place', little more than an afterthought for the Ferguson family. At first James and Elizabeth would have been able to get along. They would have saved a little while the tenement in Effingham Place came free; and at some point before 1830 the couple moved round the corner to Giffin Street, where they took a house and supplemented their income by letting out rooms.

Their immediate concern was finding work for James. Deptford was struggling again, as no new work had come to the docks. Things were so bad that a public meeting was held at the beginning of March 1830, at which people spoke about the 'very great hardships under which the inhabitants of this once flourishing place' were labouring. Hundreds of craftsmen had been retired on just £8 a year. Many had large families and had worked all their lives in the dockyards, but 'the establishment of this ancient and celebrated arsenal [was] nearly broken up' and Deptford was full of 'unemployed hands and empty houses'.[1] As the *Morning Advertiser* warned, things would only get worse for the parishes where 'the discharged shipwrights and labourers resided'.[2]

For many families, the only way to avoid starvation was to 'throw themselves on the parish', yet the one thing every family sought to avoid was claiming outdoor relief or entering the workhouse. London's workhouses had a terrible reputation. According to the journalist James Greenwood the flagstones in the workhouse in Lambeth were so encrusted with filth that he thought it was a 'floor of natural earth' and the men slept on shallow pallets with 'narrow bags scantily stuffed with hay'.[3] Several establishments ran a particularly harsh regime. Paupers were only allowed one day out a week, and often came back drunk. Those who misbehaved were thrown in the 'black-hole' for three or four hours. The overseers treated the poor with disdain. The vestry clerk at St Margaret's and St John's in Westminster despised his clients, a large majority of whom, so he claimed, were prostitutes. 'They walk the streets until they are reduced to great distress, and then apply to be taken into the house', he told the Royal Commission into the Poor Law in 1832.[4] According to the assistant overseer in Windsor, 'the wives of paupers are dirty, and nasty, and indolent; and the children generally neglected, and dirty, and vagrants, and immoral'.[5] Mr Brushfield of Spitalfields thought that the children of the poor were not only dirty and out of control and that the clothes of both children and parents were ragged – but thought the poor were to blame, as they lived 'improvident' lives, demanding nothing but the best and refusing even to patch their clothes.[6] Likewise, the assistant overseer in St George's, Southwark, thought it was 'utterly impossible to prevent considerable fraud' in providing out-relief and claimed that the majority of 'out-door paupers [were] worthless people'.[7]

It was the same in Deptford. The St Paul's workhouse lay opposite the end of Giffin Street and Effingham Place on the site of the old gravel pits in Workhouse Lane. Here 125 'paupers' were housed in rudimentary conditions, the men, women and children separated on entry. The local overseers of the poor were endlessly looking for more productive work for their charges. In 1831 they employed them building and repairing the highways, but they soon abandoned this idea and contracted Edward Pilbrow to 'farm the poor' for 3s 9d per head a week for three years. For a while the women were put to work making lace. When none of these schemes delivered results, the poor were left to pick ropes apart. The state of the St Paul's workhouse was revealed when the Poor Law Amendment Act transferred responsibility for it to Greenwich in 1834, as the new overseers found it in a 'truly deplorable' condition with a complete 'absence of good order, cleanliness and management'. Inmates were rarely bathed and kitchen waste was left heaped outside the door. They recommended that the place be closed immediately and the inmates 'be taken out as soon as possible'.[8] Later, James Pratt made a point of having always provided for his family and he and Elizabeth were proud of the fact that they had never relied on the parish. They must have come close, though.

'When sorrows come, they come not single spies, but in battalions,' says Claudius in *Hamlet*, and Deptford's experience in the 1830s proved the adage. With unemployment and poverty came disease. When 'cholera morbus' arrived in London from the Baltics in February 1832 Sir Robert Peel argued that St Paul's Deptford was 'rather a metropolitan than a county parish' and therefore ought to qualify for national funds to combat the disease.[9] When cholera hit Deptford that September, ninety people died in less than a week in a few houses at the north end of New Street and the adjoining French's Fields, not far from where James and Elizabeth Pratt lived. The government had required ships to quarantine in Deptford's Standgate Creek, but people pointed the finger at the local water supply from the Kent Water Works, which 'smelled like a cesspool and frothed like soap suds'.[10] Since there were no sewers in the area and refuse collected and saturated the land where the water pipes were laid, people believed that the water had been infected. The newly appointed local health commissioners sent notices to every house, which, 'after giving such miscellaneous advice as to the cleanliness of the houses, and as to cramps in the arms, legs, or belly ...' ended by stating that if any were 'attacked with looseness of the bowels, however slight', they were to obtain medical aid immediately either by application to the Kent Dispensary, or to the nearest of the following gentlemen: 'Mr Hatfull in Union Street, Mr Mitchell in High Street ... Mr Atkins in Union Street.'[11]

Elizabeth and James Pratt were only too aware of the dangers of disease. In the autumn of 1833, their son William Samuel fell ill and died, aged just six years and three months, and James and Elizabeth took him back to St Paul's to be buried on 3 November 1833. The distressed couple tried for another child, but when Dr Robert Mitchell attended Elizabeth in February 1835, she miscarried.[12]

The death of his employer had an inevitable impact on James, but a few weeks later came another death that affected the whole nation. At around three o'clock on the morning of 26 June 1830, George IV shat blood, clasped his stomach, leaned on his page's shoulder and shouted 'this is death'. At 3.15 his physician pronounced him dead. Two things followed in short order. First the privy council assembled to proclaim 'Vivat Rex' for George's younger and more affable brother William IV. And then, as the law dictated, there was a general election. When the new parliament gathered on 14 September, the duke of Wellington's Tories had fifty more seats in the Commons than the Whigs, but not enough to form a majority. Still rancorously split between hard-liners like Wellington and Peel and moderate Tories who had served in the short-lived coalition governments led by George Canning and Viscount Goderich, and still smarting over the Catholic Relief Act, which it had reluctantly carried in 1829, the duke's administration was in trouble – and that was before the 'Swing Riots'.

As James knew from Great Burstead, agricultural workers in England had been systematically ground into ever more abject poverty over the preceding decades. Millions of acres of grazing land on which the poor could freely graze a handful of sheep had been enclosed. Fewer and fewer families had enough land to sustain them. Corn prices fell after the Napoleonic wars, slashing rural incomes. Thousands of landless farmers found themselves out of work and migrated to the cities, like James and John.

Patience broke in 1830. The riots started with the destruction of dozens of horse-powered threshing machines in Kent in August, but unrest soon spread across the south-east of England and East Anglia. Anything that symbolised the intertwined hierarchy of Church and State became a target, especially the workhouses and the tithe barns. The campaign was well organised. Local magistrates, guardians and landowners received threatening letters pseudonymously signed by 'Captain Swing', demanding pay rises and the destruction of threshing machines. If these were ignored, hundreds of rioters gathered and attacked property. The duke of Wellington's arrogant and cack-handed response to the crisis meant parliamentary support rapidly ebbed away from the Tories. A motion of no confidence was tabled in the Commons on 30 November, which was carried. Wellington was out and the reform-minded sixty-six-year-old Opposition leader Earl Grey was in, partly thanks to the change at the Palace, as George IV had singled out Grey as the one man he could never appoint as a minister, but King William was more amenable. This change of government did not immediately bring the 'Swing Riots' to an end. They spread to Deptford in December, when it was reported that threatening letters had been sent to all the main factories in the area, stating that 700 men would march from Kent to Deptford to destroy machinery unless wages were improved. Nothing came of it, but the new government was put on notice.[13]

The driving principle behind Grey's government was reform. The list of government campaigns was lengthy. They planned to abolish slavery, slash the number of capital offences, ban employers from paying their staff with company tokens, end child labour in factories and chimneys, abolish rotten and pocket boroughs, extend the franchise in a sweeping reform of the House of Commons, reform or abolish the duties on a range of goods, amend the gaming laws, allow Quakers and Moravians to become MPs, introduce a new Poor Law and end hanging in chains. None of this was easy. The Tories fought every inch of the way but were in endless retreat. The row over the first Reform Bill delivered Earl Grey 370 Commons seats in a snap general election in 1831 and the Tories' refusal to accept the second Reform Bill delivered him

441 seats in another election in 1832. With such a Whig majority
in the Commons Grey could do virtually what he wanted. One
topic, however, was not on his or any of the reformers' list: the
laws on sodomy, buggery and homosexuality.

If anything, these laws were being applied with more vigour than
ever. The Tories were still in government when the newly created
Metropolitan Police ran a sustained campaign in the spring of 1830
to catch men cruising for sex in Hyde Park by sending out officers
of S Division in plain clothes to entrap men at night. The police had
some initial success. The newspapers were acerbic about the accused,
whom the *Morning Advertiser* called 'creatures' and 'miscreants'
charged with assaults of 'a revolting nature'. *The Times* rejoiced.
'Four more of the miscreants who infest Hyde-park at night were
brought up in custody from the watch house', it reported at the end
of March, detailing how James Byrne, a 'very respectable looking
young man', a clerk in the India House, had allegedly assaulted
police constable Michael Cannon and claimed in his defence that
he was 'rather tipsy'.[14] Over the next few weeks more than a dozen
other men were caught, including 'a genteel looking young man,
fashionably dressed in a blue frock coat', a 'servant out of place',
a 'stout-built, respectable-looking tradesman', and 'a middle-aged
man, dressed in livery'.[15] The men were terrified. Several gave false
names and addresses when they appeared before the magistrates.
Others claimed they had been drunk or pleaded for mercy.
However, the police campaign met with scepticism and hostility.
The Queen Square magistrates decided to let several of the 'Hyde-
Park Gang' off with a £5 fine, but others were sent for prosecution
at the Westminster Sessions. Lawyers repeatedly attacked the
police in court. When a 'respectably dressed' fifty-year-old man,
Richard Reeves Childs, was charged at the Westminster Sessions
with assaulting a police officer, who was 'dressed as a servant' and
had placed himself near a clump of trees close to the Serpentine and
coughed to get Childs' attention, Childs' lawyer rounded on the
police for 'being sent in disguise into the Park, to lure and entrap
persons into the commission of an offence at which humanity and
nature revolted'. It was, he claimed, 'an encroachment on the rights,
the liberties, and the immunities of the people of England'.[16] Yet

the jury found Childs guilty and he was sentenced to six months in prison. In another case the defence lawyer, Mr Charles Phillips, 'expressed the utmost indignation against the demoralizing system of policemen disguising themselves to ensnare crime'.[17] Another attorney said that 'such a mode of employing police-officers was most degrading, and was calculated to bring the present system into public odium'.[18] Apart from anything else, it seemed to fly in the face of Peel's comments when he set up the Metropolitan Police. 'God forbid,' he told the Commons, 'that he should mean to countenance a system of espionage.'[19]

The police campaign sent a chill through the hearts of gay men. The Hyde Park Gang campaign was not the only danger for the likes of James, John and William. Sir Richard Birnie was still in post when two soldiers, William Humphreys and Thomas Cheer, complained to the police about what they had seen in the Bull Inn off the Strand. When Humphreys returned to the Bull with undercover police, they saw men 'behaving with great impropriety' and when a sixty-year-old man called William Trimmer squeezed Humphreys by the hand 'and was proceeding to take other liberties' they gave the signal for uniformed officers to raid the pub. Two men ran upstairs and hid underneath beds, but were arrested. Others managed to escape. But six appeared in the dock the following day.[20] *The Times* noted that their appearance 'excited the greatest disgust, two of them having paint upon their cheeks, with their hair curled in drop ringlets, such as women wear'.[21] Barnard claimed this was all a plot got up because he had refused to stand Cheer a pint, but Birnie committed them for trial at the next assizes. The *Evening Mail* also noted that three of the prisoners were recognised as 'old offenders'.[22]

So it went on. In July a thirty-six-year-old labourer and father of three called John Stammers was charged with an 'unnatural crime' at the Essex Assizes in Chelmsford on the evidence of a witness called John Cook. Stammers claimed innocence but the judge, Sir William Garrow, a baron of the exchequer, came down heavily on Cook's side and, while pronouncing the death penalty, inaccurately told Stammers 'The law of this, and, I believe, of all other countries, punishes the crime of which you have been convicted with death, and I cannot see any reason that the sentence of that law should not in your case be carried into effect.'[23] They hanged Stammers on 13 August 1830. The following year a soldier called James Edwards was sentenced to two years with hard labour for committing sodomy on the Isle of Sheppey, and Joshua Gibson was sentenced to two years at the Wakefield House of Correction when he pleaded guilty. In 1832 William Wilson was accused of catching hold of a young linen-draper in St Paul's Churchyard East and trying to force him into an adjoining court to commit an 'unnatural offence'. The *Morning Post* was coy about precisely what happened. 'The particulars ... are totally unfit for publication,' it pronounced, condemning Wilson as 'a mean dirty-looking fellow'. Wilson's defence, that he was drunk and did not know what he was about, did not impress Alderman Anthony Brown, who bound him over for prosecution.[24] When Wilson appeared at the Sessions in September, it was revealed that he had given a fictitious name 'in order to avoid disgracing his friends, who are highly respectable' and Sir John Silvester, the lugubrious recorder of London, sentenced him to two years in prison.[25] Yet more serious was the case of John Howarth, who was accused of 'an unnatural crime' at the Lancaster Summer Assizes in 1833, when the lord chief justice, Sir Thomas Denman, pronounced the death sentence on him. The *Manchester Times* reported, 'The prisoner, who has a most forbidding countenance, manifested a slight degree of nervousness during the progress of the trial, which was increased to tears when his fate was announced to him.'[26] He was hanged alongside an attempted murderer on 31 August.

Two prominent trials in 1833 showed that justice was inexplicably partial when it came to social standing. The first was that of the wealthy MP for Guildford, Charles Baring Wall, who had large homes at 44 Berkeley Square and Norman Court in Hampshire, and was accused of trying to seduce a policeman called John Palmer in Harley Street in the early hours of 28 February 1833. Everyone sprang to Baring Wall's defence. Nineteen prominent figures stood character witness for him on 12 May, including the dean of Salisbury, the earl of Darnley, Viscount Morpeth and Lord Auckland – and the jury did not even let Sir Thomas Denman sum up, preferring to pronounce Wall not guilty without the benefit of the lord chief justice's wisdom. But none of Wall's friends can really have been surprised at his arrest. He liked a man in uniform. Speaking of the new uniformed police to his friend and confidant Ralph Sneyd, he said he wished he lived in a more disturbed area of town so that he might see more of them and admitted, 'I delight in every one'.[27] The novelist Emily Eden, who envied Wall's luxuries and riches, also admitted, 'if he is a little ridiculous, it is no business of ours. Heaven help Mrs Wall, if there ever should be one. But there never will.'[28]

One of Wall's friends got into similar trouble that year. William Bankes was one of the most famous explorers of the age and a very conservative Tory MP, but on 6 June 1833 he was caught in a toilet by Westminster Abbey with a soldier called James Flowers, whose braces 'were undone in the front'. Bankes had the same defence lawyer as Wall, Sir James Scarlett MP, the former Whig attorney-general who had recently defected to the Tories over the Reform Bill, which he opposed.[29] Bankes also recruited a phalanx of supporters, including the duke of Wellington, to whom he had been aide-de-camp, the earls of Liverpool and of Ripon, six other peers, a couple of clergy, a surgeon and several other friends and relatives. A soldier got a laugh when he gave evidence that Flowers 'was never suspected of anything of this kind; he was quite the reverse – the other way'; and a surgeon's report that he had treated Flowers for gonorrhoea seemed to suggest that he was more commonly in the company of 'disorderly women, as the generality of soldiers are'. The lord chief justice did sum up this time, but left the matter entirely to the judgment of the jury, who returned a verdict of not guilty after fifteen minutes. The press reported that 'the verdict was received with considerable applause, which was, however, instantly checked'.[30] It was clear that juries were unlikely to convict a man of a degrading crime if he had a high social standing, a good lawyer and respectable friends. Yet when the twenty-seven-year-old soldier George Cropper was accused of committing an unnatural crime with Charles Pike in Deptford, the jury swiftly convicted him on Boxing Day that same year and he was hanged at Maidstone on 16 January 1834. In a sign of the manifest hypocrisy of the age, the authorities were so worried that a crowd would demonstrate their moral repugnance that they altered the normal hour of execution. It was said that 'he walked to the gallows with a firm step, and was kept in view for a few minutes alive. On the drop falling he struggled very violently, but the executioner soon ended his mortal agony.'[31]

William Bonell's first-floor room was at 45 George Street, off Great Surrey Street in the parish of Christ Church on the Surrey side of the Thames.

These well-publicised events must have played on the minds of gay men, who would have gone to considerable lengths to protect themselves, especially if their personal circumstances did not afford them the luxury of privacy.

William Bonell was fortunate in this sense. By 1834 he was a widower with no dependants, and having carried on working into his sixties he had set enough aside to be able to rent a room of his own. So, in July he moved in to a first-floor room at 45 George Street in the parish of Christ Church on the Surrey side of the Thames. It was a half-and-half kind of parish. To the east lay the bishop of Winchester's autonomous fiefdom of the 'liberty of the clink' and the parish of St Saviour. To the west lay the Archbishop of Canterbury's manor and palace in the parish of Lambeth. Like its neighbours, Christ Church had been a place of industry, entertainment, adventure, prostitution, crime and incarceration for centuries. Much of the land lay below high-tide level and regularly flooded, so it offered cheap land for the noisome and foul-smelling industries that the capital needed. Foundries, smelting yards, glass workshops, vinegar distilleries, breweries, timber yards and tanneries belched out effluent and noise on the south bank of the river. The rules were more relaxed here, too. It was a place for pleasure gardens and bawdy houses. The well-heeled of Westminster and London preferred not to have to step through the muddy detritus of these industries, or to witness the depravities of those who lived and worked there. They preferred them tucked away, out of sight and beyond the reach of the most delicate nose – but close enough for easy access.

Fortunes changed for Christ Church when the new 'William Pitt Bridge' was built in 1769. Soon renamed after the old Blackfriars monastery which had stood on the north bank, the bridge and its impressive new approach road, Great Surrey Street, joined up with other new roads south of the river enabling carriages, mail-coaches, wagons and post-horses to speed along the major roads through the open fields that spanned out like spokes of a wheel to the rest of Surrey, Kent, Sussex, Hampshire and beyond. The district had architectural and social aspirations. Houses were knocked down to expose the fine Italianate church to better view.

The popular preacher the Reverend Rowland Hill and his brother Sir Richard built the Surrey Chapel (and reputedly made it round so that the devil would have no corner in which to hide) as a venue for concerts and religious services. An obelisk was placed at the new St George's Circus. The next few years also saw a rush of house building in the parish and by 1800 most of it was laid out with a grid of new streets, replete with plum-coloured brickwork, fanlights, moulded architraves and pediments, sash windows, wooden surround doors, wrought-iron balconies and railings. Even the street names aspired to royal approval – hence Charles, John, Edward, William, Brunswick and Great and Little Charlotte Streets and, two years after the battle of Trafalgar, Nelson Square.

George Street lay in the midst of this grid, having been started in 1776 and completed and tenanted by 1780. It was a street of respectable artisans: a hatter, a carpenter joiner, a tailor, a clerk, a leather draper, a couple of French polishers, three stonemasons, a laundress, a pastry chef, a bedstead manufacturer and a newsagent. There were two pubs, the George and the Crown, and there was a surgeon, William Deighton, at no. 33. The writer Mary Wollstonecraft had lived there between 1788 and 1791. Several residents were in the printing and book trade, including Edward Mullins at no. 50, who advertised that he made 'all sorts of Presses, Ploughs, Pressing-boards &c. for Stationers & Book-binders ... in the completest manner and on the most reasonable terms'.[32] George Jacob at no. 40 published the *Atlas*. Richard Cox, at the largest private house in the street, no. 57, was a sheriff's officer. George Street also had proper sewers – even if, as a sanitary report complained, 'the outfall of sewerage [was] into a tidal river passing through the heart of a densely populated metropolis'.[33]

George Street did not always live up to its pretensions. In March 1834 an inquest was held into the death of Mrs Dickenson, a baker's wife, who had thrown herself out of the second-floor window at no. 34 after trying to slit her husband's throat with a razor. The inquest was told she 'was addicted to drinking, and when in a state of intoxication she acted like a mad woman'.[34] In September Inspector Hagan of M division of the Metropolitan Police, was called to no. 55 where he found a seven-year-old girl,

Caroline Hanks, 'worn almost to a skeleton, her bones nearly protruding through the skin ... pale and emaciated'. When her father was brought before the local magistrates, a neighbour said she had seen the child 'in the yard, nearly naked, picking the potato peelings out of the dust-hole and eating them'.[35]

No. 45 George Street was a corner house, but like all the others in the street, it was three storeys high and had basement windows partly above ground level. It was one of the larger houses in the street, rated at £30 a year, and it was substantial enough for the owners, John and Jane Berkshire, to run a thriving business, selling and delivering coal from a shop on the ground floor, renting horses from the stables at the back, organising house removals and letting out at least three rooms.[36] William Bonell's first-floor room was not luxurious, but it was respectable. It was about ten feet square, with a fireplace in the corner. It had a turn-up bedstead, a table and a couple of chairs. It had its own door with a lock – and unlike many tenants, he possessed the key. He was no longer working, but at the age of sixty-four he had afforded himself a degree of privacy.

As for John Smith, he remains as hidden from view in the 1830s as he was at his birth. Apart from his two years working for Thomas Phillips, all we know is that by the summer of 1835 he was scratching a living as a labourer and sending money back to his elderly mother. The indictment at the Old Bailey described him as 'late of the parish of Christchurch, in the country of Surrey', but since the court used the same description for James Pratt, who lived in St Paul's Deptford, and since there is no other evidence for where John Smith lived, it seems unlikely that he enjoyed as comfortable or as private a lodging as William. Many men found occasional work and even more occasional lodging. It was a precarious life and even more so if you knew you were not as other men.

James Pratt, meanwhile, took what work he could find. For a while he too worked as a labourer on a daily rate. He also applied to his old employer, William Scott Preston, who recommended that his mother take him on. Nothing came of that, but at some point between 1830 and 1835, he secured another important position, as footman to the Reverend Dr Samuel Cole, the chaplain of the Royal Hospital at Greenwich. This was James's most prestigious appointment. Cole was extremely well connected. He was one of five Cornish brothers, all of whom had achieved fame in the service of their nation in the Royal Navy, the British Army or the Church of England.[37] He had joined the Royal Navy as a chaplain in 1790, and had seen plenty of action. He was on board Admiral Sir John Colpoys's flagship, HMS *London*, at Spithead in 1797 when Colpoys ordered marines to fire on mutinous sailors demanding better pay; and when the mutineers overpowered Colpoys and forced him to surrender, Cole was one of the officers whose life was spared, and he was put ashore. Later that year Cole was also chaplain on Vice Admiral Richard Onslow's flagship, the 74-gun third rate ship of the line, HMS *Monarch*, which played a decisive role in Admiral Duncan's famous victory over the Dutch at the battle of Camperdown. Cole's career brought him into direct contact with the duke of Clarence (before he became William IV), who appointed Samuel as one of his domestic chaplains and secured him the post of resident chaplain of the Royal Hospital at Greenwich in 1816. It was a lucrative appointment, bringing in £300 a year, plus £10 4s 6d in lieu of small stores and 10 chaudrons (360 bushels) of coal; and in 1820 William ensured Cole was made vicar of Sithney in Cornwall, which brought in an additional £19 11s 4½d. The chaplaincy was prestigious. The Royal Hospital for Retired Seamen occupied beautiful Baroque buildings in Greenwich designed by Sir Christopher Wren and his assistant Nicholas Hawksmoor. Its pensioners dined in a 40,000-square-foot hall with a beautiful allegorical painted ceiling. There were houses for the officers, wards for the sick and disabled, a school, an exercise yard and a beautiful chapel, which had been rebuilt after a fire in 1779. Residents were fed and cared for and had to attend divine worship daily in the chapel, where Cole preached from a high pulpit. Just to make the retired sailors feel at home, the altar was dominated by a large painting of St Paul's shipwreck in Malta.

James was part of a large establishment at the Hospital. It employed surgeons, assistant surgeons, physicians, dispensers, clerks, cashiers, a gardener on £160 a year, staff to cut up meat and prepare butter. Alexander Rance, the master shoemaker, was on £40 a year; Robert France, the porter to the infirmary, was on £30, even though he couldn't read or sign his own name, as was John Carey, a labourer in the store; while the boatswain Joseph Welsh, who could read and write, received £35 plus £20 for 'gymnastic instruction'. Even retired figures like Joseph Flavier, the former boatswain's mate, were on £5 a year.

The Hospital was eminently respectable, but James may have found his new master pragmatic when it came to personal morality, as Cole prided himself on being a mainstream Anglican. He had no truck with nonconformists, dissenters or Catholics and disliked the excessively enthusiastic moralistic tone adopted by fervent Evangelicals. He prevented Evangelical tracts from circulating on board ships, and when the duke of Clarence was briefly lord high admiral in 1827 all Royal Navy chaplains were instructed to refer any matters regarding the discharge of their duties to Cole and 'to prohibit the reception and circulation of all religious tracts, or other scriptural books' on board their ships, unless they had his express approval.[38] One such tract, *Statement concerning Certain Immoral Practices*, which was published anonymously by Admiral Edward Hawker in 1821, denounced the widespread practice of allowing prostitutes on board warships when they were in harbour and claimed that the argument that this would stop men from engaging in other 'unnatural crimes' was immoral. 'What can be more unnatural, more contrary to all the feelings of our common nature, than the open, undisguised, unblushing, promiscuous concubinage, which now takes place on board his Majesty's ships of war?' he asked.[39] Hawker's main target was female prostitution, but he also condemned the fact that sailors 'huddled promiscuously together without an adequate means of separation or privacy' and lived 'in the sight and hearing of all around them … in the unrestrained indulgence of every licentious propensity'.[40] His hatred of homosexuality permeates the work, but both Cole and Rear-Admiral Sir Thomas Hardy, who was the flag captain at the battle of Trafalgar to whom Nelson addressed his dying words, 'Kiss me, Hardy' and who served as first naval lord in Lord Grey's Cabinet from 1830 before becoming governor of the Royal Hospital, seem to have disliked such moralising and preferred a more relaxed attitude to on-board sexual discipline. Evangelical zealotry was not Cole's style.

Admittedly, the Royal Navy's public position as stated in the Articles of War of 1749 stipulated that 'if any person in the Fleet shall commit the unnatural and detestable sin of buggery or sodomy with man or beast, he shall be punished with death by the sentence of a court-martial'. Thus, some sailors and officers were lashed or executed for homosexuality. Some people also believed in a vengeful God. The Puritan preacher Cotton Mather, for instance, held that 'many a vessel has been lost in the Salt-Sea, because there have been Sodomites on board [as] God will have those dogs to be Drowned'.[41] Yet, despite the fact that a naval expedition would involve many long months cooped up in the sole company of other men, there were remarkably few courts martial for 'unnatural offences'. Only eleven sailors (out of 70,000) were court-martialled for sodomy during the Seven Years' War. Four were acquitted and the other seven were sentenced for lesser offences like 'uncleanness'. Some historians have therefore concluded that homosexuality was very rare in the Royal Navy at this time, or at least that the lack of privacy on board ship made sailors especially circumspect. However, an alternative conclusion[42] is that the navy turned a blind eye to sailors' indiscretions unless and until they became too flagrant, as yet another example of the hypocritical cloak of secrecy of the age. It is difficult not to agree with Jeremy Bentham, who privately found this entirely hypocritical, writing that although many crimes committed in the Royal Navy incurred the death penalty, including burning the fleet and betraying it to the enemy, only sodomy was excluded from mercy. As he sarcastically pointed out, 'the safety of the fleet and of the Empire were in the eyes of the legislator objects of inferior account in comparison with the preservation of a sailor's chastity'.[43]

Whatever the public position, the Royal Navy mostly seems to have eschewed zealotry in favour of turning a blind eye. Perhaps this was a lesson James learnt at the Royal Hospital. For some reason, though, Cole only kept him on for eight months and he was again looking for work. We don't know whether James had been required to live in the Hospital, but in the summer of 1835, he was back at home with his wife and daughter at 27 Giffin Street in Deptford. It was a bit cramped. Susan (or 'Ann') Turner and her sailor husband George had one room, and Mary Orchard and her ship-caulker husband another. But it was home.

PART II

6

Saturday 29 August

Henry Buckler's shorthand notes of the trial record that at ten o'clock on the morning of Saturday 29 August 1835 James Pratt said goodbye to his wife and daughter and stepped out into Giffin Street on his way to central London. His destination was Swan Inn Yard by Holborn Bridge, a little over five miles away, where he hoped to visit his Irish friend Fanny Cannon.*

If James had had the money or the inclination to purchase one of London's several newspapers that day, he would have learnt that there had been a rebellion in the House of Lords against the government, which was now led by Viscount Melbourne; the partridge season was due to start on Monday; and Mrs H. H. Davis, formerly Miss Louisa Michau, had the honour to inform the Nobility and Gentry that 'her STAY in TOWN will now be PERMANENT'.[1] A tremor had made the bells ring at the Reverend Mr Clay's vicarage in Preston. On Tuesday, the Emerald Birmingham coach had been upset near Fenny Stratford, pitching five outside passengers into a hedge and killing the driver. There had been much excitement on Thursday afternoon over in Vauxhall, where the famous balloonist Charles Green, his father and a Mr Vivian, 'a gentleman of fortune', had set off in two balloons at quarter to five, only descending safe and sound after two hours in the air.[2] There had been sightings of Halley's Comet on Friday afternoon in Berlin and in Dublin – although the Royal

---

* Fanny's name is given in the Old Bailey records as Conin, but there is no record anywhere else of such a person.

Observatory at Greenwich said 'it appeared very faint'.[3] The *West Kent Guardian* added that when an Irishman boasted of having seen *two* comets, 'One may guess what produced this second sight.'[4]

There was plenty of Deptford news, too. The military review on Woolwich Common had caused much excitement in July, when the roads were thronged for hours with people eager to catch a sight of the royal cortège as it passed through Deptford, although the *Standard* commented that 'the number of the "working-classes" was smaller than we remember to have seen on any similar occasion'.[5] Perhaps, it speculated, the public houses held more allure than the sight of a regiment of foot guards, two regiments of the line, four batteries of foot artillery and one of horse being put through their paces.[6] The local coroner, Mr Carrtar, had been busy, dealing with the suspicious death in a brawl of a royal marine called Howarth Thomason, the suicide of Jane Wilmington, who had drowned herself in a water butt, the stabbing of a customer at the Golden Lion, the manslaughter of 'a woman called Flint'[7] by another woman outside another local public house and two drownings, when an oyster boat had been run down by a steamer off Woolwich and a seventeen-year-old solicitor's clerk's boat was driven against Blackfriars Bridge.[8]

James had other matters on his mind, though. Employment was scarcer than ever locally and the only prospect of work lay in central London.

James could have taken one of several coaches which ran half-hourly from the Lord Duncan in Broadway, just round the corner from Giffin Street, to the City (driving, thanks to the new Highways Act, on the left). A seat inside would have set him back 4d a mile and outside 2d. He would have found himself within the hour at the George and Gate or the Pewter Platter, both of which catered for the travelling public in Gracechurch Street. A cheaper option would have been to hitch a lift on a cart, which would have been slower but would also have deposited him at the Cross Keys tavern, whose courtyard had hosted plays in Shakespeare's time.

Given James's financial situation, though, it is more likely that he walked, not least because the newspapers reported that the weather that week had been fine and 'the heat more moderate'.[9] It was a common complaint at the time that the outskirts of London were so built over that it was 'a difficult matter to find a country walk without being tired out previous to arriving at it'.[10] But Deptford was still surrounded by countryside, its market gardens were famed for their asparagus and most of James's route that day would have felt rural, with cuckoos, blackbirds and skylarks accompanying him and one flower, the *caryophyllus pratensis*, the Deptford pink, growing in profusion on his route.

From Giffin Street he would have turned right up the High Street, past his old master's house, towards the victualling house before turning left into Evelyn Street. After a couple of hundred yards, he would have crossed the Black Horse Bridge over the Surrey Canal and set out along the new straight road to Rotherhithe that had been completed in 1830. On either side there were extensive fields and market gardens, with the Surrey Hills and the canal on the left and the docks on the right. Having paid his toll at the turnpike, on entering Rotherhithe he would have seen vast granaries and an expanse of commercial docks. On the left was the China Hall Tavern and further on, the recently expanded Rotherhithe workhouse, whose rooms were apparently very spacious, 'kept perfectly clean, and [had] a beautiful, open view of the fields opposite, of Brandram and Co.'s vitriol works, and the shipping in the Thames beyond'.[11]

If he had a spare shilling, he might have visited the cathedral-like tunnel at Rotherhithe, although the steam engine that kept it dry was very noisy and the northern end consisted of a mirrored wall so that you could get an impression of what it would look like when it was completed. If he had wanted to visit the church of St Mary's Rotherhithe, he would have had to pay the pew-openers who lived opposite, as the church was shut on a Saturday. From here the journey lay along Paradise Street, Jamaica Row, Great George Street and eventually up Bermondsey Street to Tooley Street. At first, he was walking through acres devoted to gardeners. One had grown an entire hedge of lilac and filled his garden with golden laburnum. Others had pear and cherry trees that blossomed in profusion in the spring and many cottagers sold roses, dahlias and heart's-ease to passers-by.

After he passed the elegant and costly portico of the new church of St James's, Bermondsey, though, things felt increasingly urban. Tanners' yards and glue manufactories filled the air with a smell that was considered more healthy than pleasant. There were dozens of large cisterns or tan-pits for tanning hides, but ox- and cow-horns would be turned into combs and knife handles, and offal awaited the gluepot. Bermondsey Street was almost entirely dedicated to the leather trade, and its two-year-old market was the City's 'great emporium for hides and skins'. Much of the area was even more insanitary than Deptford. James must have walked within yards of the 'rookery' or tenement slum known as Jacob's Island, whose Folly Ditch was tidal like the Thames, but ran blood-red with tanners' dye. Charles Dickens described the place two years later in *Oliver Twist*. It had 'crazy wooden galleries ... rooms so small, so filthy, so confined, that the air would seem to be too tainted even for the dirt and squalor which they shelter; wooden chambers thrusting themselves out above the mud and threatening to fall into it ... [and] dirt-besmeared walls and decaying foundations, every repulsive lineament of poverty, every loathsome indication of filth, rot, and garbage.'[12]

At the end of Tooley Street, James came to New London Bridge. Its predecessor had stood on the site for centuries as the only river crossing, but its many houses and shops had meant it was too narrow to cope with the growing traffic of pedestrians, wagons and coaches. By the turn of the century, it had been decided to replace the old bridge and on 1 August 1831 'the new bridge presented a scene of gaiety and splendour that far surpassed any spectacle we were prepared to witness'.[13] If James attended that day, he would have seen a river full of boats with streamers, waggons with awnings and seats along the approach roads, and all the banks, wharfs, timber-yards and anywhere that afforded a view, thronged with people keen to see King William and Queen Adelaide ascend crimson-carpeted steps from the royal barge to open the bridge and enjoy a cold collation on one of its five solid granite arches while the ubiquitous Mr Green ascended in a balloon.[14] Since then, the old bridge had been dismantled and the new bridge had become as crowded as its predecessor.

At this point James had a choice: cross into the City and climb Fish Street Hill to Gracechurch Street; or continue along the south side of the river through Borough until he reached one of the other new bridges, Southwark or Blackfriars. On the north side of the river, Gracechurch Street was the main terminus for south London coaches and teemed with life. Sixpence would buy you a plate of food 'of the very finest quality' in the dining rooms at the Grasshopper.[15] There were four public houses in the street, the Swan Tavern lay up a tiny alleyway and the adjoining Bell Yard was host to the Bell and the White Hart. You could get soupe des galles, 'the best substitute for Real Turtle' from H. Wayte, Confectioner, at no. 5.[16] If you were thinking of emigrating, you could book your passage on the *Agrippina* at 3 Nag's-head Court.[17] You could pick up a copy of *The Teacher's Treasure, & Dunce's Delight*, 'being a simple and expeditious method of teaching to read' at the book-sellers Darton & Harvey at no. 55.[18]

Gracechurch Street also had a well-known print shop, where an apprentice confectioner called Henry Gunter had stopped to read the duke of York's speech condemning Catholic emancipation round about midday at the end of August in 1825 and was propositioned by William Dorien, 'a young gentleman of high connections in the City'. They bumped into each other several times over the next few weeks, but when Dorien tried again in October, Gunter, who was carrying a tray of pastries on his head, threw the tray down and struck Dorien several times. Gunter prosecuted Dorien for 'indecent assault', but Dorien was well defended by his lawyer, who brought in a series of character witnesses, including the governor of the Bank of Ireland; and when he was acquitted 'the verdict appeared to give high satisfaction to those present'.[19]

From Gracechurch Street to Holborn Bridge was an easy journey. Lombard Street and Cheapside would take James to Newgate Street – and that ran straight into Skinner Street, which ended at the corner of Farringdon Street and High Holborn.

James Pratt's destination on 28 August 1835 was Swan Yard to the north of Holborn Bridge, where he had a couple of pots of half-and-half with his friend Fanny Cannon.

James's alternative route lay along the south bank of the river, past a series of wharfs to Southwark Bridge, which had been opened on a commercial basis in 1819. Most people shunned this 'Iron Bridge' because it charged a toll, so James probably continued along Bankside into Holland Street and then right onto Blackfriars Bridge. These riverside parishes displayed all the worst features of overcrowding. The area was 'lamentably destitute of breathing-spaces for the pent-up citizens'[20] and a man coming home from work would find the house filthy, the air close. 'He might be thirsty, but the broken water butt is full of disgusting green vegetation and stands beside a drain, whose foul stagnant liquids taint it; the refuse heap stands nearby, full of decaying vegetable matter; and the dilapidated privy and cesspool send up heavy, poisonous and depressing gases.'[21] The Commissioners on Large Towns commented in 1844, 'Within the rooms, close offensive smells, the atmosphere quite vitiated, the faecal smell of the cesspool is often distinguished; the courts are uncleansed and in a dirty condition.'²² Not surprisingly, the Surrey medical officer reckoned the area had 'always been remarkable for its deathly pre-eminence; in the ancient plague, as well as in the modern cholera'.²³

The moment James stepped onto Blackfriars Bridge, he had left Surrey and was in London. This bridge had also originally charged a fee when it opened in 1769, but now it was free and crossed the Thames just where the old River Fleet discharged on the north side and where the Marygold stairs had given access to watermen on the south side. It was said that the bridge commanded 'a very fine view of St Paul's cathedral, as well as of both sides of the river, including the Tower, the Monument, Somerset House, Westminster Abbey and about thirty churches'.²⁴ To the west, James would also have seen the first of the new bridges to have been built since 1750, at Westminster. Beyond it lay the remains of the Palace of Westminster, most of which had been burnt to the ground on the night of 16 October the previous year. Hundreds had gathered on the other side of the river to watch the flames soar into the night sky – and to applaud. There was no plan as yet for replacing the old Chapel of St Stephens where the Commons had sat since 1548 or the Lords' home, the Painted Chamber, but both Houses had been meeting in temporary accommodation since February and that August demolition crews were clearing the space near the river for New Palace Yard. James would have crossed the bridge at about noon, just as the Commons started sitting. That day's business concerning the Shannon Navigation Bill and tithe instalments for Irish clergy would probably not have interested him. However, the debate in the Lords the day before might have done, as Lord Denman effectively killed off a Bill to make 'offences against the person [i.e. buggery] punishable more severely than at present'.²⁵

James's destination now lay straight ahead at the north end of Farringdon Street, where Holborn met Snow Hill and Skinner Street. James would have seen a considerable change in this last stretch since he first arrived in London, as Farringdon Street followed the course of the old River Fleet. This had once been navigable, lined on either side with wharfs and spanned by four

Portland stone bridges, Holborn Bridge being the last, but the
City Corporation covered it over in 1734 and opened a new
market on top of it. This lasted just under a century, but in 1829
the old shops were pulled down and a new market was built on
Farringdon Street. Everything money could buy was available.
There were butchers, tripe dressers, herbalists, watchmakers,
cheesemongers, fruiterers, grocers, greengrocers, bakers, tailors
and bootmakers. Barclay and Sons sold Perry's essence for
tooth-ache at no. 95.[26] Mr Salmon sold Morison's pills at no. 6
and thanked those who had supported him in his recent trial, as
'TRUTH will shine with the more splendour by having to break
through the clouds of prejudice and interested opposition.'[27]
George Hodson had his wholesale and retail trimming warehouse
at no. 1, where he sold 'fancy and plain cassimeres, buckskins,
waistcoatings, cantoons, drill, merinos and gambrooms'.[28] Henry
Colwell sold strong and good trusses for labouring men at 2s 6d
at no. 20.[29] At Holborn Bridge James Cook sold poultry, Nathan
Button sold sweet delicacies, Edward Boyle sold French muslins
and Richard Dickins sold his 'celebrated British tooth-powder',
which would cure all toothache.[30]

Whichever route James took, he passed a gaol. The route across
London Bridge took him directly past Newgate and its neighbour,
the Old Bailey, where seven men were sentenced to death that
week and twenty were transported for life, four for fourteen
years and fifty-four for seven years. Four of those convicted and
sentenced that week were called John Smith. The other route took
him directly past the Fleet prison, which had been rebuilt after
its destruction during the Gordon Riots in 1780 but retained a
medieval attitude towards its 300 or so inmates, most of whom
were debtors and bankrupts. If James took this route, he would
have passed the grille through which inmates begged for alms.

This was a quirky part of old London. It had been built upon
so many times that its jumbled streets made little sense. The
surrounding lanes sounded agricultural – Field, Chick, Cow
and Cock Lane – or whimsical, like Turn Again Lane, named
after Dick Whittington. Yet its courts and alleys had a terrible
reputation. Most of Field Lane had gone when the Fleet was

covered over, but rumours abounded of how Jonathan Wild and his murderous companions had disposed of the corpses of their victims by letting them down from a back window into the 'silent waters of the Fleet', and its reputation as 'the emporium of larceny' had been inherited by the surrounding streets which were known as 'Jack Ketch's Warren' after Britain's most famous hangman.[31] Dickens set Fagin's kitchen here in *Oliver Twist*. Oliver had never seen 'a dirtier or more wretched place', he wrote. Pubs were the only places that seemed to prosper. 'Covered ways and yards, which here and there diverged from the main street, disclosed little knots of houses, where drunken men and women were positively wallowing in filth; and from several of the door-ways, great ill-looking fellows were cautiously emerging, bound, to all appearance, on no very well-disposed or harmless errands.'[32]

It was also renowned as a gay pick-up area. Mother Clap had set up her molly-house in Field Lane beside the Bunch o' Grapes and along with Fleet Street and the Strand, it was said that Holborn was 'actually thronged' with 'monsters in the shape of men, commonly designated Margeries, Pooffs'.[33]

One of the local nooks and crannies was Swan Yard, an enclosed yard to the north of Holborn Bridge, which had an aspect onto the last open part of the Fleet. In the middle of the yard stood an inn, the Swan. It had been there since at least 1637 when it was reckoned to be especially busy every Thursday with carriers from Bristol, Devizes, Watford and Marlborough, while carriers from Wendover came on a Tuesday and Wednesday and wagons from Gloucestershire would arrive most days.[34] The three-storey tavern had been converted into separate dwellings and the yard had sprouted other properties, but horses were still housed and fed beneath its clap-boarded timber barn and the Sun insurance company kept a fire engine there. This was where Fanny Cannon, later described as a 'hawker' or a 'seller of sheep's feet', lived with her husband, who was a 'carman', and their daughter Winifred.

According to Fanny, James had been drinking by the time he arrived at Swan Yard at one o'clock. There had been plenty of

taverns to choose from along the route. Farringdon Street alone
had eight, including the Hoop and Grapes, which still exists.
Fanny and James had a couple of pots of half-and-half with their
dinner and chatted with another resident, John Keeley, who was
also 'out of place'. Fanny suggested that James should stay to tea,
but he was in a hurry to leave, claiming that he was in search
of a weekly situation and had to be back home in Deptford by
six. Fanny added that he 'appeared a little affected with liquor'
and that he left at two o'clock with 'a friend'. It is possible that
this was John Smith, but none of the other witnesses in the trial
mentioned this and Fanny was not asked whether she saw the
'friend' in court. Nor do we know what James got up to for the
next two hours.

We do know from the court records that at about four o'clock,
John Smith, who was described as a 'somewhat stocky' man,
appeared downstairs at 45 George Street, where William Bonell
rented his room, and asked John[*] Berkshire if Bonell lodged
there. 'Yes, he does,' he was told, 'but I do not believe he is
within.' Undeterred, Smith replied that he had seen Bonell at the
window and without another word walked through the shop
and started up the stairs to Bonell's room on the first floor at the
back, as if he already knew the way. Berkshire then saw Smith
turn back and open the private side-door to let James Pratt in
and the two men went upstairs to Bonell's room, where they
shut the door.

John and Jane Berkshire have left a confusing paper trail.
These are the hard facts. The 1841 census says they were born
outside Surrey and gives their ages as fifty-five and forty-five,
which would suggest they were born between 1786 and 1796, but
Jane died on 6 February 1847, aged fifty-eight (suggesting a birth
date of 1789) and John died on 10 February 1848, aged sixty-
two. John left everything in his will to his 'sole surviving child',
Eliza, who married James Lord at St James, Westminster, in
1838. Later censuses suggest Eliza Lord was born in 1821 in Mid
Lavant in Sussex – and a Jane Berkshire brought a two-year-old

---

[*] The court record inaccurately calls him 'George'.

daughter Eliza for baptism in Northchapel in another part of Sussex in 1823. Only three John Berkshires (or similar-sounding surnames) appear in English baptism records between 1784 and 1786. One was baptised in Northchapel on 20 March 1784, but he was buried there in 1796. Two others were baptised in 1786 in Reading and in Wimbledon, but the former died in 1856 and the latter in 1853. Neither is therefore the 'John Berkshire of No. 45 George-street, Blackfriars-road in the County of Surrey, Coal Dealer and Carman' who died in 1848.[35] Details about Jane are also elusive. She might be Jane Branch, who married a widowed John Berkshire at St Saviour's, Southwark, in 1822, but she might not.

Whatever their origins, they were living in George Street by the middle of the 1820s. John Berkshire referred to himself as a carman and coal-dealer, but in practice that meant turning his hand to any profitable enterprise, whether that involved hauling coals and selling them to his neighbours or running a furniture removal company. It was in this latter capacity that he was charged with 'driving furiously' across Blackfriars Bridge in 1827, knocking over a Quaker lady and narrowly missing two others when his horses fell on the pavement at Holland Street. His defence was that the horses were 'unmanageable' when they knew they were on their way home, but he was fined thirty shillings.[36] In 1830 he also rented out a house and shop 'in a good thoroughfare', which he thought suitable for 'fruiterers and others'.[37] With the additional income from lodgers, the couple were able to afford a maid-of-all-work and accumulated all the accoutrements a polite household required. When Jane Smith, the sixteen-year-old daughter of a former servant, burgled the house in 1838, she made off with a large quantity of silver including three watches, thirty-three spoons, five pairs of sugar tongs, a cream jug, two salt cellars, a pepper castor, 'besides fourteen gold rings and several other articles of jewellery'.[38] In the subsequent trial at the Old Bailey, her haul was said to be worth £6 6s 4d, which in an earlier era would have been enough to see her hang. John Berkshire would doubtless have been pleased that all the press reports described him as 'a respectable tradesman'.[39] There was one other clue to the Berkshires' status. They had locking doors and their lodgers had keys to the side-door to the house and to their own rooms.

We don't know whether James, John and William already knew each other, or where they met up that day. They might have arranged a rendezvous at the George, which was run by Joshua Wall, or at the Coachmakers' Arms in Robert Street, which was the scene of a bloody attempted murder in 1838 but boasted that it 'long commanded a first-rate trade'.[40] Or they might have met in one of the pubs on the other side of the river. What seems clear, though, is that this was an assignation.

Something piqued John Berkshire's interest when he saw James and John go up to Bonell's room. During the thirteen months that Bonell had lodged there the Berkshires had noticed that he frequently took men up to his room, generally in pairs and sometimes more than once a day. Full of suspicions, John went out to the next-door stable and squeezed himself into the loft. Once he had dislodged a tile, he had, so he later told the court, a very good sight of Bonell's room, where he saw Bonell and Smith sitting on either side of the window. After a few minutes he saw Pratt sit on Bonell's knee, and when Bonell pushed him away, he sat on Smith's knee 'for five or six minutes'. It was cramped in the loft, so John soon gave up and went back indoors to his tea – and to his wife, to whom he related what he had seen.

This prompted Jane Berkshire to go upstairs and peek through the keyhole of Bonell's room. Bonell had just left in search of a jug of ale, so James and John were alone. Jane later claimed in court that she saw the two men take down their trousers and start to have sex, Pratt lying on his back on the floor, with his head up against the turn-up bedstead[41] and Smith lying on top of him. She said that she saw the 'private parts' of both men and that Smith's were 'in a state of connexion' (sic). After less than a minute, scandalised, fascinated or furious, she ran downstairs to her husband and told him what she had seen. He immediately ran upstairs, knelt outside Bonell's door and also peered through the keyhole. This time what he saw was far more incriminating than what he had seen from the stables. The transcript of the court reads as follows: 'I saw Pratt laying on his back with his trowsers below his knees, and with his body curled up; his knees were up – Smith was upon him – Pratt's knees were nearly up to Smith's shoulders – Smith's clothes were below his knees.' With that Berkshire put his shoulder against the door and burst it open. The two men immediately drew apart and started pulling up their trousers. Pratt shouted something (Berkshire claimed it was, 'Oh, my God, we are caught,' or 'caught at last') as he turned away from the door to rearrange himself and Smith tried to cover himself up. Terrified, they threw themselves on their knees and begged Berkshire to let them go, offering him their purses.

At that moment Bonell returned with the jug of ale.

'What is the matter?' he asked.

'You old villain,' cried Berkshire. 'You know what is the matter; you have been practising this in my place for some time past.'

'I know nothing of what is done in my place,' Bonell said, calmly pointing out that he had not been present and offering Berkshire a drink.

Berkshire responded with a sneer, 'No, I would not drink in any such society.'

The commotion attracted one of the other lodgers, who agreed to guard the three men while Berkshire set off in search of a police constable.

Policing was a recent and controversial phenomenon. Sir Robert Peel had created the Metropolitan Police force in 1829 to replace the old local watchmen, street-keepers or 'charlies' (named after Charles II), within an area spanning seven miles from Charing Cross (excluding the City of London), and its officers (known as 'peelers' or 'bobbies') were required to patrol the streets, 'arrest disturbers of the peace, house-breakers, reputed thieves, and beggars, and preserve good order'.[42] Some objected to this centralised force. The vestry of St Paul's Deptford wrote that its creation was 'dangerous and unconstitutional and oppressively expensive'.[43] The *Weekly Dispatch* complained that it was 'a gendarmerie'[44] and a lively meeting in St Saviour's, Southwark, concluded in 1830 that the new police force was 'a military establishment' and that its officers were 'vampires who feed and fatten upon the vitals of the country'.[45] Conscious that the new force would have to win the confidence of the public, Peel laid down strict rules. All police officers had to devote themselves to policing as a full-time profession and could never take money or even a Christmas-box without the express permission of the three police commissioners. Constables were required to understand the law, obey their seniors, and get to know their beat so well that they would recognise the inhabitants of every house. They were also expected to be 'civil and attentive to all persons of every rank and class',[46] and at all times to appear 'neat in his person, and correctly dressed in the established uniform'.[47] This involved a navy blue single-breasted tunic tied with a black leather belt, with a row of white buttons each marked with a crown and the word 'police'. He wore a heavy chimney-pot hat with a shiny leather top, and on the tight high collar of his tunic he bore the letter of his division and his warrant number. At night he wore a dark brown greatcoat, and by his side he carried a rattle and staff or baton. In summer he had white trousers and gloves and a shorter tunic. They were not the only 'police officers', as the Middlesex Justices Act 1792 had set up nine 'police offices' in Westminster, Middlesex and Surrey, at which magistrates dispensed local justice – and each of these also had a number of constables. Some thought these constables 'more expert in tracing out and detecting crime, than the common Metropolitan Police officer',[48] but the Home Office 'peelers' were the visible embodiment of the law.

When John Berkshire went in search of a Metropolitan Police officer at the police station on Southwark Bridge Street, the man he found was Sergeant Robert Horwood Valentine, a Devonian from the Stoke Damerel part of Devonport. Most police officers were single, but Valentine had married another Devonian, Catherine Leroux Pardew, not long after his twenty-first birthday in 1822, before moving to London. Robert was working as a builder in

Shoreditch when their first two children, Eliza and Amelia, were born in 1823 and 1828, but he was one of the first to sign up for the Metropolitan Police, being inducted as a police constable on 21 January 1829 and issued with his warrant card, no. 2477.

Officers were expected to serve wherever they were directed and although many single men were housed together with their sergeant, special arrangements were made for married officers like Valentine, the only stipulation being that they must live as close as possible to their district. This may explain the fact that by the time Catherine brought her son George to be baptised in 1831 the Valentines were living in Poplar Row in Christ Church, as Robert was based in Southwark. The couple moved to Brook Street in the neighbouring parish of St Mary's Lambeth by the time two more sons, Charles and Frederick, arrived in 1832 and 1834, but he was still on the Southwark establishment. He was thirty-five, but he had lost his mother in 1832 and buried his father in 1834 and he was father to five children (and four more would follow). In a later photograph he looks tall and self-confident, with a mutton-chop beard that was greyer than what remained of the hair on his balding pate.

This was almost certainly Sergeant Valentine's first case of this kind and since the 1830 Hyde Park debacle, Metropolitan Police arrests for 'unnatural offences' were relatively rare. However, his duties were clear. A constable had to arrest anyone he caught 'in the act of committing a felony, or anyone who another positively charges with having committed a felony, or whom another [person] suspects of having committed a felony', as long as he thought the suspicion was well founded, 'and provided the person so suspecting go with the constable'.[49] So, Valentine went to 45 George Street and interrogated the three men. He examined Bonell's room and the men's clothes and satisfied himself that the Berkshires' claims were well founded. Peel had also stipulated that rather than take the suspect to the divisional watch-house or police station, it was always desirable to take the prisoner 'as soon as convenient before the city magistrates, who will dispose of the case'.[50] That meant taking the men with John Berkshire to the Union Hall police office.

7

The Small Wares of Justice

It was less than half a mile, but James, John and William probably attracted a small crowd as Sergeant Valentine and the Berkshires marched them through the streets of Southwark, down George Street, right into Gravel Lane and left into Union Street. Just after the turning for Pott's Vinegar Manufactory and the vast expanse of the Anchor Brewery, whose fumes hung in the air day and night, they came to St Saviour's burial ground on the left and immediately opposite it the Union Hall police office, which had been built in 1782 to house the County Justices of Surrey but now acted as a combination of magistrates' court and police office. This is where local justice was dispensed by three paid magistrates, who oversaw a small cadre of constables.[1] It was not a large establishment. There were two clerks, eleven constables, a messenger, an office-keeper, a housekeeper and two retired constables. Yet it had sole jurisdiction over the parishes south of the river and their 300,000 or so souls, 'the principal part of the population [being] of the poorer order'.[2]

It was said you could spot the office by 'a number of sickly-looking women, and pallid gin-faced men, lurking about the doors of an unpretending stucco-fronted edifice',[3] which would explain why 'the respectable inhabitants of the neighbourhood generally resist[ed] the building of a police office ... on the ground that it would depreciate the value of property in the neighbourhood'.[4] The whole of life passed through its doors. As Samuel Leigh put it in 1830, the magistrates were required to hear and determine in a summary way (i.e. without trial by jury) 'a variety of instances

... particularly in cases relating to the customs, excise, coaches, carts, pawnbrokers ... persons charged with being disorderly, or brought for examination under charges of treason, murder, felony, fraud and misdemeanours of every description'.[5] The longest standing Union Hall magistrate, Charles Knight Murray, told the House of Commons Committee on the Metropolitan Police that the office entertained 'every possible case incident to vice, misery, and passion'. All sorts of people called on the court to recover property worth trifling amounts, which they alleged had been unlawfully withheld from them. Servants complained that their strongboxes had been withheld by their masters, people who had lent furniture to friends while they were in the country found their friends refused to hand back their goods on their return and young girls complained that their brothel-keepers retained their clothes 'for some extortionate charge'. The idea behind the Middlesex Justices Act 1792, which created the public offices, had been to improve public conduct, but according to Murray there was 'scarcely a conceivable case arising, particularly among the lower orders, which may not immediately or indirectly come under the notice of the police officers'.[6] Consequently, the value of his and his fellow magistrates' work did not so much consist in the strict legal performance of their judicial duties, 'than in [their] exercise of sound discretion, and in the considerate application of [their] feelings of humanity, as an advisor, an arbitrator, and a mediator'.[7]

The cases came in all shapes and sizes. In January John Palmer was charged with hawking spirits without a permit. He had been going house to house with large bladders full of 'very strong white spirit' claiming it was French brandy. He was fined thirty pounds and sent down for three months when he could not pay up.[8] Also that month Eliza Bray attended the office on behalf of her husband, a chimney sweep, who was summoned for employing his son, who was under the new legal working age. Eliza made out that the boy really was over twelve, but when the magistrate pressed her and asked her son's actual age, she said, 'I have been married twenty-three years, and in that time I've had twenty-two children, and surely, your Worship, you can't expect that my head is like an almanac, to bear in memory the ages of all of them.' The magistrate had little choice but to stand the case over to ascertain the boy's true age.[9] In February, 'the Indian chief' Muek Coonee, who had been exhibiting great dexterity at the Victoria theatre by shooting an apple off a man's head, was charged with attempting to violate a young girl.[10] In March an Irishwoman named Bryan was committed to the House of Correction for a month for abandoning her nine-month-old baby, her plea being that 'she had applied to the overseers [of the Poor Law] for relief, and had been refused on the grounds that she had a husband living'.[11] In April Harriet Lane, 'a woman addicted to excessive gin-drinking', was brought before Mr Wedgwood charged with cruelly assaulting her nine-year-old boy. Apparently, 'she not only pledged her own clothes, but also those of her children, to procure liquor, which she drank like water. Even her husband begged that she be kept in prison for a while.'[12] At the start of August Richard Mandeville, nicknamed 'The Pet of the Petticoats', who was described as 'a young fellow with a well-cultivated pair of bushy whiskers', was charged with dressing in women's clothes and assaulting respectable persons in the streets. It was reported that he met his match when, 'imitating the boldness of a Cyprian', he grabbed hold of a gentleman who 'gave Mandeville such a crack over the jaw as to set him a roaring, besides spoiling the shape of a green silk bonnet he wore at the time'. He was fined ten shillings for his 'pranks'.[13]

Most Union Hall cases involved mediation over civil matters between aggrieved parties, but if a minor offence termed as a misdemeanour had taken place, the magistrates could dispense summary justice, imposing a fine or a spell in the House of Correction. If there were enough prima facie evidence that a felony had been committed, which was by definition a capital offence, the magistrates could commit the suspect for trial by jury at the next Sessions of the Peace.

The Union Hall police court would not be in session until seven that evening, so James, John and William had a short wait with their accusers until the duty magistrate arrived.

This was the thirty-two-year-old Hensleigh Wedgwood. He may not have been in a good mood that evening, as he lived three miles away in Lark Hall Lane in Clapham, which involved a hard ride down the Newington Road; he was covering for one of the other magistrates, who was away for five weeks; and he generally found the evening sessions at Union Hall a waste of time. Yet Hensleigh was a compassionate and independently minded man who was fascinated by words, meanings, the spiritual life and scientific discovery.* He had spent his life in liberal Whig circles, as the fourth son of Josiah Wedgwood and grandson of the famous English potter. One visitor to his childhood home, Maer Hall in Staffordshire, reported that it was a place where there was 'no difference in politics or principles of any kind that makes it treason to speak one's mind openly', and since nothing was said there from party or prejudice, there was 'no bitterness in discussing opinions'.[14] Hensleigh's father was a keen abolitionist and electoral reformer, who sat for a single term as one of the two inaugural MPs for Stoke-on-Trent between 1832 and 1835. Charles Darwin, who was Josiah's nephew and Hensleigh's cousin, said of Josiah that he was 'the very type of an upright man, with clearest judgement. I do not believe that any power on earth could have made him swerve an inch from what he considered the right course.'[15] Hensleigh's mother Bessie was equally immersed in the liberal Whig world, as her sister Kitty married the Whig MP, Sir James Mackintosh, who led the campaign for reform of the penal code to limit the death penalty.

Thanks to the Wedgwood potteries, Hensleigh had no great need to earn a living until he married. After reading mathematics and classics at Cambridge (where he was awarded the wooden 'wedge' rather than the wooden spoon, for coming last in his year in classics), he qualified as a barrister in 1828, but he never practised. Some said it was his family's passion for public service rather than the £400 salary that inspired him to put his name forward when Joseph Hone's death led to a vacancy

---

* In 1865 he published a comprehensive three-volume *Dictionary of English Etymology*. It omits the words 'buggery' and 'sodomy'.

for a magistrate at Union Hall in November 1831, but he had been courting Sir James Mackintosh's daughter Fanny for years and it was only when the new Whig home secretary, Viscount Melbourne, appointed him as magistrate, that 'after many hopes and fears ... his marriage could now prudently take place'.[16] Fanny and Hensleigh were first cousins, but they were following in a family tradition, as two of Hensleigh's elder brothers also married their first cousins and his sister Emma married Darwin, who was prevented from attending Hensleigh and Fanny's wedding in January 1832 because he had just set sail on the *Beagle*. At first Hensleigh moved in with his wife, father and brother-in-law, but Sir James died at home in Langham Place (thanks to a chicken bone stuck in his throat) four months later. By 1835 Fanny and Hensleigh were living in Clapham and had two children, Frances, known as 'Snow', and James.

Hensleigh had proved himself a stickler for fairness. Some magistrates had a close relationship with their constables. When trade unions organised a massed march through central London in April 1834, for instance, Charles Murray positioned himself with nearly a hundred special constables and four officers of the dragoons at the Philanthropic Institution in case a disturbance required summoning the dragoons with their artillery, which were being kept out of sight in Kennington. But Wedgwood was more sceptical. He feared that police officers pressurised witnesses to press charges because they would be paid 3s 6d for attendance in court. Moreover, he had been through a particularly gruelling battle with several constables at Union Hall when local publicans, led by Archibald McPherson of the Rising Sun in Kennington, claimed that constables had been threatening them with prosecution for opening during divine worship on a Sunday if they did not pay them off. Wedgwood led the investigation, interviewed the senior constables Blackman and Skillorn, and dismissed them when he found them corrupt.[17]

All three Union Hall magistrates were frustrated by the limits of their powers and resources. The office was too informal to command wide respect. The magistrates did not wear court dress or even a wig and Charles Murray suggested 'that it should be a highly respectable court, in which the public may have confidence, and which may have every attribute of a court of justice'.[18] But according to one contemporary writer, the courtroom in which the magistrates 'retail[ed] the small wares of justice, [was] somewhat narrow and incommodious'. The law said that all courts should allow plenty of access for even the meanest member of the public, and Union Hall had ample space for the ordinary business of the tribunal, but little to spare 'for those distinguished amateurs who are in the habit of crowding the bench when any criminal of more than ordinary atrocity is brought up for examination'.[19] In other words, this was a very rudimentary court and the quality of justice it meted out was less than perfect. As Wedgwood put it: 'We very frequently witness the departure of applicants from the office under a burning sense of injustice, on learning that there was no redress accessible to them. Nothing, in my opinion, would tend more than such a jurisdiction, to encourage among the common people a habit of looking to the law for protection; a consideration which, I think, can hardly be over-valued.'[20]

One other thing stuck in Wedgwood's throat – the compulsory oath that magistrates had to swear. His religious objections to it were so strong that he nearly resigned in 1833 and only remained in post after a great deal of persuasion from his father, who reminded him that he had a family to look after.

It had been a busy week at Union Hall. The magistrates had seen fifty-one cases and sent six prisoners for trial by jury, including Thomas Cooper, who ended up getting one month in prison for larceny, and Joseph and Mary Pettit, who had stolen furniture from their lodgings in the parish of St Olave. Eighteen people had been sentenced for a misdemeanour and another twenty had been remanded for further investigation. The evening sessions were not normally busy, but it was standard practice for all the accused to be brought up and stand together in the dock without distinction. This meant the dock could be filled at any one moment with a random collection of individuals. The press commented on another occasion, for instance, that Harriet Lewis 'was dressed in the first style, with satin gown and rich velvet shawl', but cut a very curious figure in the dock, when seated amongst 'a motley group of persons, consisting of low prostitutes and ragged mendicants'.[21]

It was an equally curious combination that Saturday evening, as James, John and William were lumped in with a bunch of petty thieves. Isaac and William Cuff had stolen some apples and pears from a garden in Camberwell and were discharged. Joseph Dale was found guilty of the same misdemeanour and sent to the House of Correction in Brixton for fourteen days. Up for the second time, Thomas Cooper was alleged to have stolen a machine for sweeping chimneys which belonged to John Deaton, and was committed for trial. James Ryall, John Burridge, John White and Thomas Wall were re-examined for passing counterfeit coin but were discharged for lack of evidence. The last man up, Joseph Greenfield, was remanded till Monday for stealing a quantity of nails, 'the property of some person unknown'.[22] The only man who had not committed a property crime of any kind was John Cooper, who was charged with playing 'pitch and toss' with pennies and ha'pennies in the public highway in Camberwell, which was a new offence under the recent Highways Act. He too went to Brixton, for six weeks.

James, John and William may have taken succour from Wedgwood's treatment of the only other men up for a capital offence that day, Thomas White and Alexander Lawson, who were charged with stealing cigars from William Tucker's shop in Lambeth. Wedgwood decided to discharge them of the felony and instead imprison them for two months with hard labour for the misdemeanour of being found in a shop with an unlawful purpose.

James, John and William may also have hoped that the Berkshires would drop their allegations that evening or that Wedgwood would dismiss the case. William may have noted that Wedgwood spoke with a similar Staffordshire accent to his own. He might also have wondered whether he would be treated separately from the others. In the event, Wedgwood asked some simple questions and remanded them till Monday. The men must have spent an anxious time locked up in the basement cells that Sunday, wondering how to get news to family and friends. What explanation could they give? Shame and fear must have mingled anxiously.

The court reassembled on Monday morning at eleven o'clock, when Wedgwood was again in the chair. This time he felt he had little choice. Whatever he thought of the rights and wrongs of such sexual offences, there was prima facie evidence that an offence had been committed, so the law required that he commit the three men for trial. Everyone knew what that meant – if convicted, the death sentence. Some newspapers added to the sense of moral panic, reporting that the Union Hall office was 'occupied for a considerable time in the investigation of one of those revolting and unnatural cases, so many of which have recently been heard at the different police offices in town'.[23]

Hensleigh Wedgwood was the presiding magistrate at the Union Hall Police Office where James, John and William were dragged by Sergeant Robert Valentine.

The next Sessions at the Old Bailey were not due until 21 September, so the three men were sent to await trial at the

Surrey County Gaol, a 'massy brick building ... surrounded by a strong wall'²⁴ which lay 300 yards down Blackman Road on Horsemonger Lane, after which it was commonly known.

The gaol's grisly reputation would have struck the three men the moment they arrived. Henry Mayhew described the experience a few years later. 'We enter the gateway of the flat-roofed building at the entrance of the prison, on one side of which is the governor's office, and an apartment occupied by the gate-warder, and on the other is a staircase leading up to a gloomy chamber, containing the scaffold on which many a wretched criminal has been consigned to public execution.'²⁵ Between 1800 and August 1835, that scaffold had been wheeled out onto the flat roof for 113 hangings and in recent years it had seen more executions than Newgate. This was where the traitor Colonel Ned Despard, who was arrested with thirty co-conspirators at the Oakley Arms in Lambeth, was hanged and beheaded in 1803. It was where Sarah and Benjamin Herring were hanged for the treasonable offence of coining in 1806 in front of a vast crowd who were especially fascinated to see a husband and wife hang together. It was also where James Bartlett was hanged for sodomy in 1809.

Horsemonger Lane Gaol was also closely identified with a series of horrific recent events. It started with the disappearance of a fourteen-year-old boy called Lawrence in November 1832. When the police tracked the boy down, he told them he had been inveigled into working for a wealthy fifty-year-old captain in the 14th Infantry Regiment called Henry Nicholls, who had forced him to have sex with him. The police went to arrest Nicholls but he evaded capture with the help of a man calling himself Captain Thomas Beauclerk, who was in turn arrested at his home in Paddington on Monday 19 November 1832. Beauclerk was duly brought to the Union Hall police office, where he was charged with helping Nicholls escape. Beauclerk's young servant, John Steyne Verea, gave evidence against his employer in the subsequent trial, saying that he had seen Beauclerk and Nicholls conspiring together on the eve of Nicholls's escape and that he had slept with Beauclerk ever since he had started working for him. Beauclerk denied it all, but Charles Murray

committed him to Horsemonger Lane, where he was searched
on entry and placed in a ward on his own, where he dined at five
o'clock before being locked in his cell. That night he slit his own
throat with a penknife. When Varea was told what had happened,
he said he was not surprised, as 'he had heard the captain say that
if ever he was taken into custody, he should destroy himself'.[26]
The public was furious. Beauclerk had cheated the gallows and
Nicholls was still free.

There was then a further disappearance of a thirteen-year-
old boy called Robert Paviour in March 1833. His body was
found in the Regent's Canal 'with both arms broken' and it was
assumed that he had been murdered. The home secretary offered
a reward of £100 and a pardon for any information that led to
the apprehension of the murderer. When Frederick Marshall,
George Evans and William Taylor were charged with Paviour's
murder, the press did not attempt to disguise their sense of
disgust. Marshall was described as about twenty-six, thin and
short, with brown hair and a pointed nose. He dressed elegantly
in a black frock coat, white neckerchief and Wellington boots of a
superior make, 'evidently the left-off clothes of some person of a
higher grade in society'. The *Bucks Herald* noted 'his appearance
is rather dissipated, and when he spoke it was in an effeminate
tone'.[27] However, all three were acquitted at the Old Bailey in
April 1833 and the murder remained unsolved. Yet again the
public felt cheated.

A few weeks later, Captain Nicholls was arrested, tried, convicted
and sentenced to death for sodomy at Croydon. Anxious that he
too should not evade justice, the turnkeys searched him carefully
on his arrival at Horsemonger Lane, when they found a sharpened
nail secreted in his jacket. He seems to have been reconciled to
his sentence by the time he was executed at the gaol on 12 August
1833, but it was said that his 'highly respectable family' refused to
visit him, or even take his body.[28] Neither the law nor armchair
moralists drew any distinction between paedophilia and gay sex
between consenting adults at the time, so the story of Beauclerk's
suicide and Nicholls's execution may have made James, John
and William especially anxious as they arrived at Horsemonger

Lane. They might not have wept any tears for the last man to have hanged there, Frederick Finnegan, who at twenty-eight had drowned his twenty-month-old daughter Charlotte Matilda in a ditch in a fit of fury when he discovered his wife was having an affair. They might, however, have read of Finnegan's execution shortly before nine o'clock on 1 December 1834, when 'immediately the party arrived at the top of the prison, a tremendous shower commenced, which in one minute drenched everyone present'. It was said that Finnegan, who was a muscular man, had hoped for forgiveness until the very last, but James, John and William might have speculated whether someone would soon write the same of them: 'The last solemn offices of preparation and of religion having terminated, the platform fell, and the unfortunate man died in the presence of an immense number of spectators.'[29]

In other regards Horsemonger Lane Gaol compared well with the majority of contemporary prisons. George Gwilt the elder had built it between 1791 and 1798 to house 300 prisoners according to a set of principles laid down by the prison reformer John Howard. It formed a three-storey quadrangle, three sides of which housed criminals, mostly awaiting trial, the fourth side being reserved for debtors. Round the outside was an extensive kitchen garden. The poet Leigh Hunt had been imprisoned there from 1812 to 1814 for supposedly libelling the prince regent, and received much-publicised visits from a number of luminaries who disagreed with his incarceration, including the fellow-poets Thomas Moore and Lord Byron. One of Hunt's visitors, Cyrus Redding, said that his apartment 'was cheerful for such a place, but that only means a sort of lacquered gloom after all'. He added, 'if the place was not unwholesome, it lay close upon the verge of insalubrity'.[30] Similarly, William Dixon was scandalised in 1850 that some of the prisoners 'clearly prefer their present state of listless idleness: with hands in their pockets, they saunter about their dungeon, or loll upon the floor, listening to the highly spiced stories of their companions, well content to be fed at the expense of the county – upon a better diet, better cooked, than they are accustomed to at home – without any trouble or exertion on their own part'.[31] Horsemonger Lane visitors reported to Parliament in

1832 and 1833 that they 'invariably found … every thing relative
to the prison and its officers in a state of cleanliness and good
order'.[32] Each prisoner had his own bed. Towels were provided
twice a week, soap and combs were made available on request and
those awaiting transportation washed the prisoners' linen. Meals
were basic but adequate, as each male prisoner was allocated 24
ounces of bread a day, 5¼ ounces of meat, with a pint of soup
and a pint of gruel three times a week. The bread was said to be
'good wheaten household bread, of a former day's baking' and
the soup was made from 'the clods and stickings of good ox beef
without bone, thickened with Scotch barley and vegetables from
the prison garden'.[33]

There were problems. Two turnkeys were dismissed in 1834 for
'clandestinely conveying articles to the prisoners',[34] and another
resigned during 1835 for twice getting drunk and trying to pick a
fight with an inmate. Although the health of the prisoners was said
to be good, diarrhoea prevailed in the prison 'to a considerable
extent' in May 1834; in September that year four prisoners got
cholera and two died. The biggest problem in 1835, though,
resulted from 'the unemployed state of the prisoners', and the
'inevitable corruption of the morals of the better disposed'. Only
weeks before James, John and William arrived there, it had been
decided that some of the prisoners should be employed in picking
oakum and 'in scraping the iron-work of the prison previously
to its being painted'.[35] The chaplain was sceptical that this would
deliver the expected improvement in morale and complained of 'a
gradual, almost a frightful, increase in the number of the prisoners
in the gaol'. Yet he said that the prisoners were devout, attentive,
submissive and obedient to the authorities, although he regretted
to say that he could speak less favourably of the female prisoners
than the male.[36]

This was the men's home for three weeks. Visitors were allowed
between twelve and two every day, but they had to stand on the
other side of a double iron grating at the end of the airing-yard, with
a prison officer standing in between. Explaining his predicament

to Elizabeth cannot have been pleasant for James. Did he protest his innocence? But it must have been equally harrowing for her. She had her own shame with which to contend. Would she admit the nature of her husband's crime if anyone asked her? Would she deny all knowledge of his 'unnatural crime'? There would be little privacy to ask James the many questions that must have been running around in her head. She would have been searched on entry – perhaps for the first time in her life. Yet she would also know that with no facilities to wash clothes, James relied on her to bring fresh linen – and she may even have done the same favour for John.

Visiting hours for condemned prisoners at Newgate were limited, but James's wife Elizabeth stood by him and organised a petition among friends and neighbours in Deptford, pleading for his life.

Practical matters may also have consumed their thoughts. James was the breadwinner in the house and the law required that a felon be deprived of his property when he was hanged. It had been a source of public anger that James Bartlett, who was hanged for sodomy at Horsemonger Lane in 1809, had managed to convey more than £1,500 to his daughter before the trial. And one newspaper commented on Finnegan's execution that he was 'possessed of some property in Camberwell'.[37] When David Myers was hanged for sodomy in 1812, his wife found herself and her family 'bowed down into the dust by affliction, and utterly unable to raise themselves from their prostrate state without assistance'.[38] Fearing losing her millinery business, she appealed to the public, who raised more than £251 on her behalf. But she had a string of wealthy clients and local worthies to assist her, unlike Elizabeth Pratt. Neither John Smith nor William Bonell seems to have had any dependants, but as the three men awaited trial, James and Elizabeth must have worried that his disgrace might bring destitution to his wife and daughter.

All three men must also have shared another emotion in varying degrees. When John Church was imprisoned for two years for attempting sodomy in 1817, he wrote, 'all was dark within … horror overwhelmed me, and I sunk low at the footstool of divine mercy; I feared, I trembled, I was brought low, I was troubled … What a state to be in!'[39] He was a clergyman and turned to his faith, but James, John and William must have felt similar feelings of shame, horror, depression and fear.

Hell above Ground

On Saturday afternoon on 19 September 1835, James, John and William along with twenty-one other Surrey prisoners were marched 'Newgate fashion', cuffed together in pairs, from Horsemonger Lane Gaol to Newgate in preparation for their trials, which would start the following Monday morning. All bar three were men. They were committed for fraud, embezzlement, theft, burglary, counterfeiting, breaking and entering and stealing a mare. Jane Jackson, a twenty-eight-year-old 'spinster' was charged with stealing a pillow worth 5s. Lucy Nelson was said to have stolen a bonnet and 'monies' worth 30s 6d. Mary Jones was charged, with her husband, a baker, of counterfeiting forty-six half-crowns and four crowns. Only one other prisoner in the Surrey chain-gang was up for a sexual crime, a forty-nine-year-old hot-presser called Charles Parr, who was said to have assaulted Mary Ann Parr with intent 'feloniously to ravish and carnally know her'.[1] It was commonplace for prisoners who were charged together to be cuffed together, but James, John and William may have been kept apart or treated to ribald comments about holding hands. The one-and-a-half-mile journey cannot have taken much more than thirty or forty minutes along Horsemonger Lane, down Borough Road to the obelisk at St George's Circus, straight up Great Surrey Street (passing George Street on the right), across Blackfriars Bridge, up the gentle incline of New Bridge Street, turning right onto Ludgate Hill just before the Fleet Prison, then left into Old Bailey, past the Sessions House until they reached

Newgate Gaol. These were streets James Pratt had walked down on 29 August.

The journey would have been unpleasant, as crowds took every opportunity to jeer at criminals bound for Newgate and pelted them with whatever came to hand. But the men must also have quailed at the sight of the gaol itself. The building was not especially old. A predecessor had been burnt to the ground during the orgy of senseless violence known as the Gordon Riots in 1780, so the edifice was just fifty years old. But its 297 feet of regimented, dark, unornamented high stone walls inspired fear. As one writer put it in 1829, 'the exterior appearance of no structure ever better corresponded with the purpose for which it is intended; there is a sort of gloomy grandeur and terror-striking uniformity in its outer walls, which would at once point it out as the abode of crime or misery.'[2] Another said that it loomed 'grim and grimy' and that 'every one of the rugged weather-beaten stones ... seem[ed] eloquent of its purpose'.[3] Charles Dickens never forgot the 'mingled feelings of awe and respect' he felt when he gazed on its 'rough heavy walls and low massive doors' as a schoolboy.[4] The knocker on the prison door was said to be the deepest shade of black imaginable. Criminals would swear 'Newgate seize me' as an oath akin to 'on my children's lives' and there were dark rumours of a 'Newgate monster' within its walls. Even short prisoners had to stoop to enter, as the outer door puncturing the four-foot-thick walls was just four feet six inches high. It seemed designed to let people enter, but never leave. Above it, iron spikes and bars were across every window. Curious passers-by would often spot someone standing just within the outer door and leaning over the spiked railings: 'an ill-looking fellow, in a broad-brimmed hat, belcher handkerchief and top-boots ... and an immense key in his hand'.[5] Only rarely, though, would they catch sight of what lay beyond the inner door, whose hefty oak was reinforced with iron and whose brass bolt rumbled ominously when it was locked at night. As Dickens noted, thousands might pass by 'this gloomy depository of the guilt and misery of London' every day 'utterly unmindful of the throng of wretched creatures pent up within it'.[6]

What primarily earned Newgate its reputation, though, was the fact that it had been the capital city's place of execution since 1783, when Tyburn was abandoned. On either side of the main entrance stood two lodges, each with a pediment and iron-barred fanlight and steps up to a large studded door. Facing the gaol, to the right, stood the 'Felons' Lodge' and to the left, the 'Debtors' Lodge'. A separate debtors' prison had opened its doors in Whitecross Street in 1815, so Newgate's Debtors' Lodge and Yard had been reassigned, but the 'Debtors' Door' retained a grisly use. On the day of an execution, a scaffold would be erected outside the Lodge, projecting into the street of Old Bailey. At the appointed hour, the condemned prisoners would pass through the Debtors' Door, climb the steep steps to the scaffold where, in a cruel pun, they would pay their final debt to society.

Newgate's exterior was 'massive, dark, and solemn, arrests the eye and holds it'.[7] But once inside, another sensation overtook you. The place stank, as the prisoners were kept in clammy dungeons for fourteen or fifteen hours every day; the floors were so damp that some were swimming in an inch or two of water; and straw or miserable bedding was laid on the floors. The stench permeated everything, including clothes and books. One report commented, 'the atmosphere of the apartments is heavy, and when they are first opened in the morning the smell is most offensive'.[8] A turnkey was more forthright. 'The air in the morning is enough to knock a man down', he said, advising any visitor to empty his stomach and bowels, 'to carry off any putrid or putrescent substance which may have lodged in them'.[9] It was renowned for disease. The 'Black' Assizes held at the next-door Central Criminal Court in 1750 had seen sixty lawyers, jurors and witnesses infected by prisoners with the 'gaol fever' raging in Newgate and judges still insisted that the court be fumigated every day by plunging a red-hot poker into a bucket of vinegar and sweet herbs.[10] The gaol was so dark that candles and burners were used all day, and one contemporary said the darkness was so oppressive you could lean against it. Even in the depth of winter prisoners would tear away the paper covering the windows to allow in a little fresh air. The sounds that echoed round the musty walls were just as disturbing, as 'lunatics raving mad ranged up and down the wards, a terror to all they encountered'.[11] Many referred to Newgate as 'Hell above ground'.

As the Surrey prisoners waited to be processed, they sat in the 'bread-room', where the prison staff had assembled gruesome memorabilia. There were old manacles and leg-irons, including the twenty-pound set worn by the infamous burglar Jack Sheppard, who was the last man to escape from Newgate but had eventually been hanged, and the thirty-eight-pound set worn by the highwayman Dick Turpin. There were plaster casts of the heads of John Bishop and Thomas Williams, who had been sentenced to death in December 1831 along with James May for killing a young boy called Carlo Ferrari and trying to sell his body for twelve guineas at the dissecting room at King's College in Somerset House. May had been reprieved at the last minute, but the two infamous 'Burkeites' had hanged, and as Dickens put it, Bishop's features were so repugnant that they would have 'afforded sufficient moral grounds for his instant execution'.[12] Pride of place was reserved for the instruments of execution. There was the axe made for the decapitation of Arthur Thistlewood and the other Cato Street conspirators who had originally been sentenced to be hanged, drawn and quartered for high treason in 1820. It had never been used – the decapitation was done with a surgeon's scalpel – but the leather belts used for pinioning prisoners before their execution had been used. One was long enough to circle the largest waist and clasp the arms and hands close to the body and the other would serve to hold your legs together in case you kicked.

From here on in, the gaol was a series of tortuously winding high-sided corridors, dismal passages, numerous staircases, cast-iron gates and gratings, tiny windows, narrow paved yards and dank wards and cells.

The English prison system was a scandal, but campaigners for penal reform had been active since the 1770s, and John Howard[13] and his brother-in-law Samuel Whitbread MP in the eighteenth century and the Quakers Elizabeth Fry and her brother Joseph Gurney in the early nineteenth century had won several victories that benefited James, John and William. Most notably, manacles and leg-irons were now outlawed; and Sir Robert Peel's Gaols Act of 1823 stipulated that men and women were to be incarcerated separately, prison staff were to be paid, doctors and chaplains were to look to the physical and moral condition of their inmates and every gaol was to provide education to inmates.

Newgate, though, was still unreformed. It was overcrowded. Roughly 3,000 prisoners were committed to it every year and although its numbers ebbed and flowed, there were normally about 300 prisoners awaiting trial, transportation or execution, serving out a sentence or imprisoned at the command of the House of Commons for a breach of parliamentary privilege. There was little attempt at hygiene. Each yard had a single washing-place – a cold-water pump, with no sink or basin – and a single, very public, place 'to make water'. Prisoners complained that new inmates often arrived covered in vermin. No linen was provided, nor enough soap to wash so much as a shirt, so inmates had to hope that visitors would bring them fresh linen. Security was lax, too. Warders subjected visitors to rudimentary searches, but so many were admitted every day that all sorts of banned objects got through, including playing cards, tobacco, saws and files. Meat pies, whole joints of meat and virtually every kind of delicacy also found their way in. The prisoners' desire to supplement the prison diet was understandable, as it consisted of a pint of gruel for breakfast and on alternate days, half a pound of beef or a quart of soup for dinner.

Nor was there any attempt at rehabilitation. On the contrary, with no privacy, no employment and no education, prisoners were left to stew in their own juices. The men huddled together around the fireside, miserable, anxious and bored. One lad might be in his employer's livery, another would be dressed in a vast greatcoat and top-boots, a farmer might be in his smock-frock. The one thing that united them was that they were 'all idle and listless'.[14] Some people thought 'serve them right', but others reckoned the system was counter-productive. As the duke of Richmond, who chaired a Select Committee on prison discipline in 1835, told the House of Lords, 'men who at first went into prison comparatively innocent were, by the present system, returned upon their parish with increased power of mischief, and with more depraved dispositions than before'.[15] Others claimed that 'extensive burglaries and robberies were plotted in Newgate, and notes were forged and coining was carried on within its gloomy walls.' In short, it was 'a school and nursery of crime', and 'the most depraved were set free to contaminate and demoralise their more innocent fellows'.[16]

People had been complaining about it for decades. Alderman Sir Richard Phillips, who was responsible for the gaol as one of the sheriffs of London, admitted in 1808 that it was a disgrace. 'The shameless victims of lust and profligacy', he said, 'are placed in the same chamber with others who, however they may have offended ... still preserve their respect for decency and decorum.'[17] The MP Henry Grey Bennet also urged the City to act to 'rescue the metropolis of this great empire from the well-merited stigma of having the worst-regulated prison in the kingdom' in 1818.[18] But the gaol was a particularly hot topic of debate when James, John and William arrived. The philanthropist William Crawford, who had long argued as a member of the London Prison Discipline Society for a more humane prison system, reported to Parliament in 1834 on the beneficial effects of individual cells he had seen in penitentiaries in Pennsylvania in the United States of America. Then the duke of Richmond's Committee on Gaols reported on the terrible conditions in many English gaols and the home secretary Lord John Russell brought in a Prison Discipline Bill 'for effecting greater uniformity of practice in the government of the several prisons in England and Wales', which was enacted on 25 August, just days before James, John and William were arrested.[19] The new Act introduced the first paid commissioners or inspectors of prisons, whom Russell appointed on 14 September, making Crawford one of the two commissioners responsible for the Home Counties, including London, along with the Reverend Whitworth Russell, the former chaplain of the Millbank Penitentiary, who also believed prisons should be a place of education and reform as well as of punishment. The inspectors immediately set to work and made Newgate their first port of call, arriving when James, John and William were there. The commissioners were shocked. Newgate was, they said, 'an institution which outrages the rights and feelings of humanity, defeats the ends of justice, and disgraces the profession of a Christian country'.[20]

The Middlesex magistrates were also furious about Newgate that autumn. Their chairman was Benjamin Rotch, an independently minded Whig, who had been born in France to American parents with a whaling business in Nantucket. He had sat as a reformist MP for Knaresborough from 1832 to 1835 but had stood down to focus on his work as a lawyer and magistrate. In October he condemned Newgate as 'one of the most ill-conducted gaols in the kingdom' and suggested that the annual return made to Parliament by the City of London showed 'a mixture of deceit and insufficiency'.[21] The only reform of Newgate worth talking about, he added, 'would amount to a total demolition of it'.[22] This led to a fierce row with the lord mayor, Henry Winchester, and with Alderman Thomas Wood, who attacked Rotch's claims as a 'tissue of wilful and deliberate falsehood'.[23] Rotch overplayed his hand when he challenged Winchester to an illegal duel and Winchester retaliated with a threat of arrest for breach of the peace, so by the end of the year Rotch had apologised, resigned and been replaced by a thrice-wounded hero of the Peninsular War, General Sir John Scott Lillie.

James, John and William would have known little of these controversies, but they rapidly came to know the horrors of Newgate. On the Saturday night they were searched by a junior turnkey and were admitted to the receiving ward, where they stayed until Monday morning. This brought a cursory examination by the popular thirty-six-year-old prison surgeon, Dr Gilbert Macmurdo, who had a 'fair patrimony and a fine personal appearance' and also worked as the assistant surgeon at the Royal Ophthalmic Hospital at Moorfields.[24] Next was a brief meeting with the ineffectual governor, William Wadham Cope, before the men were introduced

to the real power in the gaol, the 'inner gatesman', a convicted
prisoner who allocated prisoners to their accommodation and was
also a 'wardsman' in charge of one of the wards.

This was their first introduction to the endemic corruption in
the prison. Things were not quite as bad as in the old days when
prisoners were told that they had to pay a 'garnish' on arrival
or else surrender their clothes to pay the debt. Then the inner
gatesman's command had been 'strip or pay', and many prisoners
had no choice but to go virtually naked. There was still no prison
uniform, but by 1829 destitute prisoners were clothed at the
expense of the City, to the tune of 12 shillings apiece. The Gaol
Act 1815 was unambiguous: 'No money under the name of garnish
shall be taken from any prisoner, under any pretence whatsoever.'[25]
But although the turnkeys, who were direct employees of the
gaol, observed the Act, the wardsmen ignored it and enjoyed
special privileges: a bedstead and a flock mattress, double rations
from the stores and the freedom to drink, smoke, take snuff and
avoid chapel. A wardsman could make life very unpleasant for
anyone who refused to pay his 'dues'. He could lodge a formal
complaint to the turnkeys, he could give a prisoner his soup or
gruel in a pail instead of a bowl, he could keep him from the fire,
he could refuse to allow him to make his own coffee and thereby
'vex and distress a fellow prisoner who resisted the exaction of
a weekly fee'.[26] So powerful were the wardsmen that Governor
Cope openly admitted that a prisoner 'of weak intellect' who had
been severely beaten by a wardsman did not dare to complain,
simply because he feared the wardsman's ability to do him harm
far more than he trusted the governor's ability to protect him.
The inner gatesman's tyranny was even more absolute, as all the
prisoners were in his power. As one report put it, 'If a man is poor
and ragged, however inexperienced in crime, or however trifling
may be the offence for which he has been committed, his place
is assigned among the most depraved, the most experienced, and
the most incorrigible offenders.'[27] In practice, that meant charging
exorbitant 'dues' for mildly better lodging.

As for James, John and William, since their crime was considered
one of the worst offences, they were automatically sent to Chapel

Yard, which had three wards, nos. 10, 11 and 12. Here too the bedding, crockery, cutlery, kettles and saucepans belonged to the wardsman, another convicted prisoner, who charged his inmates 2s 6d per week, roughly the same as William had paid for his room in George Street. The only option for an inmate who could not afford these 'dues' was to do without essentials and beg from his friends and family when next they visited. Despite being housed with the worst and most violent offenders, there were benefits to being in Chapel ward. It was just as dank as the rest of the gaol, but there was a supply of books and a newspaper was delivered daily, which might have been of interest to James and William, but not to John, who could not read. Much to the dismay of the new prison inspectors, there was also a copy of John Robertson's book, *On Diseases of the Generative System*, which had been published by the pornographer John Stockdale and was described as 'a book of a most disgusting nature, and the plates are obscene and indecent in the extreme'.[28] There were also playing cards, a cribbage board and a set of draughts, and the governor's son ran errands for inmates for a penny a time.

One problem would have reared its head early on. The vast majority of prisoners slept on rope or hemp mats 'worked with a portion of tar, to prevent the lodging of vermin', laid on the floor with two rugs to cover them.[29] These were rolled up and put away or hung on the wall during the daytime, but Chapel Yard was so overcrowded with fifty or sixty prisoners that each man had just eighteen inches to lie down in at night. Those accused of 'unnatural' offences were often viewed with contempt or suspicion. When the House of Lords Select Committee on Gaols took evidence from the principal turnkey at Newgate, Matthew Newman, they were horrified to hear that there was no means of keeping prisoners charged with 'unnatural attempts' separate from the rest. They also asked him whether he thought that with so many men sleeping together in the wards and with no segregation of those charged with 'unnatural acts', they 'contaminate[d] one another'. The reply shocked them: 'I should think they do.'[30] In other words, men were having sex together. The overcrowding meant that it was almost impossible to stop them. As Norman put it, 'The wardsmen must sleep; the rooms are dark; and if men are disposed to avail themselves of the opportunity, nothing can keep them from it.'[31]

This may explain why those charged with the 'abominable crime of buggery' do not seem to have received a worse reception from their fellow inmates, and even senior gaolers reckoned that 'the disgust of such characters soon wears off, from being associated with them'. When James, John and William arrived in Chapel Yard, Robert Salter, a thirty-eight-year-old servant, who had been convicted of a 'disgusting assault upon Edward Hall at a print-shop on the corner of Lawrence-lane in Cheapside on the 30th of May', was in ward 12, three months into a twelve-month sentence.[32] Apparently Salter spent all day in the company of another prisoner under 'a similar atrocious charge' in a neighbouring ward. This could be one of two men convicted on the same day the previous December. The first was John Mills, a seaman for the East India Company, who had been an invalid in the Royal Hospital Ship lying off Greenwich in November when he made an indecent approach to the young lad in the hammock next to him, Daniel Chambers. The lad initially asked to move to another part of the ship, but the boatswain's mate persuaded him to lodge a formal complaint, which led to the charge. Mills appeared in court as 'a person respectably attired'[33] and protested that nobody had ever previously impugned his integrity, but he was convicted of assault with intent to commit an unnatural crime on 5 December 1834 and sentenced to two years. Salter's friend may also have been Elias Hill, 46, who was convicted of an attempt to commit an unnatural crime with a nineteen-year-old, John Kraas, who, according to the *Sun*, was half-German and 'in a state of starvation' when he met Hill in Whitechapel and was induced to expose himself 'for the sake of a penny'.[34] Since both men were consenting but there was no evidence of buggery, they were both sent to prison – for two years and one month respectively. Whichever of the two men it was, Mills or Hill, he and Salter would meet up, walk together in the yard and, as the prison inspectors resentfully pointed out, 'even the other prisoners did not feel indignant at their offences, or avoid associating with them!'[35] It is tempting to think that the friendship lasted after they were released, although Salter, now described as a cheesemonger, was back in the penitentiary in 1841.

Such miserable conditions must have come as a shock to the three men, and James's only relief that week is likely to have been a visit from Elizabeth, as visitors were admitted to those awaiting trial on Mondays, Thursday and Saturdays, when they could bring in whatever provisions they liked, apart from poultry and fish. Elizabeth must have quailed at the prospect of visiting Newgate. It was a much longer walk from Deptford than to Horsemonger Lane. She would have to queue up with 100 to 150 people whom the prison commissioners called 'persons of notoriously bad character, prostitutes and thieves'.[36] But she stood by James, despite the indignity. That must have been some comfort. We know of no such visitors for John or William.

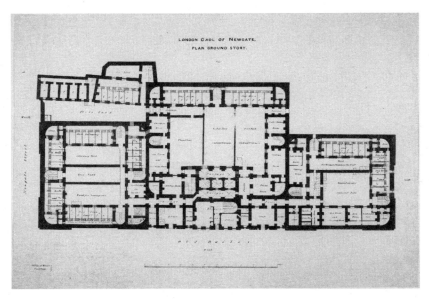

Newgate Gaol was rebuilt after a fire in 1780, but it was described as 'Hell above ground'. Top left lie the press-yard and condemned cells. Just left of centre at the bottom is the Debtors' Lodge and Door where prisoners paid their 'last debt to society'.

9

The Old Court

Nobody had anything good to say about the irascible and cantankerous lord mayor. Henry Winchester had started out as a stationer and made enough of a fortune out of government contracts to be able to purchase a house in Buckingham Street, demolish and rebuild his father-in-law's house in Hawkhurst in Kent and launch himself into politics, first as the Tory and anti-reform MP for Maidstone (for a year) and then as an alderman in the City of London. He sowed bitterness wherever he went. There were allegations of corrupt electoral practices and dodgy finances. He had become lord mayor by process of rotation and was sworn in on 8 November 1834, but he was now a laughing stock. People joked that he wanted a peerage as 'Baron Foolscap' and that he was about as stupid, cowardly and two-faced as he was corrupt – witness his terrible mismanagement of Newgate.[1] His private life was no happier. He fell out with a brother-in-law and his son-in-law so badly that they separately took him to court; and his youngest son died at the Mansion House that summer. Within three years Winchester would be declared bankrupt and confined to Dr Sutherland's lunatic asylum after attacking his remaining son with a poker; in the asylum, 'the symptoms became more alarming and he expired'.[2]

That was still to come, but on the morning of Monday 21 September 1835 Winchester donned black stockings, silk breeches, waistcoat and court coat, a ruffled jabot and buckled shoes, a scarlet robe with grey fur facings and his gold chain of office and processed from the Mansion House to the Old Bailey behind the City's sword-bearer, who was equally resplendent in a black silk damask robe bordered with velvet, with pendant tassels about the sides and sleeves and 'a curious fur cap in form not unlike a Persian caftan'.[3] After a big breakfast in his mirrored dining room, Winchester took his place in the Old Court of the Central Criminal Court at ten o'clock, 'looking as cool as the Lord Mayor can look, with an immense bouquet before him, and habited in all the splendour of his office'.[4] Thus he opened the eleventh Sessions of Oyer and Terminer and Gaol Delivery for London, Middlesex and the parts of Essex, Kent and Surrey within the jurisdiction of the Central Criminal Court. By his side were two senior judges, Sir John Gurney and Sir James Williams, and the other officers of the City, also attired in their scarlet robes of state: the recorder, Charles Ewan Law MP; his deputy, the sergeant at law, William St Julien Arabin; the common sergeant, a Welshman, John Mirehouse; and twelve aldermen. A keen eye might have spotted several former mayors, whose robes were lined with taffeta and edged with grey marten fur known as amis, rather than the green taffeta lining and calabar squirrel fur worn by the lesser aldermen.[5] This pomp and ceremony was not accidental; it was designed to impress the dreadful majesty of the court upon the criminal mind, but a few satirical commentators liked to remember the poet Samuel Butler's comments on a seventeenth-century alderman: 'His fur gown makes him look a great deal bigger than he is, and like the feathers of an owl, when he pulls it off, he looks as if he were fallen away, or like a rabbit, had his skin pulled off.'[6]

The Old Bailey was an ancient institution, but it had changed. The original medieval courthouse was lost in the Great Fire in 1666 and its 1673 replacement had been remodelled in 1737 and 1774. The courtroom, once open on one side to the elements, was now fully enclosed. The facilities for court officials, once rudimentary, were now opulent. The passage through to Newgate was now hidden behind brick walls. Spectators no longer had to crowd around in the yard, but were now allowed into the courtroom. The biggest administrative change, however, came in 1834. Until then, the Old Bailey had dealt with cases from the City of London and from the county of Middlesex separately. Since everyone was entitled to be tried by their peers, the Sessions always started with these two jurisdictions empanelling separate grand juries made up of property-owning men aged between twenty-one and sixty who lived in their respective areas. The London grand jury would then meet in the Old Bailey and the Middlesex grand jury would meet at the Middlesex Sessions House on Clerkenwell Green. However, that all changed with the creation of the Central Criminal Court, as the whole new district, including nine parishes in Essex, ten in Kent and twelve in Surrey, was to be 'considered as one county … for all purposes' and the court was allowed to summon juries 'indiscriminately'.[7] That meant that the grand jury and the petty jury (which heard the trial) would consist of a mixture of men from across the metropolis.

The introductory business that morning was dealt with in a couple of hours. The court was told that 186 defendants would appear before it that week, and there was a discussion about deferring a case featuring twenty-two proprietors of omnibuses who were alleged to have conspired to drive Mr Bray's omnibuses off the road and out of business. Once that was resolved, the grand jury was sworn in. Its twenty-five members were a cut above the rest. Six were listed as 'gentlemen', eleven were 'merchants', and Archibald Hunter and Charles Ellis Heaton were 'esquires', that is to say, just below the rank of knight. The latter was a barrister, a trustee and director of Alfred Life Assurance and owned a fine two-storey mansion, Bedford's, in Havering in Essex, as well as 43 Mortimer Street, and would later inherit a substantial fortune. Another juror, John Farnell, was the prominent fifty-year-old owner of Isleworth brewery. He was considered a significant philanthropist, but we can get a flavour of his views from a meeting he chaired two years later for Conservative candidates for the Middlesex seats in the general election, at which Henry Pownall declared 'the present was not a time for privacy, for it was a duty which they owed to their Creator (to whom they would be answerable thereafter) to come forward'.[8] One 'gent', Francis Joseph Humbert, lived at 239 Oxford Street and having recently withdrawn from the family hotel and wine merchant business, was a director of the Barbados General Railway. One of the 'merchants', Alfred Hardcastle, was a ten-guinea subscriber to the evangelical Wilberforce Fund, but he must have been irritated that his jury summons clashed with a civil case he had brought at the court of the King's Bench that same day. His absence meant he lost. One other grand juror was the thirty-year-old architect John Hallett, who lived at 5 Mortimer Street.

Once all twenty-five were sworn in, the recorder explained a few matters of law regarding the upcoming cases. It was not necessary to trouble them with many observations, he said, because although they were to consider charges of a most atrocious character, most presented 'no matter of difficulty in point of law'.[9] He would, however, pass comment on four, namely a complex larceny case, an arsenic poisoning, a stabbing and a malicious shooting. Then he talked more darkly about 'a case of a most serious character, as to which he would say, without attempting to enter into the details, if the facts contained in the depositions were proved before the Grand Jury, it would be their bounden duty to put the case in a course of trial'.[10] He did not name James and John, nor the charges against them, but the obscure reference to a case without a name must have left the jurors either nodding sagely or wondering what on earth he was talking about. The court then swore in jurors for the petty jury. Several people sought to excuse themselves. One said he was a schoolmaster with no assistant, another had just set up in business, and only had his young wife to help him. Another claimed that he was deaf, but provoked much laughter when the clerk asked him whether he was so deaf as not to be able to hear at all, and he replied 'I am'.[11] By the time the jurors were all sworn in, the grand jury had considered its first cases, and 'the trials of the prisoners commenced'.[12]

The grand jury was abandoned in England in 1933, but in 1835 its task was to consider whether there were sufficient grounds in each case for the accused to face trial.[13] It read the indictment and interrogated the prosecutor and witnesses for the prosecution. If it decided to certify the charge as 'a true bill', the trial would proceed in front of the 'petty' or trial jury. If the grand jury thought there was not enough evidence, or if the prosecution witnesses failed to appear, the term 'ignoramus' or 'not a true bill' was written on the reverse of the charge sheet and the prisoner was released. Many were critical of grand juries. They were accused of being so legally inept that they were the 'hope of London thieves'. Some thought their role should be given to magistrates. Many jurors found the weeklong task irksome and onerous. Their 'inquest' room was small and incommodious and the prosecutors and witnesses were crowded together outside waiting to be called in. The grand jury foreman that October complained that 'no doubt these circumstances deterred many respectable persons from appearing to give evidence'.[14] And more than 1,100 men entitled to serve as grand jurors in Middlesex had signed a petition in 1831 demanding that the criminal law be amended to remove the death penalty from property crimes where no bloodshed was involved because 'their own private feelings of humanity had at various times caused a struggle within themselves, lest, by finding persons guilty, they should be accessory to a judicial murder'.[15]

The grand jury steadily made its way through the lesser cases that week and occasionally 'ignored' a case, such as the charge of robbery laid against a Mr Myers by a prostitute called Louisa Holmes. On Thursday afternoon the judge, Sir John Gurney, asked them to turn their attention to the capital offences, but they replied they were unable to do so 'in consequence of those who had to give evidence not being in attendance'.[16] This might have given James and John a sniff of hope, but the grand jury had already considered their case on Wednesday. The only evidence it could consider was that of the prosecutors, namely the Berkshires and Sergeant Valentine. When they turned up, the outcome was a formality. It probably took just a few moments for the foreman to sign the charges as 'a true bill'.

As soon as the clerk of the court was notified of the decision, the three men were brought in to enter their plea. They had little choice. By law they had to enter a plea and the vast majority of the accused pleaded innocent – and were encouraged to do so. Otherwise neither the judge nor the jury had any room for manoeuvre. If you pleaded guilty to a felony the judge automatically had to pronounce the death sentence and no mercy

could be offered. But a trial following an innocent plea might lead
to a conviction for a lesser offence or a recommendation for mercy
from the jury. Either course might help you avoid the scaffold. So
at some point in the week the three men pleaded 'not guilty'.

Once commenced, proceedings moved quickly. Judges boasted
that they could get through sixty or seventy trials in a day.
According to one contemporary account, what passed for justice
took on average just eight and a half minutes – and some cases
took even less. Others argued that in a large proportion of the
cases 'five or six minutes are quite sufficient for each trial'.[17] Fifty
or sixty prisoners would be kept huddled together below the
dock getting more and more agitated as one prisoner after another
would go up and return after just a minute or two. Terrified by
the speed with which things were proceeding, they would try to
rearrange their thoughts and fret about how to put their defence
most speedily before the court. But this was irrelevant. Few
had a lawyer. Many said it felt like they were 'taken up to be
knocked down like bullocks, unheard'. Two-thirds of prisoners
could not remember a thing that had transpired in court and it
was not uncommon for a convicted prisoner to say afterwards,
'It can't be me they mean; I haven't been tried yet.'[18] The judges
worked in relays, so that they could make one of the two dinner
sittings at three and five o'clock, but such was the lavishness of
the hospitality that evening sessions of the court, which went on
till nine o'clock, could be very haphazard. More than one young
barrister felt 'disgust to the mode in which eating and drinking,
transporting and hanging were shuffled together'.[19]

Dickens was also struck by the 'calm indifference with which
the proceedings are conducted', as there was 'a great deal of form,
but no compassion; considerable interest, but no sympathy'.[20]
He fictionalised his experience in Magwitch's trial in *Great
Expectations*, when he described 'penned in the dock ... two-and-
thirty men and women; some defiant, some stricken with terror,
some sobbing and weeping, some covering their faces, some
staring gloomily about ... A great gallery full of people – a large

theatrical audience – looked on, as the two-and-thirty and the Judge were solemnly confronted.'[21] There were stories of judges losing their temper at a string of acquittals and summarily handing down completely disproportionate sentences, of sentences being drawn up before the trial had taken place, of 'passion, petulance, irritation and a spirit of unjust revenge' governing decisions from the bench.[22] The wealthy and elderly sergeant at law, William St Julien Arabin, who presided over several cases that week, was reckoned to be so eccentric that many of his comments from the bench made no sense at all and he boasted that he could try a case in five minutes, although 'it will take any other judge, whoever he may be, two hours'.[23]

James, John and William had a long wait. It is impossible to know what the men were expecting. Perhaps they feared the worst. But prison chatter might have pointed out that far more men had been acquitted of sodomy in the Old Bailey over the last twenty-five years than had been convicted. Since 1810 twenty-seven men had climbed the same stairs into the dock charged with sodomy or intent to commit sodomy and had walked free. Four had done so in the last year alone. James and John might have replied that those twenty-five years had also seen fifteen guilty verdicts and ten hangings, but that represented only a one-in-three likelihood of execution.

The week wore on. Early every morning the turnkeys mustered thirty or forty more prisoners in the Master's Side Yard and marched them from Newgate to the Old Bailey, along a narrow passageway, which was known as Birdcage Walk thanks to the open iron cross-bars overhead. It was a grim journey, as the warders explained that the letters carved in the walls were the initials of those who had been hanged and buried at Newgate and that their remains lay beneath the flagstones on which they now walked. This was especially ironic for James and John, as another Birdcage Walk was a renowned gay cruising spot near St James's Park. Once they arrived at the Old Bailey, the prisoners were crowded into a bail dock beneath the court measuring nine feet square. Here they awaited trial, never knowing when their turn would come and often returning to Newgate after waiting from eight in the morning until eleven at night without appearing in court. Some prisoners thought this was the worst time of all. One of those who was in prison with James and John told the inspectors 'There we are mixed up with horrid characters, and are like wild beasts in a den.' The conversation was gross and some of the men behaved as if they were going to a fair, not a trial. 'They annoy', he said, 'all those who are not of their set, and who seem alive to a sense of their situation.'[24] Prisoners were sometimes granted a moment in the open air of the bail dock yard, which was only separated from the public courtyard of the Sessions House and the open street by a low partition. Yet few made their escape.

It is likely that James, John and William went through this ordeal on Friday, when twenty-six prisoners were dealt with during the day and an additional session after dinner tried a further ten. But yet again the court adjourned that night and the three men were marched back to gaol where they had to endure another night of suspense. On Saturday morning they were back in the bail dock waiting their turn. Up above them, the recorder swore in a new jury. Eight of the jurors were from Middlesex, and two each were from London and Surrey, including the foreman, Alfred Chandler, a thirty-year-old resident of Wandsworth Road in Lambeth who followed in his father's profession as a nurseryman.[25] Unlike the grand jurors, these were men of modest property and earnest industry and it is likely that several of them knew each other. Three jurors were based in Marylebone High Street: Thomas Hayward, 'brushmaker and turner', was at no. 40, Henry Alexander Holland's tailor's shop was at no. 43 and John Herbert, who was variously described as a 'silk mercer' and 'decorative painter', was at no. 96. Two more had shops close to each other on Oxford Street. Abraham Landin, who had recently supported the parliamentary candidacy of John Cam Hobhouse, the radical MP and president of the Board of Control, ran a large grocery and tea dealership at no. 148[26] and the unmarried twenty-seven-year-old William Craig Lawrence, who was a local hotelier's eldest child of nine, had his confectioner's at no. 158. Not far away, Thomas

Lewis ran a perfume and hairdressing business out of 42 Duke Street near Manchester Square and William Ifold, architect and subscriber to the Royal Library, worked out of 33 Manchester Street. These were all substantial properties. It is unclear whether William Clark, who had served on juries throughout the week, sat on James and John's case, but perhaps he withdrew because he was a butcher from Trafalgar Road in Deptford and knew James. John Bull, a brewer from the same street in Lambeth as the foreman, replaced Clark and Edward Ingram, a bootmaker from Hanover Place and William Marriot, a successful silversmith living at 27 Fenchurch Street in the City, were added as last-minute replacements for two other jurors who had to excuse themselves.

The first case up that morning was that of Benjamin Green, a thirty-two-year-old charged with obtaining four shillings by false pretences. He had shaved off his whiskers since his arrest, in an attempt to disguise himself, but he was swiftly found guilty and sentenced to a year in the House of Correction. Next was John Knight, an eighteen-year-old who had stolen £10 worth of silverware. Juror William Craig Lawrence would have had little sympathy. He was frequently complaining about thieves stealing buns and sweets or passing counterfeit coin in his shop. Knight too was dealt with swiftly and was to be transported to New South Wales for twenty-one years.

Finally, James, John and William climbed the stairs and appeared at the bar of the Old Court. The room resembled a theatre, with all eyes on the defendants. Immediately opposite them was the witness box, behind which, in a semi-circle, sat the recorder and two aldermen.[27] In the centre of the semi-circle sat Sir John Gurney, one of the five barons of the exchequer or senior English judges. There was a large table covered in green baize for the lawyers and Henry Buckler, the shorthand writer. Four large chandeliers lit the room, and a mirror reflected sunlight from the windows directly onto the prisoners' faces, so that the jury could inspect them more minutely. Above the prisoners was a sounding board to amplify their every word. On their right sat the jury, seated close enough on three benches to be able to confer together and come to a decision without retiring. Behind and above the jury box was a gallery, from which the public could watch proceedings for a fee. James Pratt must have noticed his wife Elizabeth sitting there. He might also have noticed the herbs that had been spread on the bar in front of him to relieve the smell of the inmates of Newgate and (supposedly) ward off gaol fever, or typhus.

The three men are unlikely to have heard of their thin-lipped, beak-nosed and bespectacled judge, Sir John Gurney, who sat beneath the sword of justice dressed in crimson robes and a full-bottomed wig. He prided himself on being independently minded. He came from non-conformist stock, as his father, who was a famed shorthand writer, edited the evangelical *Gospel Magazine* and published non-conformist tracts, and his aunt was a fervent Baptist and abolitionist. He was almost a rebel in his early years, as his wife Maria was the youngest daughter of the physician William Hawes, who founded the Royal Humane Society,[28] and rather than have their children baptised in the Church of England, the couple registered each of their children's births with Dr Williams Library in Red Cross Street. But as he got older, 'high Church and State doctrines had taken firm root in his mind'.[29] Now in his late sixties, he had most notably secured the conviction and execution of two of the Cato Street conspirators in 1820. He was made king's counsel in 1816 and gained his knighthood in 1832 when he became one of the five barons of the exchequer. One fellow lawyer called Gurney 'pitiless ... almost brutal ... very harsh and severe in his administration of justice'. Another pointedly remarked that 'there exist those upon the bench who have the character of convicting judges. I do not envy their reputation in this world or their fate hereafter.'[30]

Back in 1810 Gurney had also represented the seven men from the White Swan in Vere Street. He acted as their 'counsel' and cross-examined the police and other prosecution witnesses, but then made an extraordinary speech, telling the jury that he had only taken on the task because of his oath as an advocate. However, 'he found the testimony so clear and uncontradicted, as to leave no ground of palliation upon which to make any appeal' and he thought the jury might very well conclude that 'the horrors of Sodom and Gomorrah were revived in London'.[31]

Not surprisingly, the men were convicted and sentenced to imprisonment and horrific spells in the pillory in the Haymarket (as detailed above on p. 67). In 1817 Gurney had also defended John Church, the non-conformist preacher of the Surrey Tabernacle in Borough, who was accused of attempting to commit an abominable offence 'upon' (rather than 'with') Adam Foreman, a potter's apprentice from Vauxhall. This time Gurney made 'a most eloquent appeal to the Jury to exculpate the prisoner from the charge alleged against him', but observed that if he were guilty, 'scarcely any punishment was adequate'.[32] Given this ambivalence, it is surprising that Church was only imprisoned for two years at Horsemonger Lane Gaol. It is difficult to see how Gurney could be impartial in a sodomy case.

The two aldermen sitting beside Gurney were equally unsympathetic figures. The senior of the two, the baronet Sir Claudius Hunter, was immensely wealthy thanks to a propitious first marriage and a career as a solicitor in Lincoln's Inn. When he became mayor in 1811, he revived all the pomp and ceremony he could, and held the most expensive and elaborate lord mayor's pageant in decades. He was also a thin-lipped member of the Society for the Suppression of Vice. The other alderman, Thomas Wood, had only been elected (unanimously) for Cordwainer Ward that January, but as a magistrate and the head of a 'highly respectable law firm near Southwark Bridge'[33] he had immediately taken an interest in prison affairs. In July he demanded that the eight 'insane' prisoners then housed in Newgate at the City's expense should be farmed out to the county gaols from whence they came and joked that 'nine out of ten such persons were not insane at all'.[34]

Nothing about the Central Criminal Court was familiar to the three men. Its pomp was deliberately intimidating. Its legal jargon was incomprehensible. Its officers were supremely confident of their authority and their right to judge their fellows. It must have been terrifying.

The Trial

James, John and William stood up as the full indictment was read out. It was long and repetitive, running to 585 words, and took nearly six minutes. It was loaded with pompous religiosity that would have chimed with Gurney, whose son John was a priest who wrote such uplifting hymns as 'Soon to the Dust We Speed' and 'Through Centuries of Sin and Woe'. It claimed the accused had no 'fear of God', that they had forgotten 'the order of nature' and had been 'seduced by the instigation of the devil'. The direct charges started with John Smith, 'labourer'. He had 'feloniously, wickedly, diabolically, and against the order of nature', had a venereal affair with James Pratt, he had 'carnally known' him and he had committed and perpetrated 'the detestable, horrid, and abominable crime (among Christians not to be named) called buggery' with him. All of which, besides being illegal, was 'to the great displeasure of Almighty God, to the great scandal of all human kind' and 'against the peace of our said lord the king, his crown and dignity'. Then came the charges against Pratt. He too had acted 'feloniously, wickedly, diabolically, and against the order of nature' by consenting to Smith doing all of the above to him. As for Bonell, he 'feloniously and maliciously did incite, move, procure, counsel, hire, and command' the two men to commit the felony. It was a lesser count, but the use of the word 'feloniously' intimated that he too might be up for a capital offence.

Then the trial began in earnest. It would be unrecognisable to us today. The scales of justice were horribly unbalanced. The judge

was not expected to be an impartial referee between prosecuting
and defence counsel. Often, he would lead the prosecution
on behalf of the court. Moreover, if the accused had a defence
lawyer – which was far from guaranteed – he was not allowed
to address the jury. As Mr Justice Ashurt reminded Benjamin
Russen at the Old Bailey in 1777, 'Your counsel are not at liberty
to state out of a matter of fact, they are permitted to examine your
witnesses, and they are here to speak to any matters of law that
may arise; but if your defence arises out of matter of fact, you
must yourself state it to me and the jury.'[1] The rationale behind
this was that many thought that a wily lawyer would persuade a
jury that a rogue was an honest man and if defence counsel were
allowed more freedom it would 'change the sober floor of a court
of justice into an arena for two ingenious combatants to display
their strength and agility in'.[2] The rules would change in 1836
when the government brought in the Prisoners Counsel Act, but
James, John and William had to mount what defence they could,
without benefit of counsel.

Even at this late stage it was possible that the prosecution would
collapse if the witnesses refused to appear, but John Berkshire
was the first to take the witness stand – and acted as the chief
prosecutor. The opening questions from Gurney about William
Bonell tell their own story:

Q. Have you known of any occupation that he has had? A.
Not any.
Q. Has he had visitors? A. Yes, he has.
Q. Men or women? A. Men.
Q. Frequent or seldom? A. Frequent.
Q. Have you known them come singly or in company with each
other? A. Generally two.
Q. Has there been more than one couple in the course of a day?
A. At times there have.[3]

In a few short words and without any substantiating evidence,
Berkshire had insinuated that Bonell was unemployed and had
made a habit of bringing male couples back to his room.

The questioning then moved on to the events of 29 August. Berkshire described the arrival of the three men and how he had climbed into the roof of the next-door stable and removed a tile so as to be able to spy on them through Bonell's window. He had seen Pratt sitting on Bonell's knee and then on Smith's for five or six minutes, but he was cramped and by the time he had made himself more comfortable, Bonell and Smith were both standing at the window, laughing, so he gave up and went back downstairs for his tea. A few minutes later his wife looked through the keyhole, and then urged him to go upstairs to take a peek for himself. This time, so he claimed, he saw 'Pratt laying on his back with his trowsers below his knees, and with his body curled up – his knees were up – Smith was upon him – Pratt's knees were nearly up to Smith's shoulders – Smith's clothes were below his knees.' Furious, he put his shoulder against the door and burst it open. Gurney then asked whether Berkshire had seen any 'motion'. Yes, he had, and a great deal of fondness and kissing.

At this point William Bodkin, one of the other lawyers in court, intervened. He was not acting formally as defence counsel, but Henry Buckler's appendix referred to him 'cross-examining' witnesses. Earlier in the week Bodkin's cross-examination in the case of Kezia Scasebrook, who was charged with stealing a shawl, a veil and some fabric worth £5 from her master and mistress had revealed that Kezia was being ill-treated by a 'young man' and that Mrs Edwards would happily have her back as a servant. This encouraged the jury, who found her guilty, to recommend mercy, so she was merely imprisoned for five days. Bodkin also led the prosecution that week in at least six cases, but unlike Gurney he had a reputation for generosity. As a fellow barrister put it several decades later, 'he tempered justice with mercy and combined kindness with firmness'.[4] He also knew sadness, as two of his three daughters had died in infancy in 1822 and 1824. His comments seemed designed to help the three men. He started by asking Berkshire about the keyhole through which he had supposedly witnessed events, the angle at which he was looking, whether the key was in the hole and whether there was any furniture in the way. There were two reasons for this line of questioning. Bodkin was keen to sow doubt in the minds of the jury as to what Berkshire had really seen, but he was also gently suggesting that there was something improper about Berkshire's prurience. The Old Bailey was used to stories of landlords spying on their lodgers. One woman had happily recounted how she had bored a hole in the wainscot with a gimlet so as to spy on a lodger she suspected of having stolen from her in 1753. But the very fact that the door was lockable and that Bonell rather than the Berkshires kept the key, suggested that Bonell was entitled to a degree of privacy, however limited.

Berkshire stood firm on all these points, but then Bodkin asked whether the door was locked, thereby suggesting that if the men had not bothered to lock the door there was probably a more innocent interpretation. Berkshire admitted that the door was not locked and that he could have opened it without breaking in. This admission might have felt like a victory for the three men, but Gurney interjected: 'Whatever the men might have been about, your sudden opening of the door interrupted them, and they got up?' Berkshire replied, 'Yes.' Bodkin's line of questioning had drawn a blank.

Jane Berkshire was the next witness. She had been the first to look through the keyhole and had seen the men lying down on top of each other. The court's questioning got more explicit. Had she seen the 'naked person' of either of the men? Yes, both of them. Had she seen Smith's 'private parts'? Yes. Were they 'laying down, or in a state of erection?' At this point she demurred for a moment, as if embarrassed, but when Gurney asked her again whether Smith's private parts were in a state of erection, she replied, 'Yes, my Lord.' Like her husband, she claimed she had seen the men 'moving', with Pratt's knees up, and she said 'there was every appearance of a connection between them'. After a minute or so she had gone back downstairs and told her husband to have a look for himself. This then gave Bodkin an opportunity to undermine her as a reliable witness. She had already stated that her husband had told her what he had seen through the tile, so why did she not send her husband up to look through the keyhole in the first place? Did she really think it 'a fit thing for a modest woman'? It was a damning enough question, but she coolly responded that she merely wished to see whether there was anything wrong or not.

Sodomy had still not been unequivocally proven, but the next witness was Sergeant Valentine, whose first answer was intended to be damning. 'I examined the linen of Smith and Pratt', he said. 'I found the linen of Smith in a very dirty state in front – the back part of his linen was clean.' When Gurney asked what kind of 'dirt' he meant, he said 'from the fundament'. He had asked Smith about it, who had said he 'had had the bad disorder, which was the cause of it'. As for Pratt's shirt, Valentine claimed the front was clean, but 'the back was in a very foul state' covered in 'a different matter ... of a sort of slimey, glutinous nature, and rather yellow'. When Gurney asked whether it resembled 'the seed of man', Valentine said that it did and added, 'I asked him the cause of his shirt being so dirty – he said he had been bad in his bowels.' Again, Bodkin tried to cast doubt on this evidence, asking why the substance on the inside of the lower flap of Smith's shirt was dry, but the substance on Pratt's shirt was wet. Valentine did not alter his evidence.

That was the end of the prosecution. No modern court of law would have thought it conclusive. The three men were each asked to state their defence. None of them had ever appeared in a court of law before. They had no lawyer to advise them. They had little idea of what to say. Buckler's account is stark:

Smith's Defence. I am not guilty.
Pratt's Defence. I am innocent of the charge.
Bonell's Defence. I am quite innocent.

Their 'defence' merely consisted of reciting their plea. All that remained were the character witnesses. First was Fanny Cannon, who said she had known Pratt for nine years. 'He bore a very good character for morality, decency, and everything that is good', she said, adding 'he always bore a most excellent character in all his situations, in every respect'. Next was Jacob Piggott, a drayman for Barclay and Perkins, who had met Pratt sixteen years earlier when they were neighbours in Camberwell. He repeated the refrain about Pratt's very good character and added that he always found him 'decent in conversation'. Gurney's question seemed sceptical: 'You have not known much of him for the last few years?' Piggott admitted that he hadn't, as Pratt had been living in Greenwich. Gurney put the same question to the next character witness, John Keeley, who lived at Swan Yard and said that Pratt was 'a decent, well-conducted, moral man'. Ah, asked Gurney, but how lately had he been to Pratt's house? as if to suggest that Pratt had changed. The next character witness spotted this turn of questioning and was keen to point out that he was on 'very intimate terms' with Pratt and that their acquaintance had 'continued down to the present time'. True, he had never visited Pratt's house, but 'he bore a very good character – he was very decent in conversation, and always conducted himself very gentlemanly'.

The final two witnesses were married women, Susan Turner and Mary Orchard, both of whom had shared 27 Giffin Street with the Pratt family. Susan had known them for ten years and was lodging with them when James was arrested. The two families were so close that Elizabeth Pratt tended to her when she was in labour with her daughter in 1830 and Susan's husband, a sailor, slept with James. This phrase prompted another question, probably from Bodkin: 'His sleeping with your husband, I suppose, was for convenience during your confinement?' 'Yes', she replied, 'I had but one room.' Mary came last. She and her husband, a ship-caulker, had lived at no. 27 for seven years. She had always found that 'he bore a good character for decency and morality in every respect' and she had 'never heard anything amiss'.

This was a strong list of character witnesses for James, but neither of the other two men had anyone to speak for them and it seems likely that Elizabeth had organised them, as John Keeley expressly referred to her presence in the court, effectively a silent witness to her husband's decency. Such character witnesses could sway a jury. When the Reverend Thomas Jephson was charged in 1823 with attempting to commit sodomy with a labourer called James Welch in a Cambridgeshire gravel pit in broad daylight, the jury were so blinded by the quality of his character witnesses that they overlooked the glaring evidence and acquitted him.[5]

The jury conferred for a moment and the foreman asked Gurney if they could ask Jane Berkshire a further question. 'The window of the room is a back window?' was what they asked. It seemed irrelevant. What bearing could it have on the men's guilt? But Jane replied, 'Yes, it is a corner house' and the follow-up question made plain the jury's concern: 'Might a person coming to your house see a person at the back window?' In other words, even though the events had occurred behind a lockable door, was there not a danger that public morality might be offended if someone happened to look up into the window? Jane's answer clinched that argument: 'Yes, there is a view of the window from the side street.' The jury had no need to retire and it took them seconds to return the verdict on all three men. James and John were guilty of the felony and William of the misdemeanour.

With that, the three men were taken down and returned to Newgate while the court proceeded to its next case.

There was then another hiatus. A law of 1752 dictated that murderers were sentenced immediately after their conviction, but all other convicted prisoners at the Old Bailey had to wait until the jury had delivered its verdict in the final trial of the Sessions before the senior judge and sentencing officer, the recorder, would pronounce sentence.

They would have known little about it, but the trial after theirs would have ramifications for them. This was a robbery case with a difference, as Robert Swan was alleged to have threatened his victim with exposure as a homosexual. Swan was a twenty-eight-year-old private in the 1st battalion of the Scots Fusilier Guards.[6] He was taller than James and John, at five feet eight and a half inches, with brown hair, light hazel eyes and 'dark carroty whiskers'. He bore life's scars. Acne or chickenpox had left him 'pockpitted', he had a large scar on his left hand, and his neck was marked with the signs of scrofula, the tubercular infection of the lymph nodes that some still called the 'King's Evil' because it was thought that it could only be cured by the royal laying-on of hands. Like many soldiers, he also had a tattoo on his lower left arm: 'R+S'.

His story started in Manchester, where he was born and where in 1819 troops charged on protestors in St Peter's Field. Reformers denounced that event as the Peterloo Massacre, but it and another outbreak of unrest in Lancashire in which 3,000 workers destroyed power looms in three mills in April 1826 led Swan to enlist in the foot regiment in May 1826. The regiment remained in Manchester for two years, but soon it returned to London to fulfil its regular duties as members of the household division, based in the Wellington Barracks that opened opposite Green Park in 1833. It was in Green Park that Swan met a wealthy twenty-seven-year-old Quaker from Carshalton called William Reynolds at about nine o'clock on the evening of 18 August. The two men's accounts of events differ. According to Reynolds, he had dined with a friend at the Garrick Club and toyed with going to the English Opera House, but had such a severe headache that he had gone for a walk in the park to clear his head. At one point he turned aside from the path 'for the purpose of making water', which was when a man in a light coat (the Scots Fusilier Guards wore white jackets) said 'good night' and grabbed hold of his coat tails, saying 'this is just what I wanted, you are the sort of men that get soldiers bad names'. Reynolds claimed that Swan then threatened to 'expose' him and asked 'what will you give me to let you go?' Terrified, Reynolds handed over a purse with some money, but Swan also demanded his watch, which Reynolds surrendered before Swan disappeared into the night. Reynolds did nothing about the incident, but when Swan tried to sell the watch in Long Acre a few days later the watchmaker contacted the police, Swan was arrested and after an investigation to establish the owner, the police called a nervous Reynolds in to Bow Street station to recover his watch. Swan was then charged with robbery – and when Reynolds gave his account, robbery with threats.

According to Swan, though, it was Reynolds who first approached him in the park. Reynolds said, 'this is a fine place for girls', and asked Swan whether he would like to meet one there. Swan's affidavit continued: 'we proceeded a little further, and as I thought, he turned his back to make water – I was going on, he said "Stop a bit, I am going through the Park, I will accompany you" – When he turned round again his person was exposed in a disgraceful manner, and he asked me what I thought of that.' He then tried to take Reynolds 'into custody', saying that it was men like him that got soldiers a bad name. In Swan's account, Reynolds then begged him to let him go and Swan agreed to do so on a promise that he would never insult a soldier like that again. He was adamant that Reynolds voluntarily surrendered his purse and watch and the two men agreed to meet the next day when Swan would return the watch in exchange for 'a present'.

Neither story adds up. Reynolds never fully explained what he was doing in Green Park, which was out of his way back to Lincoln's Inn, where he was staying. The parks were well known venues for guardsmen for hire. Plenty of people would have raised an eyebrow, not least because of the Hyde Park stories from 1830. They might also have asked why Reynolds did not report the theft of the watch. It all seemed a bit murky and Reynolds must have feared for his own reputation, if not his life. In another case in 1827 Richard Salisbury had charged a young gardener called John Morton with attempting to extort money by threatening to charge him with an unnatural crime. Morton was convicted, but Morton's wife and the trial jury pleaded for mercy on the grounds that Salisbury had fabricated the evidence and his 'unnatural propensities were known to the police'.[7] In the end Morton was released and Salisbury was disgraced.

However, Swan was in the greater danger thanks to recent changes in the law, which meant that a capital offence was proven if a threat of making allegations were made and property changed hands. Relying on the fact that the truth or otherwise of the threatened allegations was impermissible evidence, Reynolds was lucky that although some of the questioning in court strayed into examining Reynolds's character, the jury found Swan guilty. By the time the court adjourned for lunch at three o'clock, Swan had joined James, John and William back at Newgate as a capital convict.

GLIMPSES OF OLD NEWGATE,
BURIAL GROUND OF EXECUTED PRISONERS.

*The route from Newgate to the Central Criminal Court at the Old
Bailey lay through 'Birdcage Walk', under whose flagstones lay the
remains of executed prisoners.*

The remaining trials continued through Saturday and started again on Monday, and it was not until 4.30 on the Monday afternoon that the last case ended when the jury found 'without hesitation' that John Murphy, 'an ill-looking fellow', was guilty of assaulting four police constables when they tried to arrest him for the rape of Mary Fallen.[8] The Sessions finally over, the recorder processed into court just after five o'clock with a retinue of sheriffs, officials and aldermen. As before, he was dressed in his robes of state and a full-bottomed wig. The ceremony highlighted the recorder's importance as the City of London's senior legal officer, but Charles Ewan Law was not shy about his importance. He was a member of the legal aristocracy as the second son of Edward Law, a harsh and often unfeeling judge who had served as an MP, attorney-general and lord chief justice and was made Baron Ellenborough. Charles's elder brother Edward had spent five years in the Commons before taking their father's seat in the Lords in 1818 and had subsequently served in the duke of Wellington's Conservative administration as lord privy seal – and to complete Charles's establishment credentials, two of his uncles were bishops. The two brothers, Edward and Charles Law, had known scandal in their love lives. Charles became so enamoured of Elizabeth Nightingale (and so impatient of marrying her before his twenty-first birthday) when he was a student at Cambridge that with 'the flame of love growing hotter', they eloped to Gretna Green in 1811.[9] He had to get the dean of Carlisle to calm his father down. Likewise Edward fathered several illegitimate children by a mistress and went through an acrimonious divorce in 1830 when his wife's affair with a Bohemian noble became public. In his youth Charles had the look of a Regency dandy, his pink cherubic cheeks framed by masses of glossy curls, but now he was forty-three and had prospered on the coat-tails of his father, who trained him in the law and appointed him to his first legal posts. He was made king's counsel in 1829 and was elected recorder in 1833. His 'moderate abilities'[10] did not stop him from having stern views on other people's sexual propriety. Having just been elected as one of the two MPs for Cambridge University, he had tabled an amendment to a Bill presented by Sir John Jervis and George Pryme (which sought to *limit* the death penalty) to *toughen* the law on homosexuality. Under his proposal, anyone found to have attempted to commit the 'horrid crime of buggery' would be transported for seven years or more, or be imprisoned for up to four years, with or without hard labour, 'once, twice or thrice publicly whipped' and kept in solitary confinement throughout their imprisonment. It would also be easier to obtain convictions. Law's amendment was added to the Bill, which sailed through the Commons, but the Lords thought the measure so extreme that they effectively killed it by letting it lie on the table. A fellow lawyer, later sergeant-at-law, William Ballantine, thought Law 'dignified in manner before dinner always, and merciful, pompous and disagreeable'.[11] He possessed ability, he added, 'but it was smothered by pomposity and vulgar pride'.[12]

First Law addressed the twelve men and one woman who were to be transported for life. They would have to endure 'severe hard labour for a considerable term' before they could hope to gain a ticket of leave. Next, Law dealt with the ten to be transported for fourteen years. This should have included William Bonell, as his offence was considered a misdemeanour rather than a felony and was therefore punishable by transportation rather than execution. However Law kept him back for special treatment, because, he said, 'his offence was of so abominable a nature ... and perhaps some persons, upon whom sentence of death would shortly be passed, might have to lament that such men as he pandered for such degrading offences'.[13]

If this had been a 'maiden sessions', with no convictions for capital offences, Law would have been wearing white gloves, but his gloves were black, and having dealt with the lesser sentences, Law ordered that the capital convicts be called up.[14] Ever since the Waltham Black Act of 1723 – so named because it was enacted in response to violent crimes that had been committed by people in disguise or with their faces blacked near Waltham in Hampshire – the death penalty had been the failsafe of the English criminal code. All sorts of crimes were termed capital felonies under the Act and many more were added during the eighteenth century. You could be hanged for cutting down an orchard or damaging the banks of a river, stealing goods worth a shilling or more, shoplifting, pickpocketing, concealing a stillborn child as an unmarried mother, stealing hollies, thorns or quicksets, spending a month in the company of 'gypsies', burning a haystack or conspiring to commit any of these offences. In all there were more than 200 capital offences. The result was that, as Sir Samuel Romilly told the Commons in 1810, 'there was no country on the face of the earth in which there had been so many different offences according to law to be punished with death as in England'. He added that this was a legal nonsense, as 'not one out of six or seven who received sentence suffered the punishment annexed by law to their respective offences'.[15]

Romilly and other campaigners managed to get the number of offences whittled down. Romilly had it removed for pickpockets in 1808 and Hensleigh Wedgwood's father-in-law Sir James Mackintosh tabled a motion in 1823 that would have removed it from larceny, forgery, animal stealing and most of the Black Act offences. He reasoned that any foreigner would conclude from the operation of the English penal code that 'we were savage in our threats, but feeble in our execution of punishments' and that 'we cherished a system, which in theory was odious, but which was impotent in practice'.[16] The home secretary Sir Robert Peel would not go that far, but he compromised by removing the death penalty from a smaller number of offences and by introducing another measure Mackintosh had called for, allowing judges outside London the discretion to 'abstain from pronouncing Sentence of Death on Persons convicted of any Felonies, except Murder'.[17] They would still record the sentence as 'death' but they could impose the 'secondary punishment' of transportation instead. That did not always help men convicted of 'unnatural offences'. Sir William Garrow was the first to popularise the phrase 'innocent until proven guilty', but he refused to consider compassion in the case of John Stammers at the Essex Assizes in 1830. 'I cannot, I dare not', he told the accused as he sentenced him to death, 'recommend you to the merciful consideration of his Majesty, and, therefore, do not expect mercy in this world from man.'[18]

The campaign to limit the death penalty continued under Earl Grey's government, as Peel's replacement as home secretary,

Viscount Melbourne, and the more radical lord chancellor, Lord Brougham, steered through several further measures in 1832 that dramatically altered the face of criminal justice. First was the Coinage Offences Act, which made counterfeiting a felony rather than an act of treason and removed the death penalty.[19] Next the government supported a Bill brought forward by one of the Liverpool MPs, William Ewart, which repealed the death penalty for larceny, stealing from a dwelling-house to the value of £5 or more, and sheep, horse and cattle stealing.[20] Since the previous year had seen 162 men and women sentenced to death for sheep-stealing, 125 for horse-stealing and 100 for stealing from a dwelling-house, yet only one of these 387 capital felons had been executed, campaigners understandably claimed that they were merely rectifying a bizarre anomaly in the law. Towards the end of the session came a further measure, the Forgery, Abolition of Punishment of Death Act, which abolished the death penalty for all forgery offences except, thanks to an amendment from the Lords, in relation to the forgery of wills.[21] And on the back of the many petitions for reform that continued to pour in to Parliament, Brougham persuaded the king to set up a Royal Commission on Criminal Law with five reform-minded commissioners led by him, which was still preparing its report on the codification of the criminal law when James and John were arrested.[22]

When, therefore, Law summoned the felons up into the dock to hear their fate, he was merely acting out a formality. No judge at the Old Bailey had a choice about what sentence to impose on a convicted felon. A felony was by definition a capital offence. But Law made great efforts that day to emphasise the dreadful nature of what was in store. Again, he broke with convention. Normally all capital convicts were brought up together, regardless of their crime. But just as he had dealt with Bonell separately, so he ordered that James, John and Robert Swan be kept back while the others were brought to the bar, 'lest they, unhappy and guilty as they were, might feel degraded to appear at the same bar to receive judgement with them'.[23] He would not 'so far confound all penal distinctions as to conjoin men so different in moral delinquency' and he claimed that the three men should be kept apart, because 'their presence would disgrace and contaminate the others'.[24] Addressing the remaining eleven 'in a most impressive manner', he asked them one by one whether they had any reason why they should not suffer the death penalty. When they said nothing, he told them they had forfeited their lives, that he would 'neither hold out an expectation of an extended period of existence, nor would he alarm their fears', and that he would submit their several cases to the king in the presence of his privy council, from which they could expect 'the kindest consideration'. In truth, this not very subtle hint meant that all eleven could expect to see their sentences commuted, but Law still had to perform the courtroom ritual. Donning the black cap, he named each prisoner and pronounced sentence in the usual way, 'and the convicts departed weeping'.[25]

As if he had been saving himself for this moment, Law then suggested that women should leave the court, and as the *Morning Advertiser* put it, 'A vast number of respectable women then left the court, and the culprits were brought in to hear their doom.' We do not know whether Elizabeth Pratt was there. Perhaps the press would not have thought her 'respectable'.

Law started by asking the three men individually the standard question he had asked the eleven others: 'Why should sentence of death not be passed on you?' It was at this point that a pregnant woman could 'plead her belly' and, up until 1827, a clergyman could claim 'benefit of clergy' to evade the noose. John was first, but said nothing. Nor did James. Perhaps Law had cowed them into silence with his absurd theatrics or they were so ignorant of the law that they had no idea what might be a valid argument. Swan, though, was determined to argue his case. He claimed that although the jury had given his case a fair hearing, it had come to the wrong conclusion. The main prosecutor against him had lied and he was keen to point out that he had a wife. It did him few favours, as Law launched into a pious diatribe. 'If there is a crime which in the eye of heaven can be more aggravated than another it is one of false and horrid charges which you have made against an innocent individual,' he said. 'Under these circumstances I cannot hold out any hope to you,' he added. He would lay out all the particulars to the king and the privy council, but 'on the facts so adduced Swan must stand or fall'.[26]

He then addressed James and John. He had separated them from the other prisoners because 'however great their crimes might have been, they would have been contaminated' by James and John's presence.[27] 'Sympathy towards persons for such offences cannot be expected to be shown', he pronounced, 'for they are offences, which, in a British country, mercy can never be extended to.' He did not want to offend the ears of the audience by dilating upon the enormity of the offence but he would implore the two men to seek mercy from God, 'as they stood upon the brink of eternity, guilty of offences which hardly excite a tear of pity for their fate, and in consideration of which in a British country mercy had ever been a stranger'.[28] Everyone noted that James and John were 'considerably affected'[29] and 'wept very much during the address'.[30]

With that, the Reverend Horace Cotton again placed 'the black cap', a nine-inch square of limp black silk, on top of Law's heavily powdered wig and the recorder slowly and deliberately intoned the words that had been used for centuries. 'John Smith, the law is, that thou shalt return to the place whence thou camest and from thence to the place of execution, where thou shalt hang by the neck till the body be dead.' Like a death knell, he repeated that last word twice more, 'Dead! Dead!' He paused before ending with the traditional invocation, 'And the Lord have mercy upon thy soul.'[31] Cotton said 'Amen.' A few others in the courtroom joined him. Law repeated the formula for James, before urging the three men 'to apply the short time they had to live to God for that mercy which they could not expect to receive from the hands of a man'.[32] The lawyer and clergyman Martin Madan (who was unusual in advocating polygamy in the late eighteenth century), described this moment: 'The dreadful sentence is now pronounced – every heart shakes with terror – the almost fainting criminals are taken from the bar – the crowd retires – each to his several home, and carries the mournful story to his friends and neighbours.'[33] Law could not have made the point more forcefully. There was no hope. Cotton thought the recorder had done it all 'in a very impressive manner'.[34] In truth, though, it was a cruel and self-satisfied attempt at humiliation.

Traditionally, this was the point at which the prison executioner slipped a whipcord noose around the condemned men's thumbs. Journalists noted that only Swan bowed to the court before the three men were taken down and that he 'stood with a steady face, and left the dock with a firm step'.[35] Not so James and John.

PART III

Van Diemen's Land

Britain had been transporting her felons overseas since 1717, when parliament authorised the deportation of its criminals to serve a period of indentured, forced labour in the colonies. Convicts were sent to North America until the colonists rebelled and forced Britain to house its criminals on its own shores. The immediate result was severe prison overcrowding, which was only relieved by converting superannuated warships into floating prisons moored mastless and rudderless around the country. These 'hulks' had a dark reputation. They were originally designed 'for the more severe and effectual punishment of atrocious and daring offenders', but they were dank, lice-, cockroach- and rat-infested hovels that lowered over the local towns. A contemporary recalled seeing the prisoners' shirts hanging out to dry on the rigging 'so black with vermin that the linen positively appeared to have been sprinkled over with pepper'.[1] The death rate was high, infection spread rapidly and the convicts were kept in irons. Punishment for further misdemeanours was harsh and normally involved flogging or solitary confinement. Even the chaplains showed indifference, as one clergyman refused to bury those who had died of an outbreak of cholera until there were six corpses that could be interred in the marshes simultaneously – and recited the burial service from the poop deck a mile from the grave. Nearly everyone condemned the hulks. When Pip sees a hulk in *Great Expectations*, he describes it as 'a wicked Noah's ark. Cribbed and barred and moored by massive rusty chains, the prison-ship seemed in my young eyes to be ironed like the prisoners.'[2] But the hulks fulfilled one useful purpose, as the prisoners were employed in hard labour in 'raising sand, soil, and gravel from, and cleansing, the river Thames and any other river navigable for ships of burden'.[3] Other forms of hard labour were designed, including scrubbing decks, cleansing uniforms, loading and unloading ships and excavating ground. The hulks were meant to be an experiment, but Britain had not given up on the idea of exporting its undesirables, and when she established a colony in New South Wales in 1785, the government conceived of a new plan. Two years later it resumed transportation to a new site at Botany Bay and the hulks became a combination of transit and labour camp where convicts awaiting passage were housed and set to hard labour. In July 1835 a parliamentary committee recommended that no prisoners should serve time in the hulks, which 'should be considered solely an intermediate Station between the Gaol and the Penal Colonies'.[4]

The moment William Bonell arrived back in Newgate, he joined the other prisoners destined for transportation and on Friday 2 October the two sheriffs, David Salomons and John Lianson, signed the paperwork allowing Governor Cope to deliver him into the custody of John Henry Capper on the hulks, along with sixteen other men.[5] Their immediate destination was the *Fortitude*, which was moored in the River Medway at Chatham.[6] This was the former HMS *Cumberland*, a 74-gun third rate ship of the line, which had taken part in the battle of Maguelone in 1809 and had been converted into a prison ship in 1830 and renamed in 1833. In time of war, it would have had a crew of about 700 men. Stripped of its 32-pound cannon, on any one day it normally housed about 470 convicts and when the dukes of Richmond and Sutherland paid an official visit in June 1835 it had 640. Once a proud and elegant warship, it was now a miserable gaol.

On arrival, William had to be registered by the warders, who looked out for potential troublemakers. The main concern was security, as George Hughes and James Hartley had managed to escape on a quiet Saturday evening in March by letting themselves down a rope into the mud, but were captured again by a patrolling marine the following Monday.[7] However, the guards also kept a note of their charges' 'character'. Thomas Bennett, for instance, had been imprisoned in the House of Correction for a month, Stephen Bathurst was marked down as 'character bad, disposition orderly', John Burgan had an 'idle drunken dissipated bad character', Alfred Buxton was 'reported to be a man of idle drunken bad character' and James Boardman's entry read 'character bad connections good'. As for William, convict number 2382, his character was 'not known'.[8]

Poor hygiene and health were a constant problem on the *Fortitude*. When James Banks took ill on 30 May 1835 with 'inflammation of the lungs', he was transferred to the small hospital ship, the *Wye*, but he died on 27 June, when the coroner gave a verdict of 'died by the visitation of God'.[9] Capper had reported to the House of Commons in 1834 that 'the convicts generally have been healthy, but the State in which many of them are brought to the Hulks from the Gaols, totally unfit for transportation, will naturally account for many deaths'.[10] And just before William arrived at the *Fortitude*, Capper cited 'the great Number of Prisoners brought to the Hulks in a very infirm and decrepit Condition from old Age and frequently in a diseased State'.[11] Scrofula and tuberculosis were common. William's next appointment, therefore, was with the ship's surgeon, Andrew Robertson. This may not have been a very thorough examination. Those who ran the transport ships were concerned that 'There is, on the part of the officers of the Hulks, whose business it is to bring forward the Prisoner for inspection with a view to embarkation, *a disposition to impose upon the Surgeon of the Transport*, men in a state of health, which renders them quite unfit for the voyage.'[12] Yet William was given the all-clear for all the major ailments, whereupon he was handed a small keg or beaker for water, a tin quart pot, a wooden bowl and an iron spoon.[13] He was then taken below deck to one of the crowded dormitories, each of which provided a bunk or a hammock for about fifty men.

Life onboard was regimented under the watchful eye of a detachment of soldiers. The convicts were wakened by a cannon at 5.45 and had to lash up their hammocks by 6. After a breakfast of biscuit and skilly, the men were escorted in irons to their place of work. This either involved hard labour on land at Chatham dockyard or swabbing the quarter-deck. They would return at 11.45. Dinner was on board at 12.30 and was followed by an afternoon session back at work. Supper was at 6 and at 6.45 they were all expected to attend chapel. On alternate days there would be 'beef and broth, or bread, cheese, and small-beer, nicknamed "swipes" for dinner'.[14]

William was first transferred to a prison hulk, the Fortitude, similar to the Discovery, before transportation to Van Diemen's Land.

The *Fortitude*, though, was just a staging post. Two convict ships set sail that month. The *Susan* left Portsmouth on the 6th with 301 convicts on board and the *Recovery* got under way from Spithead with 282 convicts 'after a great nuisance on board' on the 30th. But neither of these was deemed appropriate for William, as they were bound for Botany Bay, whereas William was to go to Van Diemen's Land. So, on 1 November he joined ninety-nine

others from the *Fortitude* and 190 convicts from other hulks at
Woolwich, on board the *Asia*, a 532-ton brig with three masts
and two decks, which had been built in Aberdeen in 1818 as a
merchant ship, but was now engaged on her eighth voyage as a
convict ship. She did not set sail from Sheerness until the 8th. This
time, as convict number 2424, William was listed by the guards
as five feet five inches tall, 72, stout, with a fresh complexion, a
large oval head, a 'hairy breast', silver hair and whiskers, a high,
wrinkled forehead, brown eyes, a long nose, a wide mouth and a
large chin. Unlike most of his fellow convicts, seventy-seven of
whom were being transported for life, he had no tattoo.[15]

William was fortunate in getting such swift passage. Many
convicts spent months on the hulks. Twenty of William's
companions on the *Asia* had been sentenced at the Old Bailey back
in March, three had been waiting since 1834, and William was the
only convict from the September Sessions to be transported so
soon.[16] He was also fortunate in the ship's surgeon, the Scotsman,
Peter Leonard, who diagnosed him with a fever the day after they
left Sheerness and kept him on the sick list for five days. Leonard
was just thirty-two, but had spent three years on HMS *Dryad*
trying to suppress the slave trade in western Africa and had
made his first convict journey on the *Royal Sovereign* in 1834.
He would later become the inspector-general of hospitals and
fleets and took a genuine interest in his charges. As he put it, 'A
British seaman fears no enemy that his eye can see; he dreads not
the cannon's or the tempest's roar.'[17] What really terrified sailors
was pestilence and disease – a terror Leonard shared. There had
been fears of cholera on the *Asia*'s last journey, in 1833, when five
convicts had died in transit, and Leonard noted in his log this
time that the convicts received from Woolwich were less healthy
than those from Chatham; that 'intermittent fever' prevailed
throughout the voyage, with nearly two dozen individuals placed
on the sick list; and that several cases were 'troublesome and
debilitating and required care on a voyage in which scurvy was
so much to be dreaded'.[18] In fact, Leonard had as much trouble
with the crew as with the convicts. A private had gonorrhoea. The
one-year-old son of one of the sergeants died before November

was out. Private Hawkins' wife Catherine gave birth to a baby boy on 13 December. And just as many guards as convicts had swollen and tender gums, signifying scurvy. Two convicts died, however: Edward Southon, a twenty-one-year-old labourer, who had been convicted of burglary at the Old Bailey in March and after reprieve had been sentenced to transportation for life; and Samuel Thorley, who had been sentenced at Chester in July to fourteen years' transportation for assault with an intent to rob. The former died of fever and apoplexy, the latter of dysentery. Both had also been on the *Fortitude* with William.

Uppermost in Leonard's mind, though, was the loss of the *George III* convict ship off Van Diemen's Land on 12 March 1835. There had been rumours. Some thought the state of the ship was to blame, as she had started to strain when they turned the Cape of Good Hope and 'water poured in upon the lower decks in all directions so constantly as to keep the prisoners in a state of unceasing dampness'.[19] But others thought the 'mortality and indisposition' of the convicts on board was attributable to their being given cocoa rather than oatmeal, which had unsettled their stomachs. The voyage had been marred by constant disaster. A fire destroyed half the ship's stores, scurvy took hold and fourteen convicts died even before the captain decided to take the risky route to Hobart through the D'Entrecasteaux Channel, where he hit a rock. In the ensuing chaos, guards fired on convicts, 128 of whom lost their lives, many of these being sick in their bunks below decks. One died lashed to the mast, supposedly for his own safety. The government boasted that this was the first convict ship to be lost since the colony had been started, but in December came news of the loss of the *Neva*, with 224 lives, on her second convict journey to Australia. The *Asia* had already set sail by then, but Leonard was determined not to face the same problems. He insisted on a good stock of sulphate of quinine, and when this was exhausted, he relied on 'lime juice and ... a farinaceous diet'. He was pleased that 'the oatmeal supplied was of a great help in preventing *scorbutus*'.[20]

The loss of the *George III* must have also played on the mind of the ship's captain, Lieutenant Thomas Fisher Stead RN. He knew most of the route as well as anyone. He was forty-two, he had been a lieutenant for twenty years and had steered the *Asia* on its 126-day journey to Sydney on five previous occasions, carrying a total of 720 male and 200 female convicts. This, however, would be his first trip to Hobart and by far his most crowded journey. The ship had undergone major repairs earlier in the year, but it must have been difficult to accommodate 290 convicts, plus a military guard of thirty soldiers from the 4th, 28th and 40th regiments under Captain Irwin and Ensign Short, the ship's crew, eight women and eleven children.[21] Stead was not interested in taking risks. He and his wife Elizabeth had just baptised their second son Lewis at St Peter's in Walworth in April. He fully intended to deliver his human cargo safe and sound in Hobart – and return to the family in Camberwell.

In the main, though, order was readily maintained thanks to a system of self-policing by the convicts. The thirty-six-year-old County Antrim lad James Briggs, for instance (who had a mermaid tattoo on the inside of his right arm and a small scar on his right cheekbone, was heavily freckled over his arms and face and had a dimpled clean-shaven chin, hazel eyes and brown hair) had been court martialled and sentenced to fourteen years for desertion at Chatham, but Leonard reported that his conduct on the *Asia* was 'exemplary' and he was made chief constable of the upper deck and proved 'very useful in that situation'.[22] Likewise William Bales was transported for seven years for embezzling £21 4s from his employer, a Liverpool Street solicitor, but he too was so well behaved on board that he was made a ship's constable.

Van Diemen's Land sent a shiver down the spine of the most hardened individual. Abel Tasman had been the first European to land on the island south of Australia in 1642 and had named it after his sponsor, Anthony van Diemen, the governor of the Dutch East Indies, but it was not until the start of the nineteenth century that the British established an outpost of New South Wales at Hobart. The first to arrive were mostly convicts relocated from Australia, but Britain started sending convicts there directly in 1804. Free settlers also started to arrive in 1820, enticed by the prospect of land and free convict labour, and Van Diemen's Land became a separate colony in 1825. The *Hobart Town Almanack* published in 1831 claimed that the 'general face of the island [is] a never ending succession of hill and dale'.[23] But it was a place of violence. Its fundamental premise, in the words of one contemporary, was that it was 'indebted for its present prosperous condition chiefly to crimes committed in Great Britain'.[24] The colonists had waged the 'Black War' against the indigenous people, leaving just 300, all of whom were forced to move to Flinders Island in 1832. As for the colonial population, one lieutenant-governor, William Sorell, claimed that Van Diemen's Land held 'a larger portion, than perhaps fell to the same number in any Country, of the most depraved and unprincipled people in the Universe'.[25]

Colonel George Arthur, who was the harsh and austere lieutenant-governor between 1824 and 1836, wrote that 'the spirit of the convict is not subdued by unmingled severity. Encouragement forms part of the plan by which he is reclaimed.'[26] He claimed to be horrified when Edward Smith-Stanley, the Tory secretary of state for the colonies and future earl of Derby, ordered him in 1834 to put thirty of the latest arrivals to work on the chain gangs for seven years – a punishment Arthur thought only appropriate for recidivists. Yet Arthur presided over a severe penal regime. Convicts were minutely watched, their every misdemeanour catalogued and punished. He built special solitary confinement cells, measuring seven feet by four, where the convict was kept in complete darkness and was not even allowed a knife to cut his food. Flogging was commonplace, even for minor infringements such as putting your hands in your pockets; and one famous Chartist convict, John Frost, recorded that 'the knout was made of the hardest whipcord, of an unusual size. The cord was put into salt water till it was saturated; it was then put into the sun to dry; by this process it became like wire, the eighty-one knots cutting the flesh as if a saw had been used.' He added that the flogger was one of the strongest men on the island and 'felt a gratification in inflicting and witnessing human misery'.[27] Even more severe penal colonies were built at Macquarrie Harbour, Norfolk Island and Port Arthur, each of which gained a reputation as a new version of hell. A few complained, including James Ross, who wrote in 1831 that the effect of such brutality was 'to deaden the faculties … to extinguish the perception of right and wrong – to rob virtue of its charm and vice of its hideousness'.[28] In twelve years, Colonel Arthur ordered 260 executions.

The *Asia* arrived at Hobart on 21 February 1836 after 105 days at sea, and five days later the convicts disembarked. Peter Leonard noted, 'The convicts were in general very healthy and none were sent to the hospital on arrival but all landed in health.'[29] The local press agreed, citing Leonard's decision to serve the convicts with oatmeal rather than cocoa for their arriving 'in better health and condition than those in the generality of ships'. Yet everyone noticed the convicts' new uniform, as it was so coarse and 'so totally unfit' to protect the frames of the poor creatures in the vicissitudes of weather during so long a voyage that they looked 'the most miserable ragged set of men we ever saw'.[30] Others were more interested in the news Captain Stead brought from London, including the fact that the duke of Wellington had been indisposed, but had recovered by the time the *Asia* set sail, Lord Brougham had been appointed speaker of the Lords, with a salary, a dissenting minister from Cheshire had invented a new steam engine and the earl of Aberdeen's brother had died in Geneva.[31]

Leonard was not completely accurate about the health of his charges. On arrival in Hobart convicts were assigned indentured labour with a settler, as a servant or working on government projects. Peter Bennett, for instance, who was a cook from St Christopher in the Caribbean, was sent to work for Captain Swanston, William Bales was assigned to the office of the solicitor general, and James Bradley, a Mancunian labourer and iron turner, was despatched to the settler Michael Kennedy's employ. William, by contrast, was reckoned to be 'sick' and was not initially assigned any work.[32]

Van Diemen's Land was recognisably British. It had sheriffs, justices of the peace, a police force and Anglican clergy. It followed the same holidays. There were hospitals and schools, tanneries and soap factories. Yet life there cannot have been easy for William. He was old and in poor health. The population was overwhelmingly male – men outnumbered women two to one amongst settlers and five to one among convicts – and he must have feared discovery of the nature of his 'unnatural crime'. Yet Leonard gave him a favourable report as 'orderly' and he soon learnt to dissemble, fabricating a tidied-up version of the events in George Street. 'I was sent out by a fellow servant for some beer', he told everyone, 'and while I was gone, he, and a man, whom he brought with him, were detected in an unnatural situation.'[33] It was not the whole truth, but it was close enough.

Such a preponderance of men may have had a similar effect as was reported in another British convict colony, Bermuda, when a nineteen-year-old lawyer called George Baxter Grundy, who had been transported for forgery, wrote to the Colonial Office in 1849 to complain about the debauchery he saw. The hulks where the convicts were housed fifty men to a ward; they were, he claimed, 'seminaries of crime' and he was 'prepared to prove that unnatural crimes and beastly actions are committed on board the Hulks daily'. He was shocked that when he reported one incident the two men were lashed and fined, but the rest of the convicts and the guards ostracised him. Many men boasted openly of their sexual relations as 'marriages' and Grundy was convinced that at least a hundred men had long-term sexual partners.[34] No records survive of such experiences in Hobart, but it seems unlikely that Bermuda would be unique and the pressures of having so many men living together a long way from home may have loosened the bonds of shame.

William Bonell's only appearance in the records over the next five years occurs when he was sentenced to twenty-four hours in solitary confinement for having pulled 'a portion of the Roof from the Carpenter's Shed without leave' on 28 September 1837.[35] It was a blot on his record, but the rules specified that a fourteen-year convict could apply for a ticket-of-leave after six years, which would effectively guarantee his freedom. However, on 16 March 1841, he was admitted to the hospital in New Norfolk, a small town which Arthur had attempted to turn into the colonial capital. By the time William arrived there, the town had a handsome church, St Matthew's, the oldest in Australia, on Arthur Square next to the town gaol, and stage coaches regularly plied their trade to Hobart. The hospital had originally been established as the main general hospital for convicts on the island, but it had grown several new wings and had effectively become a mental institution. Thus the majority of William's 130 fellow patients were recorded as suffering from 'mania', such as Samuel Ashton, who had been there since July 1832; from tertiary syphilis, like Mary Byron; or from the catch-all mental health term of the day, '*debilitas*'. There was much criticism of the hospital. The head surgeon, Mr Casey, employed several inmates as a gardener, a groom, a cow-man and a house servant at his private home, all without pay. And as one correspondent to the local press put it, 'As the hospital is now conducted, a man has only to say another one is insane, and by force carry him to the hospital, where if he be not mad, the mad with whom he would be mixed will soon drive him so.' There were rumours of abuse of the inmates, too, with staff prodding and teasing them 'to shew their ravings'.[36]

We cannot know what ailed William Bonell. Perhaps his '*debilitas*' was dementia, or a stroke. Whatever his condition, he was on a full diet until 21 April, but his health declined thereafter and he was spoon-fed for eight days. On 29 April 1841 he died.

The record of William Bonnell's transportation to Van Diemen's Land
states that he was born in Wolverhampton, was 5 foot 5, and had a fresh
complexion, silver hair, brown eyes and a hairy breast.

The Press-yard

After sentencing on the early evening of Monday 28 September, James and John returned along Birdcage Walk's narrow passageway to Newgate. Their new status as condemned prisoners meant they were now consigned to the 'press-yard'. This was one of the oldest parts of Old Newgate, named after one of its grisliest practices. Criminals who refused to enter a plea because they feared that if they were convicted their family would be deprived of all their worldly goods, would be tied down on a press, which would gradually be loaded with weights on their stomachs, until they were 'either brought to compliance, or expire under the Insupportable Burthen they are obliged to bear because of their Obstinacy'.[1] This was abolished in 1772 and from 1827 a prisoner who entered no plea was deemed to have pleaded not guilty, but the press-yard's reputation lingered on. The building had a long, narrow courtyard, an upper and lower 'press-room' for the prisoners to gather during the daytime and a suite of fifteen condemned cells on three floors. In modern parlance, it was Death Row. Charles Dickens, who visited while James and John were housed there, reported that the entrance to the condemned cells was 'by a narrow and obscure stair-case leading to a dark passage, in which a charcoal stove casts a lurid tint over the objects in its immediate vicinity, and diffuses something like warmth around'.[2] Massive cell doors opened out from the left-hand side of this passage, which was replicated on two further floors. In size, furniture and appearance, they were all alike. This was a dank, dark place, and intentionally so. The prison reformer John Howard wrote in 1777 that he had been told that criminals who had 'affected an air of boldness during the trial, and appeared quite unconcerned at the pronouncing sentence upon them, were struck with horror, and shed tears, when brought to these darksome solitary abodes'.[3] Many found it a terrifying moment. When William Sheppard returned to prison after being sentenced to death for sodomy in 1761, the prison chaplain wrote, 'the most absolute despair seized his heart ... Never did I see such a picture of distress. The wildness of his looks, his streaming eyes, and knees smiting one against another, spoke the horrors and distraction of his soul.'[4] So too, fifteen-year-old Thomas Finlay, who was 'quite out his mind' as he waited for the execution of his sentence that same year.[5]

There were twelve others in the press-yard with James and John, eight of whom had not yet reached twenty-one. One lad called Moses Harris claimed to be sixteen, but his mother admitted that he was just thirteen. Three others were fifteen. Only one seemed 'a hardened old offender' thanks to a swarthy face and three days' growth of beard.[6] All bar one had been convicted for burglary or robbery. The sums involved were paltry. George Catlin had stolen half a crown at knife-point from a fellow seaman in Stepney, Robert Lavendar had burgled four cigar tubes, Joseph Coleman had stolen thirty shillings' worth of handkerchiefs. The three fifteen-year-olds, along with a twenty-one-year-old called James Cooper, had shoved a young woman into a crowded butcher's shop and stolen her purse and two gold sovereigns. Moses had smashed Mrs Mary Eddels's haberdasher's shop window in Whitechapel and snatched nine yards of silk worth £2 4s; and David Ward and Benjamin Vines had similarly broken into a draper's to steal some kerseymere and silk worth £1 3s. Robert Swan was the sole older exception.

The other eleven were oddly cheerful. But then these prisoners knew the rules of the game. They had all been sentenced to death, but the prison inspectors who made their first visit in early November noted that they 'looked forward with assurance to a mitigation of punishment'.[7] In consequence 'the generality of those who are sentenced to death', said the senior turnkey, 'treat it as a mere formal thing, quite a mockery'.[8] Dickens echoed the inspectors, as

he questioned whether there was a man among them 'who did not
know that ... it was never intended that his life should be sacrificed'.[9]
If they were lucky, they might get away with a spell in one or other
of London's Houses of Correction at Giltspur Street or Cold Bath
Fields. This was especially true for those who had someone to speak
for them. Mary Eddels, who had brought the prosecution against
Moses, had expressly asked the court to show mercy on account of
his youth and a local publican had vouched for his good character.
A builder from Holloway had likewise given William Miller a good
character and George Catlin had his ship's captain, an undertaker
and his brother to speak up for him. For more serious or aggravated
crimes, the prisoner might be transported, but that too meant
avoiding the noose. Either way, they were confident they would
live and, according to the inspectors, these convicts, plus three more
who joined them after the October sitting of the court, 'conducted
themselves with as much indifference as the inmates of the other
parts of the prison'.[10] As one visitor noted, they 'lessened the ennui
and despair of their situation by unbecoming merriment, or sought
relief in the constant application of intoxicating stimulants'.[11] That
is to say, they gambled on cards or games of shove ha'penny, they
played blind-man's buff and leap-frog, they entertained prostitutes
(who gained admittance pretending they were wives or sisters), and
they drank large quantities of beer (which was delivered every day
between noon and one).

The same was not true for James, John and Robert Swan, who
had been told in terms by the recorder that there could be no
hope for them. Sharing the press-yard with men who had every
expectation of reprieve was therefore a cruel added punishment.
There was very little supervision and the others repeatedly goaded
the three men, poked them, pushed them, called them names and
tried to start a fight. It was even worse at night, when each of the
three men was forced to share their cell with two companions,
even though, as the inspectors put it, 'there could be no excuse
whatever for not placing them in separate cells'.[12] The taunts, the
abuse and the innuendo continued throughout the night and the
three men lay awake almost as frightened of their companions as
they were of the hangman.

On Tuesday 29 September they had their first visit from
the Reverend Horace Cotton. He was a controversial figure.
After matriculating from Wadham College Oxford in 1791, he
held a series of clerical appointments as vicar at Desborough
in Northamptonshire, as schoolmaster and curate at Cuckfield
Grammar School and as curate at Hornsey before the City
aldermen elected him ordinary of Newgate in 1814, since when
his name had become so synonymous with hangings that it
was said that the condemned died 'with Cotton in their ears'.
He was in his early sixties, with two grown-up sons and two
daughters, and he was set in his ways. Cotton claimed that he
treated prisoners as reasonable beings. 'I always take off my hat
when I go into the ward', he told Henry Grey Bennet MP during
a Commons enquiry, 'and while I treat them thus, they will
treat me with respect.'[13] But if James and John had been hoping
for compassion from him, they were disappointed. Cotton had
attended their sentencing 'for the detestable crime of sodomy' (as
he put it in his notebook) and had thought the recorder's manner
'very impressive'.[14] Moreover, according to Edward Wakefield,
a jurist and politician who had spent three years in Newgate for
kidnapping a 15-year old girl and would later be a major figure
in the development of Australia and New Zealand, the main
business of the ordinary of Newgate was 'to break the spirits of
capital convicts, so that they may make no physical resistance
to the hangman'.[15] The writer Pierce Egan by contrast praised
his 'kindness, attention, and soothing conduct' for turning many
of the most hardened and desperate offenders into 'the most
sincere penitents'.[16] Either way, this was a task Cotton relished.
He was fascinated by criminality and executions and amassed a
collection of books and tracts on notorious murderers, thieves
and other villains. Many contemporaries commented on Cotton's
physical characteristics. Richard Hassell, who spent two years
in Newgate for selling anti-Christian tracts, referred to him as
'the portly-bellied, port-speaking-faced Dr Cotton'.[17] William
Ballantine, who was called to the bar in 1834, described him
as 'somewhat tall, very portly. His rubicund visage betokened
the enjoyment of the good things in life.'[18] Thomas Wontner,

who was the schoolmaster at Newgate and son of the former governor, thought no other Church of England minister was more suitable for the post than Cotton, who had 'an excellent heart' and 'sound judgement; and, above all, is a determined enemy to cant and dissimulation'.[19] But others loathed his brand of Christianity, referring to him as 'our precious dunder-headed Chaplain' and 'a perfect ninny'[20] and objecting that because he had 'an itching to become a popular preacher, he wished to be very profound ... instead of which he was – very ridiculous'.[21] After hearing one of his forty-five-minute sermons in 1836, *The Times* caustically despaired that he possessed 'neither simplicity of statement, precision of aim, nor fervor of appeal' and demanded that he should be retired 'with as little delay as possible'.[22] Many thought him vain and hypocritical and it was said that he was 'most punctual' at both the three and five o'clock dinner sittings for judges during the court sessions 'and never affronted the company by abstinence at either'.[23]

Nonetheless, Cotton was the men's only contact with authority and they poured out their hearts to him. The situation was unbearable. They were sharing cells at night with people convicted of completely different crimes. Swan begged Cotton for some place 'to retire to for the purpose of meditation and devotion'. Cotton agreed, but for a different reason. He was appalled that although the recorder had sentenced these three men separately from the rest because their presence would disgrace and contaminate the others, the gaol required them to share a cell and sleep with other men. Nothing had changed when Cotton returned the next day and the three men renewed their complaint. Swan was specific. All he heard from the other criminals was 'obscene conversation' and when he had tried to get one of them to kneel down to pray, they had burst into laughter. Cotton promised to raise it with the 'proper authorities' but still nothing had changed by Thursday when he returned again. This time Swan reported that he had persuaded some of the others to read a few hymns with him, but James and John complained about the night-time rantings of the men locked up with them, which they assured the chaplain 'consisted chiefly about their own and others robberies'.[24]

Newly (and controversially) elected as the first Jewish Sheriff, David Salomons and his colleague John Lainson ensured James and John were moved to more private accommodation in Newgate.

Cotton then bumped into the two sheriffs of the City of London and Middlesex, David Salomons and Alderman John Lainson. The former was a successful co-founder of the London and Westminster Bank, and the latter a wealthy spectacle-maker, but it is unlikely that

he approved of either of them. The vote had been unanimous when
the City liverymen had elected them as sheriffs at the Midsummer
Common Hall in June, but several aldermen had subsequently
objected to Salomons taking up office on the grounds that he was
Jewish and could not swear the statutory oath, which included the
words 'on the true faith of a Christian'. As recorder, Charles Ewan
Law had overseen the sheriffs' election but then led the campaign
against Salomons, telling the court of aldermen that 'there would
be great danger to the corporation, as well as to the gentlemen
filling the office' if Salomons's appointment were allowed to
proceed.[25] There may have been some partisan manoeuvring in this,
as Salomons and Lainson were both radical Whigs (Lainson had
stood unsuccessfully for East Surrey in the 1832 general election)
and Law was a Tory, but as his later objection to Jews being allowed
to take seats in the Commons suggests, Law opposed Salomons
primarily because he was Jewish and, as he told the Commons,
'Christianity was not only part and parcel of the common law, but
… it was the foundation of all the laws of this country.'[26] The row
was resolved in July when the Whig attorney-general, Sir John
Campbell, pushed through the Sheriffs' Declaration Act expressly
to allow Salomons to start his term of office alongside Lainson on
the day James and John were sentenced, 28 September. There had
been much cheering at the sheriffs' swearing-in on Monday, when
Lainson had worn splendid white and gold liveries while those of
Salomons had been rich but unostentatious, and the next day they
had presided over the nomination of candidates for a new lord
mayor to replace Winchester.

Cotton disapproved of any deviation from the Church of
England and thought Salomons's election a terrible innovation,
but he explained James and John's situation to them and asked
if there was anything they could do. Maybe their newness in
office or their liberal approach to criminal justice made them
more receptive to complaints about Newgate, but the *Morning
Chronicle* was not disappointed in expecting 'that a very active and
distinguished Shrievalty [sheriff's tenure] will follow that which
has just terminated'.[27] By that evening Salomons and Lainson had
arranged for the three men to be moved into the lower condemned

room, separate from the others. All three men thanked Cotton for intervening on their behalf when he next visited on the Saturday, but Cotton's capacity for sympathy was stretched beyond endurance on the Sunday when Swan told him that someone had been in to see him who had given him great hopes his life would be spared and that he could now think of nothing else. Cotton was furious and demanded to know who had told him such a thing. Swan declined to reply, which prompted a stern lecture from Cotton. He told him that the person had no warrant for what he had done, that he had acted most improperly and that it was only because Cotton feared that it might have some detrimental effect on the poor men's fate that he had not demanded that the home secretary end all such improper communication immediately.

Things were easier for James and John after the move. They no longer had to face the vaunted jollity of the other men. They had a bit more space and even a modicum of privacy. During the day they had the lower press-room to themselves, which had a fire but was 'a long, sombre room, with two windows sunk into the stone wall'.[28] It was not complete segregation. They shared the open yard with the men upstairs for washing, 'making water', exercising and getting a breath of (not very fresh) air. But at five o'clock they were locked in one of the cells either together or with young Moses. Candles were allowed till ten and the men were let out again at seven the next morning. The cells were not luxurious. They were stone dungeons measuring eight to nine feet long by six feet wide, with nine-foot-high vaulted ceilings. 'The thick stone walls were lined with planks studded with broad-headed nails for added security.'[29] The doors were four inches thick, and the double-grated window measured thirty-three inches by fourteen inches. The only furniture was a barrack bedstead without bedding. Beneath it was a rug; beside it, a Bible and a prayer book. According to Dickens, 'An iron candlestick was fixed into the wall at the side; and a small high window in the back admitted as much air and light as could struggle in between a double row of heavy, crossed iron bars. It contained no other furniture of any description.'[30] It was spartan and a harsh reminder of their predicament, as they would have been conscious that this lower floor was where condemned prisoners were prepared for their ordeal on the day of their execution. They were now the lowest of the low, metaphorically and literally.

One of the prisoners who had initially shared a cell with James or John told the inspectors that once they had been segregated, 'there was nothing then but reading and seriousness at night'.[31] But, notwithstanding Cotton's apparent determination to steer the men away from any thoughts of reprieve, neither James nor John had given up hope yet and both of them started putting together appeals to the king and the home secretary. On the 13th James wrote on black-edged paper to his former employer William Scott Preston at his London address. 'Honoured Sir, with painful feelings I address you,' he began. 'On the last of August I was decayed by drink to a house in Blackfriars Road and there charged of being guilty of an unnatural Offence.' Since then, he had been sentenced to death and only now awaited 'His majestys [sic] Pleasure'. Yet 'as a dying man' he solemnly protested his innocence, the evidence against him was falsely sworn and he implored Preston's kind assistance 'in my dying hours which are but few'. The grammar and the punctuation were awry and James got the name of the home secretary wrong, but the letter's intent was clear. 'I trust your words', he wrote, 'to Lord Melbourne Secretary of State would have great Effect I hope Sir you will use all your efforts to save a Persecuted man Whose life has been so falsely sworn away and delay no time as it is getting very short.' He signed himself 'your obedient servant and late groom' and added his wife's address in Giffin Street with the words 'An answer will oblige.'[32]

One other thing had changed, now James and John had been convicted. Visits to condemned prisoners were restricted to once a week, on a Tuesday, between half-past ten and two o'clock. This did not put off Elizabeth Pratt, who seems to have visited soon after her husband's conviction, and immediately started collecting signatures for an appeal petition, and lobbying anyone she knew who might provide an additional character reference in writing. John, by contrast, had nobody to fight his corner other than his mother, although he put his mark to a letter to his old employer Thomas Phillips.

Other than preparing their appeals for mercy, the press-yard prisoners had little to do. Boredom sometimes led to rowdiness and violence. On 12 October Benjamin Vines and David Ward were put in irons for three days for breaking the windows of the day-room, as was Joseph Coleman on 1 November for striking another prisoner. A few of the men ground down penny-pieces to make Newgate tokens, which were supposedly popular with the 'criminal classes', who would wear them as amulets, inscribed with a heart, a motto and lovers' initials, 'to preserve them from danger and detection'.[33] Cotton more or less gave up on these prisoners because he was 'so much interfered with and laughed at'.[34]

A picture of the depressing dreariness of the press-yard was provided by Charles Dickens, who was then a twenty-three-year-old shorthand writer and political journalist. He visited Newgate on 5 November with the editor John Black, who had commissioned him to compile the observational 'sketches' he had written under the pseudonym Boz for the *Monthly Magazine* into a book, which was to be published in 1836 along with five new pieces, one of which was to be a portrait of Newgate. It was a characteristically harrowing piece. Robert Swan 'was pacing up and down the court with a firm military step – he had been a soldier in the foot-guards – and a cloth cap jauntily thrown on one side of his head'. James and John, by contrast, barely moved. The light was dim, but Dickens wrote that one of them was stooping over the fire, with his right arm on the mantelpiece, and his head sunk upon it, while the other was leaning on the sill of the farthest window. Dickens noted: 'The light fell full upon him, and communicated to his pale, haggard face, and disordered hair, an appearance which, at that distance, was ghastly. His cheek rested upon his hand; and, with his face a little raised, and his eyes wildly staring before him, he seemed to be unconsciously intent on counting the chinks in the opposite wall.' Both men 'were as motionless as statues'.

Dickens' explanation for the difference in attitude between James and John and Robert was simple. Robert's fate was uncertain, 'some mitigatory circumstances having come to light since his trial, which had been humanely represented in the proper quarter'. By contrast, 'The other two had nothing to expect from the mercy of the crown; their doom was sealed; no plea could be urged in extenuation of their crime, and they well knew that for them there was no hope in this world.' Dickens added that as he left, the turnkey whispered, 'The two short ones were dead men.'[35]

THE CONDEMNED CELL IN NEWGATE.

13

The Pleas

Nobody knew when or why the custom had started, or what the rationale was behind it, or why a special status was accorded to London, but nor was there any doubt that 'no person sentenced to death within London and Middlesex, Essex and Surrey, can have execution passed on them until the Recorder shall have presented his Report to the King in Council'.[1]

Many held the 'Recorder's Report' in open derision. Lord Eldon, who was lord chancellor in an almost uninterrupted run from 1801 to 1827, was 'exceedingly shocked' at the 'careless manner' in which the meetings of the Grand (or 'Hanging') Cabinet were conducted. 'We were called upon to decide on sentences, affecting no less than the *lives* of men', he pointed out, 'and yet there was nothing laid before us to enable us to judge whether there had or had not been attenuating circumstances: it was merely a recapitulation of the Judge's opinion, and the sentence'.[2] This did not constitute justice. One critic pointed out in 1831 that 'the court hears no evidence, and is bound by no rules' and its decisions were made on the basis of little more than rumours. As one regular attendee put it, 'What a curious sort of supplementary trial this is; how many accidents may determine the life or death of the culprit!'[3] When Eldon objected to a man convicted of a robbery in Bedford Square being hanged, the king roused himself from his slumbers to pronounce that 'since the learned judge who *lives in* Bedford Square does not think there is any great harm in robberies there, the poor fellow shall *not* be hanged'.[4] Twenty cases could be dealt with in less than an hour and one of the attendees, the home secretary, was an excessively busy minister 'engaged in the harassing occupation of party politics'.[5] There were regular reports of ministers forgetting the details of the case and some doubted whether the recorder even read the paperwork. 'Let us suppose that he reads the petition – still does he remember its contents when in full Council?' asked Edward Wakefield.[6]

Sometimes the king was wilfully or unavoidably indisposed for several months, so the backlog of prisoners accumulated, rendering Newgate an even worse hell-hole. At the end of March 1816, for instance, there were fifty-eight prisoners awaiting their fate in the fifteen condemned cells. One had been waiting for five months. Yet when Henry Grey Bennet MP complained that the recorder had not been able to make his report because the prince regent was partying in Brighton,[7] the attorney-general Sir William Garrow claimed that it would be inconvenient to call the law officers to Brighton, and anyway, 'very few of these condemned wretches had any great reason to complain of the delay in deciding their fate'.[8] This so infuriated Henry Brougham MP that two days later he lambasted the prince regent and his friends 'who, when the gaols were filled with wretches, could not suspend for a moment their thoughtless amusements to end the sad suspense between death and life'.[9]

The Grand Cabinet meeting was invariably held between a levee and a dinner. It was rarely the main item on the king's mind. Sometimes he fell asleep by the fireside or stormed out while his ministers discussed the report. At Lord Ellenborough's first meeting, both the king and the duke of Wellington fell asleep and 'the duke looked like death'.[10] At another, the king was heavily dosed with laudanum. In George Cruikshank's satire 'A Levee Day', the gouty and dropsical King George IV is having a fit of the vapours while peers and politicians besiege him with their inconsequential business. At the back of the queue stands the recorder, Sir John Silvester, dressed in judicial black robes and full-bottomed wig, carrying his 'black jack's black bag' with his report on three men sentenced to death for stealing meat, bread and cheese. Silvester points to the king's tailor and his wigmaker, who are in front of him in the queue, and says 'I must wait until these weighty matters are settled.' Life was cheap compared to a fashionable new periwig.

The Commons had tried to abolish the Recorder's Report in 1834 but it was still the case in 1835 that James and John could not face execution until the recorder had reported and the king in council had assented. In other words, there was still hope.

Condemned prisoners could petition the king through the home secretary, but this was not simple. Access was strictly limited. It helped if you knew him, or another government minister, or anyone with a title, or just an MP, as long as he was well disposed and from the governing party. This too was a bit of a lottery, as the previous eighteen months had seen several political upheavals. A row about the Church in Ireland precipitated Earl Grey's sullen resignation as prime minister in July 1834. King William initially replaced Grey with another Whig, William Lamb, the 2nd Viscount Melbourne, but then summarily dismissed him in November 1834 because he did not like the senior ministers Melbourne proposed. However, Melbourne's replacement, Sir Robert Peel, could not command a majority in the Commons, even after a general election in January 1835 which delivered him nearly a hundred additional Tory seats. Peel limped on, but by the end of March it was clear that the king would have to acknowledge the parliamentary arithmetic. On 8 April Peel resigned and Melbourne was back at the head of a coalition of Whigs, Liberals, Radicals and Irish nationalists.

His home secretary – and leader in the Commons – was the thin, short, shy, fidgety and sensitive third son of the 6th duke of Bedford, Lord John Russell, known as 'Jack'. Everything was going well for him. He was forty-three and had been an MP since 1813, but he was generally reckoned to have been the main architect of the Reform Act and had consequently been 'hazzaed, cheered and hip hip hipped' round the country during the 1832 election. He had fallen in love earlier in the year, when campaigning in Torquay, with the pretty twenty-eight-year-old Adelaide, Lady Ribblesdale, whom his fellow Whig, Lord

Holland, described as 'a cheerful pretty looking young widow'.[11]
They were married on 30 March, but politics interrupted their
honeymoon after two days, as Melbourne summoned Russell for
discussions about forming a new government. King William was
reluctant to make Russell a minister, but Melbourne insisted on
appointing him as home secretary in the new Cabinet, which was
announced on 20 April.[12]

Russell was acutely conscious of differences with Melbourne,
who had been home secretary under Grey, especially regarding
the case of six men from Tolpuddle in Dorset, who had formed
the Friendly Society of Agricultural Labourers as an early form of
trade union in 1833. This had infuriated a local Tory magistrate,
James Frampton, and he complained to Melbourne, who suggested
that since the men had sworn a secret oath of allegiance to each
other, they should be prosecuted under the obscure Unlawful
Oaths Act 1797. The subsequent conviction at Dorchester of
the 'Tolpuddle Martyrs' or 'Dorchester Labourers' and their
transportation for seven years led to a national furore. The *Poor
Man's Guardian* complained, 'A grand jury of aristocrats found a
true bill. A petty jury of middlemen found them guilty. "A nation
of shopkeepers" looked on with satisfaction, and its base, time-
serving Whigs, sent the men abroad!'[13] Eight hundred thousand
people signed petitions, thousands joined a march on Whitehall
and dozens of MPs called for a pardon and the men's immediate
return to England. Melbourne had refused to help, but when a
motion came to the Commons in June 1835, Russell suggested that
he was minded to pardon at least four of the men. The motion was
overwhelmingly lost, but many of Russell's friends were among
the eighty-two MPs who voted for a full pardon for all six and
Russell promptly granted all six men conditional pardons.

Russell continued to prove a very different home secretary from
Melbourne. In October 1835 he published plans for reforming
England's prisons, he appointed the first prison inspectors, he
tabled a Bill to introduce civil marriages and he asked the Royal
Commission on the Criminal Law, which had been set up by
Brougham, to bring forward proposals allowing defence counsel
to address the jury and cutting the number of capital offences. His

was a very different agenda from Melbourne's. When he suggested appointing some 'manufacturers and persons in business' as magistrates, Melbourne said he should do what he thought fit, but airily added, 'it has hitherto certainly been considered a disqualification to be actually engaged in trade'.[14]

Two men controlled access to Russell. The clerk for criminal business, who was also superintendent of the convict establishment, was John Henry Capper, who had been clerk since the 1790s and superintendent since 1814 and was now sixty-one. His main office was in Downing Street, where he could be found from ten to four every day when he was not visiting the transportation hulks. Hundreds of pieces of paper passed before his eyes every week: sheriffs' letters from every county in England and Wales; removal notices from one gaol to another or to a convict ship; letters from the colonies regarding convicts; and hundreds of pleas for clemency in capital cases and for early release from imprisonment or transportation. It is not surprising that his quarterly reports on the hulks were cursory, often running to just two short paragraphs. Capper was later forced to resign because of the appalling conditions on the hulks, but he was so proud of his work that he wrote *The Emigrant's Guide to Australia* and his employees on the hulks commented on Capper's 'urbanity and kindness' and his 'zeal and impartiality in executing his arduous duties'.[15] In practice, though, the large number of transportation cases he dealt with every year left little time to devote to complex individual appeals against execution. Assisting him, therefore, was a barrister, James M. Phillipps.[16]

If James Pratt and John Smith were to stand any chance of a reprieve, they had to get past Phillipps and Capper. James had one advantage. Unlike Swan's wife, who died while he was in prison, Elizabeth Pratt attended the trial and afterwards set about gathering signatures for a general petition among their neighbours in Deptford. The document she submitted is impressive. It is written in fine copperplate on good paper and was presumably the work of a professional copywriter. Many parishioners in Deptford could not write or even sign their own name, so the fifty-five signatures carried an impressive weight, especially as they were respectable householders and tradesmen, reliant on local support, like the jeweller Richard Sullivan, the perfumer Joseph Ball and the undertaker William Ellis. Local butchers, grocers, bakers, tailors, corn dealers, fishmongers and drapers from Effingham Place, Giffin Street, Deptford High Street and Blackheath Hill signed the petition, which cited James's periods working for William Scott Preston, Charles Ferguson and the Reverend Dr Cole. The petitioners stated that 'up to the period of his being apprehended he was living in credit and supporting his wife and family', and that his 'moral character was never before impeached', and they humbly prayed that since James had never before been 'rendered amenable to a court of justice ... your Lordship will be pleased to recommend His Majesty in Council, that the Royal Clemency may be extended towards the said James Pratt and that his life may be spared'.[17] Both Deptford's surgeons, Robert Hatfull and Robert Mitchell, signed the petition and sent in their own letters, citing that they had assisted Elizabeth in her 'accouchements'. Hatfull added he always considered James 'a quiet, sober, honest, modest & inoffensive man'.[18]

Two things should have impressed Russell. The first two names on the petition were those of John and Jane Berkshire. We cannot know their motives. Perhaps they regretted bringing the prosecution. Maybe they had never thought it would come to this. Or they had only sought to catch Bonell. But whatever the Berkshires' reason, it was rare for a plea for mercy from the original prosecutor to be ignored.

Equally impressive was a note at the bottom of the petition from Richard Preston, who wrote, 'William Scott Preston, named in this memorial, is my eldest son and is now in Scotland. He had an opinion of James Pratt, that he, within a recent period, recommended his mother to take him into our service.' It begged the question of why Mrs Preston had not taken James on, but the very presence of Richard Preston's name on the petition was a coup. He had become a king's counsel, a bencher at the Inner Temple and professor of law at King's College, London, in the last twelve months; and although he was a Tory, he and Russell represented Devon seats when he was MP for Ashburton for six years.

Great Burstead was a bucolic Essex village when James Pratt was baptised in its ancient church on Easter Sunday in 1803, but rural poverty was endemic. James relied on handouts from the poor law guardians as a child and both his parents died in the workhouse.

WORCESTER - 1810

John Smith was born in Worcester, which had the reputation of being 'one of the cleanest and finest old cities in the kingdom', between 1793 and 1801.

The 1830s was an age of dramatic reform. Ministers like Lord John Russell had behemoths to slay and temples to pull down. Sometimes it was difficult to know which political cudgel to take up first: slavery, rotten boroughs, child labour or the death penalty.

England bristled with moral panic, as self-appointed arbiters of morality demanded tough action against adultery, indecency, fornication and homosexuality. Print-shops were a particular target, as it was said that 'pooffs generally congregate around the picture shops and are to be known by their effeminate air, their fashionable dress &c.'

James and John joined the many thousands who left the countryside in search of work in the teeming capital. Life as a domestic servant was precarious. Employers at the register office (bottom) sought men who knew their business 'and were not above it'. London was a mess of insanitary slums and rookeries, where cholera was rife and people scratched a living to pay the rent (top).

In 1822 the aristocratic Bishop of Clogher was caught having sex with a guardsman in the backroom of the White Lion in London. He fled the scene and the country but became the butt of many satires.

Sodomy was a capital crime and any form of homosexual act was fiercely denounced, but men found places to cruise, including the Royal Exchange whose porticoes afforded a degree of privacy where one could ogle a handsome young man and fondle his 'yard'.

When the wealthy Tory MP William John Bankes was caught in a toilet with a guardsman in 1833, the jury was so impressed by his long list of character witnesses, including the Duke of Wellington, that they acquitted him in fifteen minutes. When he was caught with another guardsman in 1841, he fled the country.

Wealthy men could escape the law. Henry Grey Bennet MP was married to Lord John Russell's cousin Gertrude, but the couple fled into exile when he was charged with propositioning a male servant in Geneva in 1825.

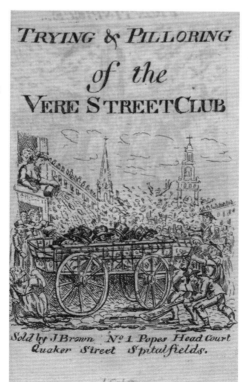

TRYING & PILLORING of the VERE STREET CLUB

Sold by J Brown No 1 Popes Head Court Quaker Street Spitalfields.

1810

The public could be vicious. When the White Swan in Vere Street was raided by the police in 1810, six men were sentenced to the pillory, where the crowd subjected them to 'a perpetual shower of mud, eggs, offal, and every kind of filth' until they were virtually senseless.

James's most prestigious appointment was as footman to the Reverend Dr Samuel Cole, chaplain to the Royal Hospital in Greenwich. He was a close friend of the King, but seems never to have appealed for mercy for James.

John worked for nearly two years as footman to Thomas Phillips, a wealthy doctor, plantation owner and philanthropist, who lived in the largest house in fashionable Brunswick Square. Phillips' bust stands in Llandovery College, to which he gave a large collection of books. He wrote that John 'conducted himself so much to my satisfaction that it was with regret that I discharged him at his own request'.

James's first job in London was as a groom to young lawyer William Scott Preston, who lived with his father in Grove Crescent in Camberwell, which lay close to London but was still surrounded by fields. His employment ended when William married.

Out of work again, James set off from the home he shared with his wife Elizabeth in Giffin Street in Deptford in search of a job in central London on Saturday 28 August 1835.

William Bonell invited James and John to his first-floor room in a house on this site in George Street in Southwark (now Dolben Street) on Saturday 29 August 1835. While he was getting a drink, James and John had sex and were spied on through the keyhole by William's landlords, John and Jane Berkshire, who burst in and summoned the police.

James and John were hauled to the Union Hall police office, where the 'small wares of justice' were meted out. The magistrate, Hensleigh Wedgwood, had little choice but to commit them for trial at the Old Bailey, but later wrote one of the most courageous letters in mitigation of their offence to the Home Secretary, Lord John Russell.

Sir Robert Peel's new police force, the 'Peelers', were a controversial innovation introduced in 1829 (here in their summer uniform). Sergeant Robert Valentine who took James, John and William to the police office and was one of the lead witnesses in court, was one of the first men to enlist as officer No. 2477.

meeting with good support

Newgate Gaol looked massive, dark and solemn and its stench permeated everything. An underground passage paved with the gravestones of executed prisoners linked it to the Central Criminal Court. The first prison inspectors, appointed in 1835 said Newgate 'disgraces the profession of a Christian country'. Others called it 'Hell above ground'.

James, John and William were sent to the Surrey County Gaol in Horsemonger Lane, where 113 people had hanged since 1800, to await trial. Visitors like James's wife Elizabeth were allowed every day from 12 to 2 p.m.

The judge in James and John's case was Sir John Gurney, described by a fellow lawyer as pitiless, 'almost brutal' and 'very harsh and severe'. In another case he had told a jury that he feared the horrors of Sodom and Gomorrah might be revived in London.

The senior London judge, the Recorder of London, Charles Ewan Law, had just been elected to the Commons, where he immediately tabled a motion to tighten the law on homosexuality. In sentencing James and John to death, he told them 'they stood upon the brink of eternity, guilty of offences which hardly excite a tear of pity for their fate'.

James and John did not have the right to a defence lawyer, nor the money to pay for one, but William Bodkin asked questions of the other witnesses that helped their case.

THE LATE SIR W. BODKIN, ASSISTANT JUDGE OF THE MIDDLESEX SESSIONS.

The Old Bailey had been formally constituted as the Central Criminal Court in 1834. The accused were brought up from the cells and stood in the dock (on the right) with a mirror reflecting sunlight on their faces and a sounding board amplifying their few words. The average case took eight and a half minutes.

No person sentenced to death in London could be executed until the Recorder of London had presented his Report to the King in Council. This 'Hanging Cabinet', including the prime minister, home secretary and chancellor of the exchequer, decided whether to reprieve the condemned or allow 'the law to take its course'. James and John's lives hung in the balance, but Charles Ewan Law and the Lord Chief Justice, Lord Denman (standing) may have had the final say.

A LEVEE DAY.

The meeting often came between a reception and a dinner, and the Recorder (here at far right in judicial robes and full-bottomed wig) had to wait in line behind the King's tailor and wig-maker. It was the final court of appeal, but it heard no evidence and was bound by no rules. It was judicial murder.

Honoured Sir

With Painful feelings I address you
On the last of August I was decoyed by drink to a house
in Blackfriars road and there Charged of being guilty of
an unnatural Offence and with 2 more men was
Committed to Horsemonger lane gaol and after
My hearing was Committed to Newgate there
I have been tried and the Evidences against me have
Sworn falsely and under those Circumstances I am
Sentenced Death and only now wait his majestys
Pleasure but as a dying man I Solemny Protest my
Innocence at the Same time Imploring your kind
assistance in my dying hours wich are but few
Wich I trust your Words to Lord Melbourne Secretary
of State would have great Effect I hope Sir you will
use all your Efforts to Save a Persecuted man
Whose life has been so falsely sworn a way and delay
No time as it is gitting very Short } Your Obedient Serv
and late Groom

Mrs Pratt
No 30 Giffen St
Deptford Kent   An Answer Will Oblige

James Pratt
Newgate Oct 13th

James wrote from the condemned cells in Newgate to his former employer, William Preston, claiming the evidence against him was 'falsely sworn' and imploring his 'kind assistance in my dying hours which are but few'. He adds that an answer to his wife at No. 30 Giffin Street, 'will oblige'.

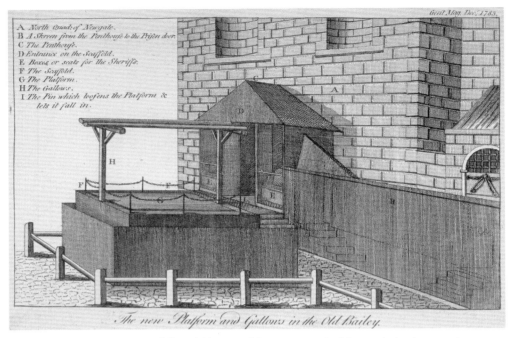

A *North Court of Newgate*.
B *A Screen from the Penthouse to the Prison door*.
C *The Penthouse*.
D *Entrance on the Scaffold*.
E *Boxes or seats for the Sheriffs*.
F *The Scaffold*.
G *The Platform*.
H *The Gallows*.
I *The Pin which loosens the Platform & lets it fall in*.

The new Platform and Gallows in the Old Bailey.

Public executions were moved from Tyburn to Newgate in 1783. Very early in the morning, the prison authorities fixed the gallows in grooves in the street in front of the Debtors' Door (where the men would 'pay their last debt to society').

The Reverend Horace Cotton, the chaplain at Newgate, assisted at so many hangings that it was said that prisoners died with 'cotton in their ears'. He also took a perverse pleasure in extracting confessions and announcing the decision of the Hanging Cabinet to the condemned prisoners.

Inside Newgate, the condemned were prepared for their execution by the hangman before being handed over to the Sheriffs (in blue) as in this picture of the execution of William Fauntleroy in 1824. Leg-irons were outlawed by 1835 but James repeatedly collapsed as he and John were pinioned by the new hangman.

Outside, vast jubilant crowds normally attended. The novelist William Makepeace Thackeray attended a public execution in 1840 and hated 'the whole of the sickening, ghastly, wicked scene'. It took a whole city to hang a man.

The Newgate undertaker Mr Barnard collected John's body and arranged his burial at Bunhill Fields off the City Road, where he lay alongside many non-conformists including the great hymn-writers Isaac Watts, William Blake and John Bunyan.

James's wife Elizabeth brought his body back to Deptford for a Christian funeral on Friday 4 December in the church where they had baptised their two children. It was the third time the words of the Book of Common Prayer were said for James: 'Earth to earth, ashes to ashes, dust to dust.'

Richard Preston's comments also meant that James's letter to William Scott Preston had borne fruit. This had been forwarded to William in Scotland, where he was staying at his wife's family home, Ernespie, near Castle Douglas, and on 18 October William wrote to Melbourne, as James requested. His letter was more tentative than James might have wanted. Preston was keen 'as a Member of the English Bar' to praise the integrity of juries and the mercy of judges and he stated that Englishmen were 'peculiarly sensitive' to the crime for which James stood condemned. Yet he had heard tell of 'so many proofs & accusations, even among the higher ranks, where the accused has been perfectly innocent & this may possibly be the case with the prisoner'. He added that James had served him faithfully for many years as a groom and that 'his wife now interests herself much in his behalf'. All of which led him to ask Melbourne for 'a respite of so awful a sentence, for a short period' so that he could make diligent enquiries. He ended by saying that he 'should be but too happy if [James] can prove the falsehood of his accusers'.[19]

Thomas Phillips also wrote to Russell on John's behalf, following representations from John's relatives. He too admitted that this was 'a most disgusting crime', but thought that 'revolting' as it was, Phillips could not refuse to proffer evidence in John's favour that he alone could give, as John had lived in his service for nearly two years and 'conducted himself so much to my satisfaction that it was with regret that I discharged him at his own request'. He could also attest that John was a good, kind and dutiful son, as he had met John's aged mother, who lived 'at a great distance from London' and 'to whose subsistence, I may almost say existence, he was the only support'. Phillips played on Russell's sense of humanity, suggesting that the 'life of a fellow creature is of too much importance not to interest you deeply' and ended by hoping that he would use his influence to bring about 'a mitigation of Punishment, as may not be inconsistent with the merciful administration of Justice'.[20]

Elizabeth Pratt was indefatigable. She persuaded a former neighbour from Effingham Place, a baker called Andrew Lawson,

Hensleigh Wedgwood's letter to Lord John Russell seeking a reprieve for James and John was the bravest in a contemporary sodomy case.

to write that he had known James for twelve years and that 'he was the last person I should have believed to be guilty of the crime imputed to him'.²¹ She secured additional letters from Mary Minikin, a painter called Thomas Haynes and a coach painter called George Parker. All wrote in near identical terms. James was 'esteemed as a man of good moral character and lived in the respect of all his neighbours & acquaintances'.[22] Elizabeth also provided her own letter, copied professionally and signed in her own hand on 10 October. Her words speak for themselves: 'Your petitioner trusting to the declaration of her husband as to his innocence of the above charge, however suspicious the appearances might have been on which he was condemned, and pleading his former character, he never having in the course of his life been before rendered amenable to a court of Justice, most humbly and earnestly begs your Lordship will take his lamentable case into your humane consideration and intercede for a mitigation of his awful sentence for which favour the thanksgivings of your disconsolate petitioner will be offered to Almighty God, ander [sic] her prayer for the happiness of your Lordship and your family.'[23]

The most striking letter Russell received came from Hensleigh Wedgwood. There is no evidence that it had been prompted by either of the men and it seems to have been the first to arrive at Mr Capper's office, having been sent from the Union Hall police office on 6 October. Wedgwood's argument is as impressive as his handwriting was elegant. His only claim to Russell's attention was that he was the magistrate who had committed them to trial, but, he wrote, 'I feel so strongly that death is not the punishment for their offence, & the dreadful situation they are in shocks me so much, that I cannot neglect a chance of saving them.' He admitted that their offence was a very heavy one against God and it showed 'a most degraded nature'. But he questioned whether it called for the spilling of blood, as it involved no violence to others. He was convinced that the only reason for the conviction and the death sentence was that it was impossible to find anyone 'hardy enough to undertake what might be represented as the defence of such a crime'. That was not all. Wedgwood was shocked by the unequal way the law operated upon the rich and poor. 'It is the only capital crime that is committed by rich men but owing to the circumstances I have mentioned they are never convicted.' This was the central injustice: 'The detection of these degraded creatures was owing entirely to their poverty, they were unable to pay for privacy, & the room was so poor that what was going on inside was easily visible from without.' He ended the letter by referring to the fact that most of those convicted of this crime were eventually spared. In consequence, 'I most earnestly hope that your Lordship will find it possible to spare their lives.'[24] It was elegant, professional and authoritative. It is shocking that it had no effect on Russell.

It was also the bravest letter sent in a contemporary sodomy case. Sir Robert Peel had received a similar letter as home secretary in 1828 when two nineteen-year-olds, Martin Mellett and James Farthing, were convicted of 'b-gg-y' at the Old Bailey. Like Wedgwood, Peel's correspondent had suggested that death was an excessive punishment for a crime that was widespread but did not seem to have brought society to any obvious state of ruin. He wondered why the law should obstruct a man in 'the free use of any parts of his own body'. But that letter was from an anonymous 'Observer', whereas Wedgwood had put his name to his letter.[25]

There are very few records of other contemporaries agreeing with Wedgwood. The radical MP John Cam Hobhouse, who was a friend of the bisexual Lord Byron, was imprisoned in Newgate on a trumped-up charge of breach of parliamentary privilege in 1819 when the twenty-six-year-old John Markham was hanged for sodomy. Hobhouse could not sleep, so he could hear them putting up the scaffold at four o'clock. He wrote in his diary, 'the tolling of the bell at eight was frightful – I heard the crash of the drop falling and a woman screech violently at the same moment – instantly afterwards the sound of the pye-man crying "all hot all hot"'.[26] A visitor told him later that Markham had committed his crime 'with a pauper in a workhouse on a coffin'[27] and the *Morning Post* recorded that 'Markham was a person of the lowest stamp in society ... a pauper inmate of St. Giles's workhouse.'[28] Hobhouse nevertheless wrote, ''Tis dreadful hanging a man for this nastiness.'[29] That too was kept private. As were William Beckford's comments on the similar execution of John Eglerton in 1816: 'I should like to know what kind of deity they fancy they are placating with these shocking human sacrifices. In a numerous list, he was the only one to be sent to the gallows; all the others were "respited during pleasure". The danger must be great indeed and everyone in the country must be running the risk of having his arse exposed to fire and slaughter.'[30]

The only other public rejection of the death penalty for buggery came from Humphry Woolrych, a fellow member of the Inner Temple with Richard Preston, who dismissed the religious argument in 1832, on the grounds that nobody still called for the death penalty for adultery or cursing your parents, as Leviticus also demanded. He believed the death penalty was singularly ineffective, as 'notwithstanding the most inexorable strokes of justice, the horrid propensity has multiplied amongst us lately'.[31] His conclusion was that 'we have no right to put any man to death, for any crime whatever, unless in the *immediate* defence of ourselves, our properties, our internal peace as a nation, and our country at large'. Only moral and political education would 'lessen this offspring of indecency', although he hastened to add in a footnote that neither sodomy nor bestiality 'is at present by any means predominant, when we consider the dense mass of population'.[32]

This last point was made by Capper's assistant, James Phillipps, who annotated Wedgwood's letter with his initials, JMP, and a table:

For this offence –	
The total charged, in 1834, was	28
Of these 8 were sentenced to death	
5 of these were transptd. for life	5
and 3 were executed	3
12 were found not guilty	12
In 8 cases, no Bill found	8
	28

It clearly proved that the majority of those convicted for buggery were reprieved. Only days earlier Russell had also accepted a plea for mercy in an out-of-London 'unnatural crime' case, that of fifty-six-year-old William Booth, who had been convicted in Chester of an offence with a mare. Russell had written to the High Sheriff of the County of Chester pardoning Booth 'on condition of his being transported ... for & during the term of his natural life'.[33] Perhaps there was a chance for James and John. Everything now depended on the Recorder's Report at the Grand Cabinet.

14

The Hanging Committee

Everyone loved Brighton. 'A visit to Brighton comprised every possibility of earthly happiness', declares Lydia Bennet in Jane Austen's *Pride and Prejudice*.[1] The journalist and MP William Cobbett, too, described the town as 'certainly surpassing in beauty all other towns in the world'.[2] And the artist and engraver John Bruce claimed that there was scarcely a building in the town that was not 'calculated for the residence of a Prince'.[3] It had been transformed in recent years thanks to George IV, who had fallen for its seaside charms as a rebellious prince of Wales and prince regent, on the basis that it was close to London but far enough from the prying eyes of his father's fusty court. It took him nearly forty years to transform a small rented lodging house into a vast oriental palace, but by the time the work was completed – and he was king – the Marine Pavilion's minarets, domes and pinnacles screamed of opulence, ostentation, luxury and modernity. It was only a shame that sickness and royal duties meant that he rarely visited this royal palace as king.

If there was ever any doubt that Brighton would retain its place in royal affections when George died, this was rapidly dispelled when his younger brother William became king. William's private life had been as unorthodox as his brother's. As a third son with few expectations of any title other than the duke of Clarence, he enjoyed more than a decade of unmarried domesticity with an Irish actress called Dorothea Bland who went by the stage name of Mrs Jordan. They had five sons and five daughters out of wedlock, but in 1811, deep in debt and under pressure to marry

when his brother George the prince of Wales became regent, he
suddenly parted with her, taking the boys with him and leaving the
girls and £4,400 a year behind on the sole proviso that Dorothea
should not return to the stage. Neither of William's elder brothers
had produced a male heir by then and they were both estranged
from their wives. When the prince of Wales's only daughter
Princess Charlotte died in 1817, William became third in line to
the throne and a good marriage became all the more important.
After several attempts at more lucrative matches, he married the
astute and accommodating Princess Adelaide of Saxe-Meiningen
in the summer of 1818. When his father George III died in 1820,
followed by his elder brother Frederick in 1827, William became
heir presumptive to his ailing brother George IV – and three years
later he succeeded him.

Brighton thrived under royal patronage again, as William
regularly held court in Brighton and although the king and queen
were both already in their sixties, they enjoyed being seen in
public and preferred a relaxed and informal style of entertaining.
In their wake came a flurry of politicians, dignitaries, socialites,
aristocrats and ambassadors, bringing yet more business to the
up-and-coming seaside resort. The 'vigilant hand of improvement'
continued to bring 'innumerable and splendid additions'.[4] New
hotels like the Royal York, the Albion, the Bedford and the
Norfolk Arms had a hundred beds apiece and entertained their
guests with concerts, balls and fine dinners. You could hire a
bathing machine on the beach for a shilling, take a 'douch' or a
shower in the new bathing machines at the end of the Chain Pier
for 1s 6d or take a season ticket to swim at Lamprell's, Williams's,
Wood's or Hobden's Royal Artillery Baths. Most luxuriously, Mr
Mahomed, 'a native of India', welcomed persons 'afflicted with
chronic diseases, stiff joints, rheumatic and paralytic afflictions,
contractions, sprains &c' to his shampooing baths and promised
'extraordinary success'.[5]

Royal patronage had brought prosperity, so it was not
surprising that William was considered locally as 'one of the
most popular Monarchs that has ever graced the throne of this
country'.[6] Or that Brighton put on a good show for the arrival

of the king and queen at 5.20 p.m. on Tuesday, 3 November 1835, when a large proportion of its 40,000 or so inhabitants, 'including a great number of fashionables',[7] turned out to greet their majesties as they passed through the Palace Gates, with the pealing of the parish bells and 'the loudest acclamations of assembled thousands'.[8]

Brighton was not just a resort, though. William conducted business in the pavilion most mornings and on Thursday the 19th the *Brighton Gazette* announced that the king would hold 'a Council at the Palace to-morrow'. This would involve a meeting of the privy council to discuss important matters in the Empire, followed by the 'Grand Cabinet' at which the recorder would present his report. James and John had already been waiting fifty-two days since their sentence.

The first privy councillor to arrive in Brighton that Friday was Henry Petty-Fitzmaurice, the 3rd marquess of Lansdowne, who had been lord president of the council almost continually since 1830. Now aged fifty-five, he was the son of a former prime minister and had made his name as a supporter of Catholic emancipation and the abolition of slavery. He checked in to the Royal York Hotel at 3.30 p.m. and made his way round the corner to the palace for 4 p.m., by which time the other privy councillors were already robed and gathered. Seven others had been summoned. Alongside Melbourne and Russell were Viscount Palmerston, the foreign secretary; Thomas Spring Rice, the chancellor of the exchequer; Lord Denman, the lord chief justice; Charles Grant, Baron Glenelg, the colonial and war secretary; and Sir William Fremantle, the treasurer of the household.

The first piece of business was an audience with Mustafa Reşid, the Ottoman ambassador to Paris, who was staying at the New Steyne Hotel, and his colleague, the Ottoman minister Nourri Effendi. These pleasantries over, the council meeting started at 5 p.m. in the 'most superb and elegantly ornamented apartment' in the palace, the rotunda. The cornice seemed to be made of solid gold, the curtains were crimson and gold, the vast chimneypiece was decorated with richly ornamented Chinese pilasters and vases and numerous ottomans and chairs were draped in ruby silk fringed with gold. If Russell had looked up he would have seen an eighteen-foot chandelier suspended from a flying dragon wreathed in serpents.[9] First they dealt with privy council matters from around the Empire: slavery in St Vincent, royal appointments in Saint Lucia, the vice admiralty court in Quebec, arrangements in some parish churches and chapels in Middlesex, some proclamations for Jersey and Guernsey, requests for new legislation from Caribbean governors and a new royal railway charter.[10]

Then they moved on to the Recorder's Report, for which by tradition the recorder sat on a small stool by the king's side and the other ministers stood behind the king. Charles Law's report came in the form of a large sheet of paper, folded in four, simply headed 'List of Capital Convicts to be Reported to His Majesty in Council the 20th day of November 1835', in which he listed the name of the felon or felons, the nature of their crime, the substance of the petition and the name of the person (if any) recommending mercy. Most seemed inclined to leniency. Robert Lavender prayed for a favourable consideration of his case on the grounds that 'he was in great distress when he committed the offence and an entire stranger in the neighbourhood, whither he had proceeded in the hope of procuring employment'. The prosecutors against seven of the prisoners were now pleading for mercy, in consideration of 'their former good character', their youth or, as Moses Harris's father argued, the fact that this was 'his son's first Offence'. Only Michael Collins and Joseph Coleman had no petitioner on their behalf, nor a reason they should be reprieved, but since nobody was hanged for 'burglary' any more their reprieve seemed a foregone conclusion.

The inside back page of Law's report was devoted to James and John, and in a separate line, Robert Swan. Law had ominously ended his original note to Russell by claiming that their cases would, he regretted to say, 'require a detailed statement to His Majesty'.[11] His report now read as follows: 'Letter of Wm Wedgwood Magistrate of Union Hall Police Office in favour of the Prisoners, and other applications for a mitigation of their Sentence on the ground of their former good Character.' Leaving aside the fact that he got Wedgwood's first name wrong, Law made no mention of representations from James's wife. Nor did he report that the chief prosecutors, John and Jane Berkshire, had petitioned on the men's behalf. The only reference to the trial pointed to page 728 of Henry Buckler's published account, which merely stated that they had been convicted of 'b-g-y' and sentenced to death. Law was more effusive in Robert Swan's case, reporting 'numerous documents in the prisoner's favour, and several others reflecting on the character of the Prosecutor'.[12] James and John had amassed far more names and petitions between them than Robert, but Law said nothing of that. Whether this was negligence or antipathy to their cause, it did not augur well and, as the jurist Edward Wakefield commented, there was always the danger that if there were any saving facts in the petition that were omitted from the report, 'the man was murdered by neglect, or, if you please, by the system'.[13]

Few of the assembled privy councillors were agnostic on the subject of the death penalty.

Lansdowne had been home secretary from July 1827 to January 1828, when twenty-seven executions had been sanctioned across England. It was said of him that unlike Sir Robert Peel, whose longer practice or tougher fibre enabled him to go through this abrasion of the nerves 'with more tranquillity and apparent indifference', Lansdowne was so acutely alive to these distressing scenes, that not one occurred during the period he held office 'which did not draw showers of tears from his sensitive nature'.[14] Perhaps he would support a conditional pardon for James and John.

Lansdowne's friend, the tall, imposing and sociable lord chief justice, Thomas, Lord Denman, mixed the law and politics throughout his career, but his political allegiance was never in doubt. He sat as a liberal-minded Whig MP from 1818 to 1832, he helped draft and defend the Reform Act as attorney-general and

repeatedly tabled and backed motions for the abolition of slavery
and the emancipation of slaves. In 1822 he narrowly won election
as common serjeant of the City of London and acted as deputy
to the recorder, Newman Knowlys, until 1830. It was not an easy
relationship. Knowlys was renowned for his severity, while few
were as dedicated to reform of the penal code as Denman, who
openly declared that 'the severity of the criminal law defeated
itself'.[15] He fumed that prosecutors were paid more if they
charged a prisoner with a capital felony than a misdemeanour,
and he regularly complained that the accused had no counsel to
defend them.

Denman's liberal instincts did not, however, extend to
homosexuality. When he was still common serjeant he criticised
the police for their deliberate entrapment of men in Hyde Park,
but declared the magistrates who had substituted a fine of £5
instead of sending the accused to be tried by jury for the felony
'had not only acted illegally, but they were a disgrace to the bench,
and contaminated the purity of justice'.[16] Denman also showed
no leniency when he presided over the case of John Howarth
at the Lancaster Summer Assizes in 1833, who was convicted
of sodomy on the basis of the evidence of 'three young men of
unimpeachable character' and offered no material evidence in his
own defence. Denman had the power to pardon, but he did not
hesitate to don the black cap, saying Howarth had been convicted,
'upon the clearest proof, of an abominable and hateful crime'.
Howarth was reduced to tears, but Denman was unmoved.[17]

Denman was at least aware of the need for vigilance, as he had
made a decisive intervention in the case of a post office 'letter-
carrier' called Job Cox who was convicted of stealing a £5 bank
note from a letter in May 1833. Knowlys sentenced Cox to death
at the Old Bailey, and then presented his report at the Grand
Cabinet, which Denman attended as lord chief justice. Denman
was shocked to read over breakfast at home in Russell Square
that Cox was due for execution. He complained to one of the
under-sheriffs, who informed him that it was true. Knowlys had
sent his black-sealed warrant for Cox's execution to Newgate on
Wednesday, and Horace Cotton had notified Cox 'to prepare for

the worst'.[18] Denman was incensed and perplexed. 'Impossible!' he said. 'I was myself one of the Privy Council present when the report was made, and I know no warrant for the execution of any one was ordered.'[19] The under-sheriff immediately went to Mr Capper, whose black book clearly recorded the decision that Cox was to spend twelve months in Newgate with hard labour before being transported for life, and Melbourne, as home secretary, sent a countermanding warrant. Cox was delighted, as he had spent twenty-two hours convinced 'that die he must upon the scaffold'.[20] The liverymen of the City of London were furious when they met the following Monday. Knowlys was 'assailed with hooting and hissing' and he was told to his face that he was 'an old man, imbecile, and utterly unfit to perform the duties of the office he held'.[21] The Court of Aldermen promptly resolved that this was 'the result of some mental infirmity incident to his advanced age' and that 'he ought forthwith to retire'.[22] Knowlys resigned within days, to be replaced by his deputy, the common serjeant, Law. After that everyone would have expected Denman to keep an eagle eye on proceedings.

The same could not be said for the lanky, sandy-haired and pale-faced Charles Grant, a former MP, chief secretary in Ireland and president of the Board of Trade, who had been created Baron Glenelg that May. He was an early riser and worked his way through a vast number of dispatches as secretary for war and the colonies, but he and his brother had a reputation for turning up late and ever since he and Melbourne had fallen asleep at a dinner, *The Times* had taken to calling him 'the sleeping secretary' and imagined him 'stretched out on an easy couch in luxurious listlessness'.[23] Other papers followed suit, referring to him as 'His Somnolency', 'the 'drowsy Lord' or, even worse, this 'piece of official still-life'. The *Morning Post* added that he must have been born under a 'drowsy star', as he not only fell asleep in the Lords, but was 'the cause of sleep in others'[24] and suggested that at its next exhibition the Royal Academy should pair 'a portrait of Lord Glenelg' with 'Still Life'.[25] His political allegiance wavered. Thomas Babington Macaulay, who started his career under him, wrote to his sister Hannah that Glenelg had a mind 'that cannot

stand alone. It is,– begging your pardon for my want of gallantry,–
a feminine mind. It always turns, like ivy, to some support.'[26] That
may explain why he served in both Tory and Whig governments.
Yet despite his father's membership of the Evangelical Clapham
Sect, he consistently supported Catholic emancipation; and
Macaulay 'found him very liberal and tolerant' on the matter of
religion.[27] If Glenelg stayed awake, his tolerance might stretch to
James and John.

More consistently radical, liberal and Whig was the chancellor
of the exchequer, Thomas Spring Rice, a short, bald, spry,
chatty, quick-witted and industrious man who had briefly been
his mentor Lansdowne's deputy at the Home Department in
1827. Glenelg's brother James Grant described Spring Rice as
'somewhat of a dandy' and reported that he wore 'a profusion
of rings on his fingers', a green surtout, a smart black stock and
an exceptionally high collar that was in danger of cutting off
his ears. The overall effect was of 'a prim appearance, both in
manners and dress'.[28] Like Lansdowne and Denman, Spring Rice
supported the attempts to limit the death penalty and in addition
to his support for the abolition of slavery and the introduction of
free universal education he was so appalled by the government's
response to the Irish famine in the late 1840s that he almost
bankrupted himself trying to support his own Irish tenants. His
compassionate nature suggested he too might look kindly on
James and John.

As for the foreign secretary, Viscount Palmerston, 'Harry' to
his friends, he was so abrasive that others called him 'Lord Pumice
Stone'. His views on the penal code varied. In 1853 he stated as
home secretary that nobody had ever been wrongfully executed,
yet he reduced the maximum period of solitary confinement from
eighteen months to nine and ended transportation to Van Diemen's
Land. And when the headmaster of Harrow School, Dr Charles
Vaughan, was accused of sending love letters to one of his pupils,
Palmerston intervened as prime minister (and ex-Harrovian) to
offer him the post of bishop of Worcester. His primary interest
up until this moment, however, was in foreign affairs – and he was
unlikely to play a determining role in the decision.

That just left the sixty-nine-year-old Sir William Fremantle, who had been treasurer of the household since 1826. The *Morning Post* wrote that Fremantle was 'a humble but consistent member of the Church of England, religious without bigotry, and most moral and exemplary in every act of his life, without ostentation or hypocrisy'.[29] That was little comfort to James and John, since the Church universally condemned homosexuality and supported the death penalty. But Fremantle may have been more interested in the party politics of the meeting, as he was no friend of the Whigs. He was a Tory MP from 1806 to 1827, his attempt to return to the Commons in 1830 had been thwarted by Earl Grey and he described Russell's Reform Bill as 'the commencement of revolution' under 'the supremacy of the demagogue faction'.[30] His nephew had served as one of Peel's ministers when William sacked Melbourne. More importantly, Fremantle may have hoped for a short meeting as he knew dinner had already been laid.[31]

If Lansdowne, Russell, Glenelg and Spring Rice were minded to be merciful, that might be enough to secure a pardon for James and John. However, six things might swing the decision the other way.

Firstly, there was the prime minister. Melbourne had signed off 164 executions during four years as home secretary. He was proud of his lack of squeamishness, as became evident when his brother George Lamb died in 1834, leaving a vacancy as his under-secretary at the Home Department. Earl Grey immediately suggested that his own son Lord Howick would be a suitable replacement, to which Melbourne responded that he hoped Howick was 'not infected with any of these wild notions … respecting the awfulness of inflicting capital punishment. If he is, it surely is a decisive objection to his accepting the place.'[32] Grey agreed. Howick would obviously want to limit the number of capital punishments to the minimum possible, but he had, so his father wrote, 'none of that morbid sentiment that would reject them altogether'.[33] Many thought Melbourne lackadaisical, but his political motto was clear enough. 'The whole duty of government', he pronounced, 'is to prevent and punish crime, and to preserve contracts.'[34]

Secondly, this meeting of the Grand Cabinet was unusual in that there was no lord chancellor. Normally the lord chancellor played the defining role in the meeting, giving legal advice and swaying the meeting one way or another. Lord Chancellor Eldon claimed that he had taken special care to examine every case minutely before the meeting. But Melbourne had blamed the last Whig lord chancellor, Henry, Lord Brougham, for the collapse of the Whig government in 1834, so he had refused to reappoint him in May 1835 and had left the post in commission in the hands of three senior lawyers. Since Brougham was already engaged in an attempt to reform the bloody code, it is probable that he would have argued for a reprieve for James and John, but in the absence of a lord chancellor, the recorder's views could predominate.

Thirdly, there was the recorder. Law believed in the death penalty and had made his views on homosexuality abundantly clear at sentencing. Other criminals had to be protected from being 'contaminated' by James and John and mercy could never be extended to unnatural offences. His report gave no explanation of the case, it omitted key aspects of the men's pleas and it reads as if he had already made up his mind. Law also had something to prove, as every single prisoner whom he had sentenced to death at the Old Bailey had been reprieved. If James and John were not to hang, would he ever secure a hanging?

That takes us to the fourth point. Law's father Lord Ellenborough had complained about the inequality of punishment meted out by the Grand Cabinet when he was lord chief justice. On the one hand a man might be hanged because there were only a few on the list and it was some time since an example had been made for this particular offence. On the other, a guilty man could get off if there was what he called 'a heavy calendar, and there are many to be executed'. His main concern, though, was not that there were too many executions, but that there were too few. 'There were at least ten cases in which the punishment of death ought to have been inflicted', he wrote after a Recorder's Report in 1828, '[but] we chose only six.'[35] The duke of Wellington similarly moaned that hanging 'only six' was poor considering there were so many 'atrocious cases'.[36] As Ellenborough put it, this meant that 'the actual delinquency of the individual is comparatively little taken into consideration. Extraneous circumstances determine his fate.'[37] This may have been decisive for James and John. The very fact that there had not been a hanging at Newgate since April 1833 – nor a hanging for sodomy at Newgate since 1823 – told against James and John. Some might argue against holding three hangings on the same day, but that would only save Swan.

Hence the fifth point. Swan's case was ambiguous. He was guilty of robbery and of making allegations about William Reynolds – but there were suggestions that these allegations were true. This doubt led to a protracted discussion in the Grand Cabinet, but it also told against James and John, as their case was clear-cut by comparison. The prosecution argued that it had proved penetration and emission of seed. There were two eyewitnesses. Whether the law was right to condemn men to death for sodomy, or whether the men had been allowed to make a proper defence, was immaterial. No man could lawfully consent to sex with another man.

Finally, this was not a serious court of appeal; it was a capricious assembly of nine men who loathed one another. The king was fuming because he felt the Whigs had been foisted on him and consequently, according to the secretary to the privy council, Charles Greville, he abhorred 'all his Ministers, even those whom he used rather to like formerly' and had spent the summer picking fights with them.[38] He hated Russell the most, but he and his queen 'could not bear Glenelg' because he had opposed a grant of £25,000 for Adelaide's coronation outfit.[39] Both William and Fremantle were also still smarting at the fact that Melbourne had made it a condition of accepting office that members of the royal household, who had formerly voted in parliament as they saw fit, must always support the government. In addition, Law was a Tory MP and repeatedly voted against Russell and Melbourne's bills; Lansdowne and Spring Rice had only joined the government reluctantly at the last minute; Palmerston, who was a former Tory, was having an adulterous affair with Melbourne's sister, Emily,

Lady Cowper; and it was rumoured that Glenelg, who never married, was engaged in an affair with Emma Murray, another of Palmerston's lovers. These men had neither the time nor the inclination to look into every case with compassion. They never saw the letters from Hensleigh Wedgwood and James and John's former employers, nor were they made aware that the Berkshires had pleaded for mercy, and that Elizabeth Pratt had worked ceaselessly on her husband's behalf. They made their decision on James and John in the twinkling of an eye and without all the facts. Their appeal was denied. They were to hang. It is difficult not to conclude that this was judicial murder.

The discussion on Swan's case meant the meeting went on longer than usual and only broke up at 8.30 p.m., when the ministers dispersed to their hotels to dress for dinner back at the palace, at which the 'celebrated linguist'[40] Mr Urquhart acted as translator for the Turkish ambassador. It was a convivial evening. Covers were laid for fifty, and the guests included Emily, Lady Cowper, Melbourne's younger brother Sir Frederick Lamb and Russell's uncle, Lord William Russell. Afterwards, 'the company adjourned to the music room, where the Queen's band were in attendance'.[41] Most of the ministers stayed in Brighton overnight. Melbourne and Palmerston had audiences with the king the next morning and attended divine worship in the chapel with the Ottoman ambassador. The choir sang the anthem 'Why do the heathen?', but Mustafa Reşid took no offence and returned as ambassador to London the following year. Lansdowne, Spring Rice and Russell were back in London by mid-afternoon.

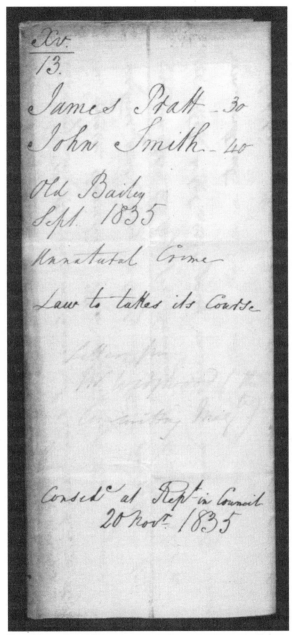

The bundle of letters and petitions seeking a reprieve for James and John was annotated with the harsh words 'Law to takes its Course' (sic) after the Hanging Cabinet had met.

15

The Drop

Law did not stay overnight in Brighton, but 'immediately came to town and made known to the authorities at Newgate the result of the Council'.[1] By this time the seventeen men in the press-yard would have caught wind of the council meeting. They also knew that the recorder was meant to deliver the news to the governor swiftly and in person. However, despite reports that the governor 'lost no time in communicating [the news] to the convicts whose cases had been reported',[2] they had to endure another anxious night. James, John and Swan must have been especially desperate to know their fate. Such an unexplained delay made the prisoners angrier and angrier as they imagined all sorts of possible outcomes. Friends and family gathered outside the gaol, in as much suspense as the prisoners, and when they detected a delay they started inveighing against the recorder, the home secretary, the privy council and the king. Some of those whose lives were spared understandably later expressed 'a wish to murder the Recorder for having kept them so long in suspense'.[3]

Finally, before breakfast on Saturday morning, Governor Cope had the turnkeys gather all seventeen condemned men into the upper room of the press-yard, where they forced them to kneel in a circle with their heads bent as if in prayer. Once they were all suitably submissive, Cotton came in, dressed in his long black gown and preaching bands. This was his moment. He was the messenger of hope and the harbinger of doom. Life and death were in his hands – quite literally, in the shape of a sheet of parchment. He knew that fourteen of the men were almost certain that they would be reprieved, so he turned to the other three first. Looking straight at James and John, who were kneeling next to each other, he said, 'I am sorry to tell you it is all against you.' Then he turned to Swan. 'I am happy to tell you that your life is spared,' he said, and continued almost as an afterthought, 'and I am very happy to tell all the others their lives are spared.' There was an eruption of joy in the room, but James and John were thunderstruck and one of them was so overpowered by his feelings that he collapsed. Despite his reprieve, Swan seemed equally upset and asked Cotton if he could remain with James and John 'until the last, that he might read with them'.[4] Cotton then required them all to recite a general thanksgiving to God and to the king before they could have their breakfast.[5] James and John were conducted back to the condemned cells. From then on they were afforded a cell each.

The following day was Sunday and the prisoners gathered in the chapel at ten o'clock for the 'condemned sermon'. This long-established feature of the ritual of execution was a macabre charade of Christianity, as the 'proceedings had the appearance of a show rather than solemn religious service'.[6] The two sheriffs Salomons and Lainson attended in their ceremonial robes and gold chains of office. Behind them stood two liveried young footmen. The public were admitted and such was the excitement about setting eyes on the now definitively condemned men that tickets went for a shilling apiece and the galleries were crowded with well-dressed voyeurs. It was said that one nobleman had attended condemned sermons so often that although he was not remarkable for his attendance at church, 'yet he was a constant chapel goer'.[7]

The chapel was grim. As Dickens put it, 'the meanness of its appointments' emphasised the desultory nature of the proceedings. The pulpit was 'bare and scanty' and had 'paltry painted pillars on either side'. The women's gallery had a heavy curtain to protect them from the men's attentions and the men's gallery had unpainted benches and a dingy front. The altar was a 'tottering little table' and the ten commandments on the wall above it were 'scarcely legible through lack of paint, and dust and damp'. The place was completely 'unlike the velvet and gilding, the marble and wood, of a modern church'.[8] But what really distinguished the chapel was the condemned pew immediately in front of the pulpit. This was 'an oval-shaped sable-coloured box, constructed with a due regard to the effects of religion without morality, as it is sufficiently capacious to accommodate thirty individuals'.[9] Once the rest of the congregation – or audience – had been seated, the deputy governor and an assistant turnkey escorted the prisoners to the condemned pew, where they were gazed on by the morbidly prurient, who inspected them in the most minute detail, looking for signs of mental agony, distress, remorse or sangfroid. The family and friends of the condemned also looked on. It is likely that Elizabeth Pratt attended, possibly with her daughter. The service started with the morning hymn, proceeded with the 'Lamentation of a sinner' and ended with the service for the dead. When it came to the responses, Cotton said, 'From the Gates of hell', and the congregation replied, 'deliver their souls, O Lord'. James and John were participating in their own funeral.

They still had to endure the 'condemned sermon' itself. It was a routine Cotton had gone through many times – and many thought he enjoyed it too much. Dressed in a black cassock, a clean white surplice and a black preaching scarf, and with his knuckles covered in rings, he ascended the pulpit and stared down at the men. He slowly and deliberately took a large helping of coarse snuff before he started. He had a stock of favourite texts. One was from Galatians: 'Be not deceived, God is not mocked; for whatever a man soweth that shall he also reap.'[10] Another, which seemed a cruel reference to the manner of execution, came from the first epistle to the Corinthians: 'Let him that thinketh he standeth, take heed lest he fall.'[11] His aim was to force the men to repent in earnest, so he expatiated for forty minutes on the evil of sin and the vengeance of the Lord of Hosts. Finally, he paused and lowered his voice to little more than a stage whisper and addressed James and John directly: 'you, my poor fellow mortals, who are about to suffer the awful penalty of the law'. What followed was ten minutes of 'crimes, punishments, bonds, shame, ignominy, sorrow, sufferings, wretchedness, pangs, childless parents, widows and helpless orphans, broken and contrite hearts, and death to-morrow for the benefit of society'.[12] James and John must have felt the intensity of what Cotton was saying – and the eyes of everyone watching them. Some thought the whole rigmarole degrading and distasteful. 'I could not perceive anything like humanity, in thus publicly annoying poor devils, who were evidently worn to the bone by misery,' wrote William Haley.[13] Some complained that 'religion is ever mixed up with our national brutality, a war or an execution, it is all the same.'[14] Lord Brougham loathed this 'base traffic of pandering to the prurient curiosity of the more foolish and idle part of the public'.[15] Despite having assented to James and John's execution, Lord Denman despised prisoners having 'their every gesture, their expression, their manner, their deportment ... watched in this way'.[16] And the marquess of Clanricarde told the House of Lords that it was wrong 'to desecrate the Liturgy of the Church by placing a man in that position before an assemblage of spectators watching to see what effect the solemnities of the Church might produce on him'.[17]

The sermon concluded, James and John were led out from the chapel. As they left, they wished a final farewell to their former press-yard companions. It was also a moment for James to hold Elizabeth.

That week the press debated the men's impending execution. On Tuesday, the *Morning Herald* reported that Prussia was removing the death penalty for all offences other than murder. 'Would we could say so of England!' it proclaimed, before commending the king's 'merciful anxiety' for the fact that there had been no execution in London for two and a half years. It was therefore disappointed that 'two criminals are now ordered for execution in the county of Surrey'. The paper did not mention the nature of their crime, but it fumed against the execution. 'Their crime and the remembrance of it ought to be buried in the silence and seclusion of the prison-house,' it stated. An execution merely

The hangman, William Calcraft, had already hanged thirty-one men and three women at Newgate by the time of James and John's execution.

attracted the curiosity and attention of the public. People hawked reports of executions round the streets and 'disgusting details are given to gratify a vicious curiosity'.[18] The *London Courier* copied this article and concluded that 'a private execution' was 'undoubtedly the most appropriate punishment'.[19] The *Morning Herald* went further on Thursday. 'Our Whig rulers', it stated, were engaged in a 'disgusting and pernicious spectacle'. They were 'returning to a practice which had been interrupted, and interrupted – we presume it had been found worse than useless – because it had been found to be offensive to public decency'.[20] Secret executions were not the answer. They were a characteristic of tyranny. It recommended instead 'the *restraint and seclusion of a prison*'.[21] The *London Courier* also returned to the matter that day, publishing a letter from 'Scrutator' who claimed that 'no such execution has been ordered by the Privy Council since the year 1822 – that is, for a period of thirteen years.'[22] The implication was clear. Both newspapers thought the government had made the wrong call. Interestingly, Russell kept a copy of that edition of the *London Courier* in his private papers.[23]

Unknown to James and John, there was another row. Since the creation of the Central Criminal Court with its expanded jurisdiction, it had been expected that condemned criminals would face execution in the county where their crime had been committed, which should have meant a return to Horsemonger Lane Gaol.[24] But when Law sentenced them, he omitted the requisite words 'in the respective counties where their offences are alleged to have been committed'. Several 'municipal authorities' took umbrage, but Law persuaded the other judges that the men should hang where their judgment was pronounced.[25] So he would get a hanging at Newgate, after all.

On Thursday evening James and John received another visit from Horace Cotton. The sheriffs had asked him whether a 'dissenting teacher' with 'a regular congregation near town' could see the men. He had visited them several times since their sentence and hoped to comfort them on the eve of their execution. Cotton was not impressed. 'I saw no necessity for it,' he wrote in his diary. He had complained bitterly earlier in the year when 'a person of the name of Berry' had been allowed to give religious instruction to prisoners, despite being 'of some sect dissenting from the Established Church' and was delighted to report when he first met James and John that both of them 'wanted no dissenting teachers'.[26] He thought it was his business alone as the Church of England ordinary to bring the men to a full acceptance of their wickedness, and he was as impressed that 'Smith scarcely denied his guilt all along' as he was infuriated that Pratt continued to deny everything. Thomas Wontner was equally dismissive of 'obtrusive visits' from dissenting clergy. '*One* person, and *only* one, should be admitted to give religious instruction,' he wrote. How else could a man prepare to meet his maker?[27]

Despite this, when James and John said they would like to see the preacher, Cotton allowed him to be admitted, along with 'some other parties'.[28] The *Morning Chronicle* claimed that 'the Reverend Gentleman exhorted [James] to repentance, and implored him not "to cover his sin"'. But James would have none of it. Not enough had been proved legally, he said, and although he was a great sinner in need of mercy, he was not guilty as charged. However, the moment the minister left the press-yard and Pratt's cell was bolted shut, James apparently told Swan, whose request to stay with James and John to the end had been granted, 'I am sorry I have told that gentleman a lie.' Swan immediately had the preacher recalled, whereupon Pratt 'made a confession of his guilt, and the justice of his sentence, lamenting that down to the last hour almost he should have cherished a false hope'.[29] In Cotton's account, James added 'that he had been addicted to these abominable practices from his youth'.[30] Whether this is precisely what happened, or whether James ever confessed at all, is a matter for conjecture. This was, after all, the outcome the ordinary of Newgate always sought – a last-minute confession. It proved that the system worked. In a similar vein, *Bell's New Weekly Messenger* claimed that although James and John's conduct had been exemplary in many respects, they appeared to have been 'insincere, and had recourse to subterfuge, rather than a real repentance' right up to the last minute. The paper was all the more delighted therefore to report that James finally 'declared that his crime is abhorrent, and his punishment just'.[31] It had one remaining niggle. 'There exists a little doubt,' it reported, 'that they became leagued with a gang of miscreants. Upon this, however, they were doggedly taciturn.'[32] Nobody liked to think that other homosexuals might have escaped the rigour of the law. Cotton and the press may have deliberately exaggerated for their own reasons, but it is possible James admitted that he had always known which way his affections lay and perhaps it was because he had thus 'disburdened his mind' that he became 'more tranquil', as *Bell's* put it.[33]

Neither of the two Church of England clergy who knew James before his arrest seem to have shown any interest in him. The vicar of St Paul's Deptford, who had baptised both Elizabeth and William Pratt, Thomas McGuire, had died in 1834, but the man who had taken his place, his former curate, the Reverend Benjamin Ffinch, was from a long-established Deptford family and he would have known the Pratt family. Yet he was one of the prime movers in the recent creation of a Conservative Association for Blackheath, Greenwich, Woolwich and Deptford, which was launched at the Red Cow in Deptford. Church, Crown and the established order, that's what Ffinch believed in, not the liberal nonsense coming out of the new Whig government. Ffinch's creed was the same as that of his fellow Conservatives who wanted to retain the death penalty and purge society of immorality. Perhaps it is not surprising that James preferred the ministrations of an independent dissenting minister. This may well have been Richard Aldridge, who was the clerk and minister at the Independent Chapel in Deptford High Street for more than forty years. Aldridge counted many shipwrights and artisans in his congregation, including James's brother John Pratt, as well as the wealthy shipbuilder Edward Barnard, who lived at Deptford Green and had been elected as one of the two 'ultra-radical' Liberal MPs for the newly enfranchised borough of Greenwich in 1832. Aldridge regularly got into skirmishes with local Conservatives, who saw his chapel as a nest of radicalism, but he also had a sense of humour. When asked in court whether his congregation could turn him out if he misconducted himself, he replied, 'If they were deranged, they might.'[34] Aldridge might have been a more sympathetic person to whom to unburden himself.

James might have hoped that even at this late hour Dr Cole of Greenwich Hospital would speak up for him. A simple word might have sufficed. He might not even have needed to put anything in writing. Considering how hard Elizabeth laboured on James's behalf, it seems likely she would have tried to persuade him to help. But Cole seemingly kept his own counsel.

This leaves the question of why James's brother John did not sign the petition for mercy. Perhaps he was one of the 'other parties' who visited on the eve of execution. Or perhaps he was so disgusted that he wanted nothing to do with his younger brother. We can only speculate.

As the extreme penalty of the law approached, the criminal justice system continued to ram home its message. If James and John managed to sleep at all on the eve of their execution, the loud ringing of a handbell would have woken them in the middle of the night, as it had been customary since 1612 for the sexton of the church on the other side of Old Bailey, St Sepulchre's, to ring 'twelve solemn towels [tolls] with double strokes' at midnight on the eve of an execution. With the tolling of the bell came a dirge, bellowed out to the prisoners who were due to die for their 'wickedness and sin'. It urged them to keep that night in watching and prayer for the salvation of their souls and to repent of their sins in the hope that they might not be sent into the eternal flames. The next morning the great bell of St Sepulchre's would toll for them, 'to the end that all godly people hearing that bell, and knowing it is for you going to your deaths, may be stirred up heartily to pray to God to bestow his grace and mercy upon you whilst you live'.[35] Cotton would have heard the bell in his house next door to the gaol, as would the governor, Cope, all the prisoners and the occupants of Swan Yard, including Fanny Cannon. Many must have thought, in the words long attributed to the sixteenth-century evangelical preacher John Bradford, when he saw criminals being led to the scaffold, 'There, but for the grace of God, go I.'[36]

Very early on the Friday morning, a team of horses drew the gallows out of the Sessions House on wheels, and the prison authorities fixed it with posts in grooves in the street in front of the Debtors' Door and hung it in black. Seats were set for the sheriffs on either side of the steps up to the scaffold. There were galleries for officers and attendants and a railing to keep the public five feet away. In the middle of the scaffold, underneath the gibbet, which projected straight out from Newgate, was a six-inch platform measuring ten feet by eight, which was supported by two beams held in place by bolts. This was where the condemned men would stand. When the hangman pulled the bolts, the platform would give way.

Few people gathered outside Newgate that Friday, which was unusual. Ever since executions had been moved there from Tyburn in 1783, the streets around Newgate had thronged with mawkish spectators from early in the morning on the day of an execution. Nearby pubs and hotels rented out window seats and people clambered on wagons and roofs and hung out of windows to get a good view. All sorts of people made a day of it. Publicans and pickpockets, surgeons and stockbrokers, bucks and swells, matrons and ingénues, and members of both Houses of Parliament. Wealthy aristocrats could wangle a place in the press-yard with the governor, for a fee. So many apprentices and masters considered it a holiday that tradesmen including master coach builders, frame makers, tailors and shoemakers 'who had engaged to complete orders within a given time' reminded their clients 'that will be a hanging-day and my men will not be at work'.[37] For those who could not attend, extensive reports were produced and such was the fascination that the *Newgate Calendar* sold ten times more copies than the *Spectator* or the *Manchester Guardian*. The crowd could easily become a mob. Arthur Griffiths described execution crowds as 'a ribald, reckless, brutal mob, violently combative, fighting and struggling for foremost places, fiercely aggressive, distinctly abusive'.[38] When two men were hanged at Newgate in 1807 for the murder of a lavender-seller, the crowd of 80,000 was so vast that thirty people were killed and nearly seventy were injured. The authorities were so frightened of a repeat of this when John Bellingham was executed for the murder of the prime minister Spencer Perceval in 1812, that they put up posters all around Newgate saying 'Beware of entering the crowd! Remember thirty poor persons were pressed to death by the crowd when Haggerty and Holloway were executed!'[39]

Large crowds had also been reported in sodomy cases. They started gathering at Newgate at three in the morning when the scaffold was brought out in 1822 for the execution of John Holland (who was married but had 'a very effeminate voice') and William King, and the moment the bolt was drawn 'the mob shouted loud execrations repeatedly and there were cries of "Where's the Bishop?"', in reference to the bishop of Clogher.[40] A couple of months later, 'considerable numbers of spectators' assembled there again for the execution of 'the wretched culprit' William North, who 'appeared to have grown at least ten years older during the five months he has been in a condemned cell'.[41] Likewise, when a servant, Thomas Rodgers, was hanged at York at noon on 12 April 1834 for 'an unnatural crime' – or, in the words of the trial judge, for 'giving vent to unbridled lust'[42] – it was said that 'the number of spectators was very immensely great, probably more than five thousand'.[43] By contrast, the *Sussex Advertiser* reckoned that 'the spectators upon the melancholy occasion' of the most recent execution for sodomy, that of the nineteen-year-old labourer John Sparsholt at Horsham in Sussex on 22 August 1835, 'were fewer in number than we remember to have seen at former executions at Horsham, there being not more than 300 persons present'.[44] The *Brighton Gazette* added, 'and not the slightest manifestation of feeling was observed among the spectators'.[45]

Several contemporaries detested the public's ghoulish excitement at a hanging. Edward Wakefield thought the whole thing was counter-productive, as 'the effect of the punishment is to excite sympathy for the criminal and hatred of the law'.[46] William Makepeace Thackeray agreed. Long before he acquired fame as a novelist, he attended a hanging at Newgate in 1840, when a Swiss valet called François Courvoisier was executed for cutting the throat of his master, Lord William Russell, in his bed. The story had wound London to fever pitch, not least because the victim was Lord John Russell's uncle, and 'half the world went to sleep expecting to have their throats cut before morning'.[47] Estimates put the crowd at 40,000. But Thackeray hated the 'whole of the sickening, ghastly, wicked scene'. Much of the time he closed his eyes. Afterwards he felt he had been 'abetting an act of frightful wickedness and violence' and prayed that it would soon 'be out of the power of any man in England to witness such a hideous and degrading sight'.[48] Dickens was also there. He had never felt his fellow-creatures to be so odious, as he had not seen 'one token in all the immense crowd; at the windows, in the streets, on the house-tops, anywhere; of any one emotion suitable to the occasion. No sorrow, no salutary terror, no abhorrence, no seriousness; nothing but ribaldry, debauchery, levity, drunkenness, and flaunting vice in fifty other shapes.'[49] There is no record of Dickens turning up at Newgate on 27 November 1835.

Myths abounded about prisoners' final meals. It was said that Nathaniel Parkhurst, who had murdered a fellow-prisoner in the Fleet in 1715, 'demolished a roast fowl at breakfast on the morning of his execution, and drank a pint of liquor with it'.[50] Cockneys supposedly referred to hanging as breakfasting on an artichoke (or hearty choke) with caper sauce. But James and John had just had a cup of tea when Horace Cotton arrived at the condemned cell at seven o'clock on Friday morning. He said they seemed so completely exhausted that he ordered them some warm wine, which they drank before being taken through to the press-room, where they met the hangman and his assistants.

Hangmen fascinated England. Often they were thought of as little better than common criminals, for the good reason that in some cases they only agreed to perform the role in exchange for a respite of their own death sentence. In one seventeenth-century instance, the judge offered a pardon to a father and his two sons who had been convicted of horse-stealing at the Derby Assizes, on the condition that one would act as executioner of the other two. The father declined, as did the older son, but the younger one agreed – and after hanging his father and brother he became the regular local hangman. Likewise, John Price, who was appointed hangman for the City of London in 1714, ended up on the scaffold for rape in 1718. And Jack Ketch, whose duties in the reign of Charles II included several executions of traitors by hanging, drawing and quartering, achieved such universal notoriety for his barbarous inefficiency that all subsequent executioners were referred to by his name.

The 'Jack Ketch' on 27 November was William Calcraft. His life had followed a similar pattern to that of James Pratt. Born in 1800 in Great Baddow in Essex, and married there in 1824, he made his way to London with his wife Louisa in search of a living. He had a trade, as a boot- and shoemaker, but by the end of the 1820s he was earning a precarious living as a night watchman in Reid's brewery in Clerkenwell and selling meat pies in the streets of the City. Somehow this brought him into contact with John Foxten, the elderly and illiterate long-standing hangman at Newgate, who took him on as an assistant. He was paid ten shillings a week to flog young inmates for misdemeanours. Foxten had been ailing for years, thanks, so he claimed, to performing his duties over forty years in all manner of foul weather; and on 14 February 1829 he died. On 17 March the *Morning Post* announced that the aldermen of the City of London had appointed Calcraft as the executioner for Middlesex and London on a salary of a guinea a week plus a guinea for each execution. Calcraft's first official duty at Newgate was a difficult affair, as he had to restrain Esther Hibner in a straitjacket while she screamed for revenge before the sheriffs escorted her up onto the scaffold. Such was Hibner's widespread reputation as an 'Evil Monster' – she had starved her nine-year-old apprentice Frances Collpitts to death – that the moment she appeared on the platform, the many thousands who had gathered 'rent the air with shouts of exultation'. One newspaper reported that Calcraft's every movement in fixing the noose and cap was 'hailed with shouts of applause' and the moment the drop fell, the applause bestowed on him was 'greater than before'.[51] Some claimed that the cheers went to Calcraft's head. He would never say that he enjoyed his work. He always put 'boot and shoe maker' as his trade rather than hangman on the census returns. He liked to be thought of as a 'mild-mannered man of simple tastes, much given to angling in the New River, and a devoted rabbit fancier'.[52] But there was a feeling that he enjoyed entertaining the crowd. And in addition to his *per capita* fees, it was said that 'he also appropriates whatever property might be on the persons of those he executes, including the clothes they die in'.[53]

By 1835 Calcraft had hanged thirty-one men and three women at Newgate, but James and John would have known his terrible reputation for incompetence. Part of the problem was the 'short drop' method he and others used. Many believed that the hanged died of 'apoplexy', but the Scottish anatomist Dr Alexander Monro told Samuel Johnson that 'the man who is hanged suffers a great deal', that it was not that different from being suffocated with a pillow and that 'for some time after he is thrown over he is sensible and is conscious that he is *hanging*'.[54] When the lever was pulled and the trapdoor gave way, the prisoner fell just three feet before the rope snapped taut, which was rarely enough to cause the 'hangman's fracture', instantly snapping the neck at the C2 vertebra. Sometimes the condemned would twist and flail around for several minutes before the rope finally fell still. If they were lucky, their windpipe was so restricted that they were asphyxiated and passed out within seconds. More commonly the cord pressed on the jugular veins or the much deeper carotid arteries. The prisoner's face would fill with blood and go blue for lack of oxygen; their tongue would stick out. The capillaries would burst and the pressure would build on the brain until they had a stroke. Even after the brain died the heart would keep on beating and the body would shudder with involuntary spasms. Hopefully, the prisoner would have lost consciousness within a minute, but it was a painful death. It helped if the rope and the drop were longer, especially for smaller, lighter prisoners. If the knot of the noose were placed carefully beneath the chin rather than to the side, that too might help despatch the prisoner more humanely. It was said that some prisoners bribed the hangman to guarantee a swift end. When James Ings was about to be executed as one of the Cato Street conspirators in 1820, he told the hangman, 'Now, old gentleman, finish me tidily … Pull the halter a little tighter round my neck, or it'll slip.'[55] He was wise to ask. Things went badly wrong when Calcraft hanged the three members of the 'Fields Lane Gang' in 1829, including their leader, 'a small man with a clean muscular frame', Thomas Birmingham, as the noose slipped under Birmingham's chin, throwing his head back but not drawing the cord tight. As Calcraft pulled on Birmingham's legs from under the scaffold, 'the yells of the crowd, mingled with the screams of women, were terrible, and it was at least five minutes before the unfortunate man dropped his hands'.[56]

James and John were taken into the press-room at 7.30 a.m. Calcraft, Cope, Cotton and a small group of spectators who had paid for the privilege were waiting. Reports suggested that James and John were weak and dejected, and that when Calcraft's assistants started pinioning John, James 'appeared to suffer dreadfully' and his groans could be heard throughout the gaol.[57] Soon John's hands were tied in front of him so that he could pray, and a second loop was passed round his elbows. Then Calcraft's assistants started on James, who repeatedly collapsed and had to be held up. Finally, Calcraft placed a noose round each man's neck, with the loose end wound round his waist. Cope then started walking the two men in solemn procession through the prison, while Cotton recited prayers and biblical texts. Contrary to some accounts, they did not walk down Birdcage Walk, which would have taken them to the Sessions House at the Old Bailey. Instead, they had a tortuous route through the gaol, through a narrow doorway into the Common Side yard, down a long narrow passageway, which passed through a series of arches, each narrower and shorter than the last. Passing through another narrow corridor under the chapel, they reached the Debtors' Lodge, whose large studded door opened onto the street. Here the execution party gathered.

There was one further convention. The governor was required formally to surrender the prisoners at the Debtors' Door to the sheriffs. Normally this formality passed without comment, but Salomons was still embroiled in his battle with anti-Semitism, as he had only just stood to be alderman for Aldgate ward, 'for the purpose of exhibiting in his own person the progress which sound liberal principles were making in this country'.[58] The *Morning Advertiser* had backed him, saying that 'London has done itself immortal honour by electing Mr Salomons to the high office of Sheriff' and hoping that it would now 'secure to enlightened freedom another great triumph'.[59] Salomons had won the election by seven votes on 19 November, but this provoked another row, as the former sheriff and lord mayor, Alderman Anthony Brown, tabled a motion three days before James and John's execution, barring Salomons from taking office. Brown disingenuously claimed that he could not possibly entertain 'a more profound respect – indeed he might almost say veneration' for Sheriff Salomons,[60] but others saw through his hypocrisy. Salomons was immeasurably better than 'the scoundrel-crew of aldermen that made his religion a pretence for rejecting him',[61] wrote the *Poor Man's Guardian*.*

James and John probably knew little of these events and cared even less, but this was the first time Salomons and Lainson had been required to escort condemned men to their execution. They carried an air of authority as they came out through the Debtors' Door dressed in their bright blue gowns trimmed with sable, their gold chains of office and their tricorn hats, but they must have been shocked and disturbed by the reception they received, as the small crowd started hissing the moment the prisoners appeared. Salomons might have wondered whether this was directed at him.

Cotton, by contrast, had been doing this for twenty-one years. He had assisted at 344 executions at Newgate and had kept a notebook with details of each one. He believed the death penalty was justified and necessary. Perhaps he remembered the extraordinary scenes at the first execution he attended in August

---

* Salomons had to wait for another change in the law before becoming an alderman in 1847, and had to go through the same rigmarole when he was elected MP for Greenwich in a by-election in 1851. Despite winning 63 per cent of the vote, he was removed from the Commons, disqualified and fined and although he was a very successful lord mayor in 1855, it was not until 1859 that he was able to take his seat in Parliament.

1814, when six men were hanged. It was said that one of the condemned, John Ashton, 'either affected, or suffered, complete insanity' from the moment he was convicted of highway robbery and when Cotton tried to get him to pray on the scaffold Ashton began to dance, shouting, 'Look at me; I am Lord Wellington!' The under-sheriff had then begged Cotton to dispense with the usual ceremonies and give the customary signal immediately. There was a momentary pause when the drop fell, but almost immediately Ashton rebounded from the rope and started dancing and clapping his hands next to Cotton while shouting 'What do ye think of me? Am I not Lord Wellington now?'[62] The hangman had to climb back up the scaffold to shove Ashton back through the trap to his death. Perhaps, too, Cotton recalled the spectators' shudders back in 1823 when he had signalled for William North's execution. That was reported to be 'one of the most trying scenes to the clergymen they had ever witnessed – never appeared a man so unprepared, so unresigned to his fate'.[63] But, as Cotton recorded in his notebook, John had never really denied his crime and James had finally confessed. In Cotton's mind they deserved to die.

At precisely eight o'clock, Salomons and Lainson marched John up the ten steep steps to the scaffold and placed him under the wooden beam. They then came back for James. They could hear the great bell of St Sepulchre's tolling dully and remorselessly across the road. Two coffins had been placed on the scaffold and they could hear Cotton reciting the words of the burial service. 'We brought nothing into this world, and it is certain we can carry nothing out ... The Lord gave, and the Lord hath taken away ... Deliver me from all mine offences, and make me not a rebuke unto the foolish ... Man that is born of a woman hath but a short time to live, and is full of misery ... Deliver us not into the bitter pains of eternal death.'

The hissing apparently continued while Calcraft passed the rope over the beam and tied it back on itself. There was a custom that those about to be hanged could address the crowd, but neither James nor John made to speak, so Calcraft tied handkerchiefs round their eyes and placed white caps over their heads lest they jump when they saw him pull the lever that released the trapdoor. The hoods also meant the spectators were spared the worst sights as prisoners' tongues often protruded, engorged and contorted. Calcraft then went back down the steps, leaving Cotton alone with James and John on the scaffold. The bells at St Sepulchre tolled all the while.

When all was ready, Calcraft looked to Cotton, who started reciting the Lord's Prayer and waved a white handkerchief. Calcraft pulled the bolt. The drop fell.

Executions were money-spinners, not least for publishers like Thomas Birt, who produced this broadside with supposed details of John's confession.

An hour later they took down the bodies. One of the Newgate wardsmen reported that 'some little awe was produced by [an execution], but not much. It formed the subject of conversation just before it took place; some effect continued on a few; but the majority went to their breakfast immediately after it was over as if nothing had happened.'[64] Governor Cope went off to breakfast with Cotton and the paying spectators. The crowd dispersed.

There were two more duties to perform. Prisoners' corpses were no longer disposed of on the premises at Newgate. So that same day, the two bodies were taken 'dressed as before death' to Mr Barnard, the undertaker who was based across the road from the gaol and whose duty it was to dispose of the body or hand it over to the families.[65] The next day Barnard led John's burial five feet under in the lower section of Bunhill Fields off the City Road.[66] This was licensed as a non-parochial burial ground by the City, but was not consecrated by the Church of England. Consequently, according to the poet Robert Southey, writing in 1830, 'Dissenters regard [it] as their "Campo Sancto".'[67] But the City also used it to dispose of those for whom a consecrated spot was thought unsuitable, including convicted felons. Ironically, this meant John Smith lies in the company of the great hymn-writers Isaac Watts, William Blake and John Bunyan.

Elizabeth Pratt's work was not yet done, either. She took possession of her husband's remains from Barnard and persuaded the Reverend Benjamin Ffinch to give James a Christian burial at St Paul's, Deptford the following Friday, 4 December. It was the third time the words of the Book of Common Prayer were said for James: 'Earth to earth, ashes to ashes, dust to dust.'

Epilogue

The press loved to report two things after an execution: whether the condemned had struggled and whether they had shown contrition or penitence. The one satisfied the public's morbid curiosity, the other its righteous indignation. Thus, it was reported that John Ashton 'seemed to meet his fate in great agony, and died in strong convulsions',[1] whereas William North 'never struggled after he fell [and] expired in less than a minute'.[2] Likewise, John Howarth, executed at Lancaster gaol for 'an abominable and hateful crime' in 1833, 'died almost without a struggle',[3] but George Cropper 'struggled very violently' at Maidstone in 1834 before 'the executioner soon ended his mortal agony'.[4] Sometimes two men hanged simultaneously would have different outcomes. Thomas Rodgers was observed to struggle longer than the other more 'athletic and powerful' man to hang alongside him at York in April 1834,[5] and when Thomas Mellon and Michael Byrne were hanged at Newgate for the murder of Thomas Hanlon in 1830 'Mellon died almost without a struggle, but Byrne seemed to endure great agony for some minutes.'[6] As for Calcraft and Cotton's most recent execution at Newgate, that of George Coney for burglary on 23 April 1833, it was said that Coney showed no emotion and his struggles were of 'short duration', although he was a fine young man and his conduct at Newgate 'had been exemplary in the extreme'.[7]

As for death itself, the press preferred to deal in euphemisms. Joseph Charlton was 'launched into eternity' for his 'unnatural crime' in 1819,[8] as were John Holland and William King in 1822,[9]

and John Sparsholt in August 1835. The Nottingham rioters in
1832 were carried 'from the tribunals of man to appear at the bar
of heavenly justice'.[10]

Most newspapers covered James and John's execution. All
commented – in almost identical words – on how dejected the
two men seemed, especially James. None named their crime.
Some simply stated that 'the sentence of the law was carried
into effect'.[11] Some commented on the fact that they had been
hanged at Newgate rather than Horsemonger Lane. *The Times*,
by contrast, complained that James Pratt seemed to have had
'recourse to subterfuge' since his conviction, 'instead of what God
and his country required – an open confession'. It enthusiastically
related the story of the dissenting minister's visit and pronounced
that James and John had 'expiated their heinous offence by the
forfeiture of their lives'. When the trap fell, it recorded, it 'closed
the world upon them'. Others commented on the hissing from
the crowd, but *The Times* differed. 'The crowd was excessive,' it
wrote, 'but exceedingly decorous.'[12]

The execution was a money-spinner. Piemakers and pickpockets
plied their trade around the crowd. William Calcraft sold pieces
of the noose. Thomas Birt, who with his wife and sister ran a
wholesale and retail song and ballad warehouse in Great Andrew
Street in Bloomsbury, rushed out a broadside later that day.
Entitled 'Particulars of the Execution of James Pratt & John
Smith', it carried a crude drawing of the two men hanging outside
the Debtors' Door. It barely mentioned the charges, but claimed
that the 'evidence against these wretched men was so conclusive,
that not the least shadow of doubt remained of their guilt'.
It approved of the recorder's sentence of death and stated that
James and John had left the dock in tears. 'After condemnation',
the broadside claimed, 'every exertion was made by the Rev.
Clergyman to bring them to a just sense of their awful situation
& to acknowledge the justice of their sentence, which they did,
devoting most of their time in prayer.' It also purported to carry the
text of John Smith's last letter, written on Wednesday. Addressed
to an anonymous 'William' living in the neighbourhood where he
resided, it is unconvincingly elegant for a man who could not read

or write. 'The awful period is nearly arrived', it started, 'when the offended laws of my country demand the forfeit of my life for the crime I have committed.' It carried on in similar vein, confessing that his crime was 'the most heinous and disgraceful', expressing amazement at what had possessed him. He could only attribute it to 'the baneful effects of liquor and bad company, which must have rendered me void of every feeling of decency'. It ended with religious sentiments typical of the era. 'The grave will soon close over me, and my name entirely forgotten', he wrote. Yet he died 'a sincere penitent' and hoped his friend would offer prayers up 'to the Throne of Mercy for that forgiveness which I have anxiously prayed to receive'. He signed off, 'That the almighty may bless you is the sincere prayer of Your Lost Friend, John Smith.'[13] It seems unlikely that John Smith ever wrote such a letter and it is difficult not to hear the pious self-justificatory words of Horace Cotton throughout. Birt knew his business – confessions sold well.

There was just one newspaper that refused to jump on the self-righteous bandwagon. *Bell's New Weekly Messenger* called their crime 'revolting', but added that 'no man of sense and humanity in the present age will venture to say it ought to be punished with such dreadful severity – severity exercised, I believe, by no civilised nation upon Earth but our own'. It begged the government to go further in 'temper[ing] the edge of justice' and urged the home secretary 'that our criminal code, much as it has been already mitigated, is still susceptible to further mitigation; and that as regards the present subject it rests upon an insecure and untenable foundation'.[14]

Russell started the process of further limiting the death penalty in 1836 and abolished the Grand Cabinet and the Recorder's Report in 1837. He warily supported the abolitionist campaign led by the Tory MP, Fitzroy Kelly KC, the judge and Whig MP, Dr Charles Lushington and the longstanding liberal William Ewart. Thus he opposed Kelly's first Bill to abolish the death penalty for all but murder and treason in 1840, but when Kelly reintroduced it the following year Russell voted to keep the clause ending the death penalty for rape and sodomy and to send the Bill to the Lords (unlike Russell's opponent Sir Robert

Peel, his successor as Home Secretary, Sir James Graham, and the future Liberal prime minister William Ewart Gladstone). Kelly's Bill became law, but thanks to an amendment from the proselytising 10th Earl of Winchilsea, which was taken without debate, the reference to sodomy was removed from the Bill in the Lords, so Section 15 of the Offences Against the Person Act 1828, under which James and John were convicted and executed, was not repealed until section 61 of the Offences Against the Person Act 1861 replaced the death penalty with penal servitude for life or for any term not less than ten years. That change passed through Parliament without a word of comment. Nobody who was convicted of buggery in the intervening twenty-five years was hanged, but buggery still demanded the death penalty and judges were required to don the black cap for each 'unnatural crime'. When David Pikesley, aged nineteen, was convicted of 'b-----' at the Old Bailey in November 1839, he was sentenced to death, but was immediately reprieved and sent to New South Wales for twenty-one years the following March. So too George Dimond (fifty-three), Henry Johnson (twenty), James Morrison (twenty), Joseph Page (twenty), Charles Peden (thirty), Charles Carter (thirty-nine), Henry Allen (eighteen) and a string of others who were spared the noose. The judge in James and John's case, Sir John Gurney, pronounced death on the tattooed sailor, William Beveridge, for 'b-g-y' in August 1844, but reprieved him in favour of twenty-one years on Norfolk Island, where he twice absconded. When the sixteen-year-old John Williams was convicted of 'b-----' with William Johnson in 1857, he too was sentenced to death but was merely confined for twelve months. Thomas Silver was fourteen (and just five feet two inches tall) when he was convicted of 'an unnatural offence' in 1859, but despite having the sentence of death recorded, he was sent to jail for three years and released early on licence.[15] He was the last man convicted of buggery under the threat of death.

Men faced other charges throughout this period – attempting to lay hands on another man with intent to commit buggery, unlawfully meeting with intent, assault with intent, unlawfully meeting in a public place and committing indecent acts. But men were sent to the House of Correction or transported for all these misdemeanours – and for buggery. None was hanged.

What happened to those involved? Elizabeth Pratt had tried her best to get James reprieved and it is likely she turned up at the Debtors' Door to see James one last time. No doubt many of her neighbours would have pitied or sympathised with her, but others may have shunned her as the widow of a notorious criminal. She stayed in south-east London, though, and on 28 June 1840 she married a bricklayer by the name of Jasper Sidery, who was one of ten children and was employed by his older brother William in their father's firm. At first, they and James and Elizabeth's daughter Elizabeth lived in Marine Street in Bermondsey, but by the time of the 1841 census the three of them were living at 1 Boon Street in Lee. It is impossible to know what James and Elizabeth's daughter Elizabeth thought of her father, but when she married William Hards, a miller, at St Paul's, Deptford on 24 August 1844, both bride and groom registered their fathers as 'servant' in the newly standardised marriage register. As for her mother, Elizabeth and Jasper moved one more time, to 15 Bath Terrace in Greenwich, which is where Jasper died in 1868. And on 25 April 1873, Elizabeth Sidery died of 'paralysis' at the Union workhouse in Greenwich, aged seventy-six. It seems her in-laws, who were wealthy enough to employ a housekeeper and a housemaid, were not prepared to support her.

It was not the Berkshires' last visit to the Union Hall police office and the Old Bailey. In 1838 they accused Jane Smith, a sixteen-year-old recently orphaned girl 'of prepossessing appearance',[16] who had briefly lived with them, of breaking into their house and stealing a haul of silver and jewellery, which was found at Smith's friend Mary Gunn's house. The Union Hall magistrates committed Smith and Gunn for trial at the Old Bailey, where Smith was convicted and sentenced to ten years in Van Diemen's Land.[17] The Berkshires remained at 45 George Street, selling coal, driving horses and renting out rooms. In 1841 they had seven others living with them, including two stonemasons, a furrier, a copper plate printer and an errand boy, but Jane died of asthma and diarrhoea in 1847, and John died of asthma in 1848, aged sixty-two. He left everything to their sole surviving child Eliza, who had married a farmer's son, James Lord, in 1838.

Sergeant Robert Valentine had a successful career in the police and regularly appeared in the courts. At the end of December in 1835 he gave evidence that Dennis Sullivan 'was a notorious character; he had been tried for highway robbery; he was also a pugilist and, of course, the associate of the worst of characters'.[18] In 1837, by which time he had been promoted to inspector and he and his wife Catherine had moved to the East End of London, he was involved in the case of 'a desperate virago' called Anna Bonnell, a servant who was accused of assaulting her mother's landlady 'in a most furious manner', striking her on the head with a saucepan in the washhouse and when that was taken off her, using another saucepan to smash eighteen windows. Bonnell was far from contrite, shouting 'I am sorry I did not give it her ten times more.' As she was taken down, she shouted at the court, 'You shall all catch it when I come out.'[19] Most of his cases were assaults, robberies and thefts. James and John were the only people hanged on the basis of his evidence. He and Catherine had nine children, all of whom lived into adulthood. Their eldest, Eliza, married Henry Spon, a professor of music, and ran a school in Surrey. She died in 1912. Their son Frederick married and stayed in Lambeth where he died in 1930. Their sons George and Frankland emigrated respectively to Australia and New Zealand where they married in 1854 and 1858. After retiring, Robert and Catherine moved several times around Stepney and Dalston, which is where Robert died on 5 May 1868, aged sixty-seven. Catherine outlived him by nearly twenty-nine years and died at the age of ninety-two.

The politicians' careers are a matter of record, but Palmerston and Russell both went on to become prime minister and died respectively in 1865 and 1878. As for the officers of the court, Sir John Gurney continued as a baron of the exchequer until ill health forced him to resign in January 1845. When he died two months later at his home in Lincoln's Inn Fields, some commented that 'his anxiety to dispense the strictest justice caused him occasionally to overlook those claims which might perhaps, in a mind differently constituted, have led to more lenient sentences'.[20] This was certainly the case when he sentenced John Hughes to twenty years' transportation for taking part in the Rebecca Riots in October 1843. Gurney was buried in a large sarcophagus in Old St Pancras church but was moved to be with his wife, Maria, in Highgate Cemetery in 1849.

The lawyer William Bodkin flirted with politics and was elected by just two votes as the Conservative MP for Rochester in 1841, but lost his seat at the subsequent election in 1847, whereupon he returned to the law, securing a seat on the bench as a judge of the Middlesex court of sessions in 1859. One of his enduring passions was reform of the poor laws and it was his Settlement Bill in 1845 that ended the practice of removing paupers from one parish to another where they had not lived for many years. He was knighted in 1867 and died in 1874, aged eighty-three, his wife Sarah having predeceased him in 1848.

The prison inspectors William Crawford and the Reverend Whitworth Russell continued to campaign for better conditions in Britain's gaols and laid the foundations of many important improvements. Both died in 1847. Crawford, who never married, collapsed on a visit to Pentonville Prison in April; and in August apparently believing himself terminally ill Russell shot himself in the boardroom at Millbank Penitentiary, where he was the chaplain.

Charles Ewan Law remained both an MP and recorder until he died, 'not much beyond the prime of life',[21] at his home in Eaton Place in August 1850. Five of his children predeceased him. He continued to oppose changes to the death penalty or to transportation, voted to keep the death penalty for sodomy in May 1841 and claimed in the Commons that there had never been a period in Britain's history 'when the constitution of this country was otherwise than a Christian constitution'.[22] One newspaper commented on Law's death that he 'was a man of some consequence, although in a comparatively contracted sphere'. It added that although he was the second son of Lord Ellenborough, 'it is not always that talent is transmitted from father to son'.[23] By the time of his death he had pronounced the sentence of death on eighteen more prisoners who were hanged after James and John.

The Reverend Horace Cotton retired with an annual pension of £300 in 1838, when he moved to Reigate in Surrey and started selling off his extensive book collection, which included 'an extraordinary collection of tracts relating to criminals, lives of notorious thieves, felons, &c'.[24] His wife died in 1842 and he followed her on 7 June 1846, aged seventy-two, leaving his estate to his two sons and two daughters. Although he was barred from keeping private notes and he told a Commons committee that he did not keep a journal, he detailed every convict he attended in a handwritten personal diary of Newgate executions, together with comments on the manner of their death. He included sketches of himself in action, administering the sacrament to prisoners, delivering the fatal decision of the Grand Cabinet on the Recorder's Report and praying with a man who is already pinioned prior to execution. In all he had helped launch 347 prisoners into eternity, including ten for sodomy.

William Calcraft continued as hangman for another four decades. He hanged the husband-and-wife murderers, Frederick and Maria Manning, in front of a crowd of 30,000 on the roof of Horsemonger Lane Gaol in 1849; he performed the last public hanging in England, that of the Fenian terrorist Michael Barrett, in 1868; he hanged the mass murderess Mary Cotton in 1873; and he performed his last hanging at Newgate on 25 May 1874 before retiring with a pension of 25 shillings a week. By the time he died on 13 December 1879, he had hanged at least 430 people, including 34 women.

Robert Swan was transported on the *Strathfieldsaye* to New South Wales where he arrived on 15 June 1836. Here he was assigned to an E. C. Close and put to work as a machine maker. In June 1837 he spent a period in Sydney Gaol, but in 1843 he married Margaret Jennings, a twenty-one-year-old domestic servant from Devon, who had emigrated the year before. The following year he was granted his ticket of leave, but he and Margaret set up home in the tiny rural village of Hinton in New South Wales, where they had a daughter and three sons. Robert died there in 1850 and

Margaret died in 1902. None of their children seem to have had children.

Hensleigh Wedgwood lived the longest of those involved in this story. After wrestling with his conscience for years, he resigned as a Union Hall magistrate in 1837 over the issue of the compulsory oath because, as he told his father, 'I think it very possible that it may be lawful for a man to take a judicial oath, but I feel that it is not lawful for me, and there is no use in letting £800 a year persuade one's conscience.'[25] His finances were restored by the nine years he spent as registrar of metropolitan carriages, but his intellectual pursuits led him to found the Philological Society in 1842 and publish a *Dictionary of English Etymology* in 1857. He died at his house at 94 Gower Street on 2 June 1891, aged eighty-eight, when he left his £123,694 estate (worth roughly £17 million in 2022) to his devoted wife Fanny and their five surviving children, including the feminist novelist Frances 'Snow' Wedgwood. By then the compulsory oath, public executions and the death penalty for sodomy had been abolished.

Appendix

Date	Name and age if known	Place
26 August 1803	Joseph Bird	Warwick
8 February 1804	Methuselah Spalding	Newgate
13 August 1806	David Robertson	Newgate
27 September 1806	James Stockton, 50	Lancaster Castle
	Joseph Holland, 50	Lancaster Castle
	John Powell, 45	Lancaster Castle
4 October 1806	Isaac Hitchen, 62	Lancaster Castle
	Thomas Rix, 47	Lancaster Castle
31 March 1808	William Billey, 45	Penenden Heath
26 November 1808	Richard Neighbour, 26	Suicide in Newgate
4 April 1809	James Bartlett	Horsemonger Lane Gaol
21 April 1810	Adam Brooks, 42	Lancaster Gaol
31 August 1810	Samuel Mounser	Moulsham Gaol
7 March 1811	Thomas White, 16	Newgate
	John Hepburn	Newgate
4 May 1812	David Myers	Peterborough Fengate
1 April 1813	George Godfrey	Penenden Heath

Date	Name and age if known	Place
18 August 1814	Henry Youens, 33	Penenden Heath
	John Ottaway, 21	Penenden Heath
26 July 1815	Abraham Adams, 51	Newgate
17 April 1817	Samuel Jacobs	Warwick Castle
21 August 1817	George Siggins	Penenden Heath
14 April 1819	Joseph Charlton, 26	Morpeth
29 December 1819	John Markham, 26	Newgate
3 February 1820	Duncan Livingstone, 34	Rochester
3 May 1820	Thomas Foster	Penenden Heath
25 November 1822	John Holland, 42	Newgate
	William King, 32	Newgate
21 March 1823	William Arden, 35	Lincoln Castle
	Benjamin Candler, 36	Lincoln Castle
	John Doughty, 35	Lincoln Castle
13 August 1824	Charles Clutton, 25	Northampton
20 April 1825	Joseph Bennett, 30	Ilchester Gaol
	George Maggs, 22	Ilchester Gaol
20 December 1826	Daniel Woodward, 48	Hertford Gaol
13 August 1833	John Howarth, 41	Lancaster Gaol
26 December 1833	George Cropper, 27	Maidstone
22 August 1835	John Sparsholt, 19	Horsham
27 November 1835	John Smith	Newgate
	James Pratt	Newgate

Abbreviations

BL	British Library
HC	House of Commons
HL	House of Lords
LMA	London Metropolitan Archives
PP	Parliamentary Papers
TNA	The National Archives
ADM	Admiralty
CRIM	Central Criminal Court
HO	Home Office
PC	Privy Council
PROB	Prerogative Court of Canterbury

Notes

PREFACE

1. John Wardroper, *The World of William Hone*, London, Shelfmark, 1997, p. 233.

INTRODUCTION

1. https://www.nbcnews.com/nbc-out/out-news/texas-pastor-says-gay-people-shot-back-head-shocking-sermon-rcna32748
2. *Address to the public, Part the first*, London, Society for the Suppression of Vice, 1803, p. 23.
3. Ibid., p. 27.
4. *Orthodox Churchman's Magazine*, vol. 2, January to June 1802, p. 146.
5. However, the seventeenth-century chief justice Sir Edward Coke falsely claimed that the word was Italian and referred to sexually aberrant moneylenders from Lombardy.
6. See Francis Grose, *A Classical Dictionary of the Vulgar Tongue*, London, S. Hooper, 1785.
7. Sir Edward Coke, *The Third Part of the Institutes of the Laws of England Concerning Treason*, London, M. Flesher, 1644, pp. 58–9.
8. William Blackstone, *Commentaries on the Laws of England*, London, 1767, pp. 215–16.
9. *Chester Chronicle*, 2 September 1814, p. 2.

10. *Old Bailey Proceedings Online*, May 1806, trial of David Robertson (t18060521-50), www.oldbaileyonline.org, version 8.0, accessed 17 July 2022.

11. *Public Advertiser*, 11 April 1780.

12. *London Advertiser*, 12 April 1780, p. 2.

13. *Morning Post*, 13 April 1780.

14. *Public Ledger*, 21 September 1809, p. 3.

15. *Bury and Norwich Post*, 23 October 1824, p. 2.

16. *The Age*, 16 June 1833.

17. *Public Ledger*, 5 August 1772, p. 3.

18. *Bingley's Journal*, 12 October 1771.

19. *Daily Advertiser*, 2 July and 4 July 1777.

20. *Irish Independent*, 1 May 1895, p. 2.

21. David Douglas, ed., *Familiar Letters of Sir Walter Scott*, Boston, Houghton Mifflin, 1883, vol. 2, p. 121, Sir Walter Scott to his son, 6 July 1821.

22. *Morning Post*, 9 June 1868, p. 3.

23. *Globe*, 11 April 1812, p. 4.

24. *Annual Register*, 1833, pp. 245–7.

25. No copy of the book has survived, but the text can be found in the indictment at TNA KB 10/29, as explained by Hal Gladfelder, 'In Search of Lost Texts: *Thomas Cannon's Ancient and Modern Pederasty Investigated and Exemplify'd*', *Eighteenth-Century Life*, vol. 31, no. 1 (Winter 2007), pp. 22–38; and Hal Gladfelder, ed., 'The Indictment of John Purser, Containing Thomas Cannon's *Ancient and Modern Pederasty Investigated and Exemplify'd*', *Eighteenth-Century Life*, vol. 31, no. 1 (Winter 2007), pp. 39–61.

CHAPTER ONE

1. Psalms 51:5.

2. William White, *History, Gazetteer, and Directory of Staffordshire*, Sheffield, Robert Leader, 1834, p. 360.

3. TNA HO 17 120/00431.

4. William Pitt, *A Topographical History of Staffordshire*, Newcastle-under-Lyme, J. Smith, 1817, p. 174.

5. George T. Lawley, *History of Bilston*, Bilston, Price & Beebee, 1868, p. 59.

6. Price, Joseph, *An Historical Account of Bilston, from Alfred the Great to 1831*, Bilston, Joseph Price, 1835, p. 179.

7. White, *Staffordshire*, p. 222.

8. Ibid., p. 231.

9. Cited in Marie B. Rowlands, 'Industry and Social Change in Staffordshire: 1660–1760', *Transactions of the Lichfield and South Staffordshire Archaeological and Historical Society*, vol. VIII, 1967, p. 47.

10. White, *Staffordshire*, p. 231.

11. John Stanley, *Stanley's Worcester and Malvern Guide Book*, Worcester, John Stanley, 1852, p. 17.

12. T. Eaton, *A Concise History of Worcester*, Worcester, T. Holl, 1808, p. 26.

13. Ibid., p. 28.

14. Ibid.

15. Ibid., p. 43.

16. *Penny Magazine*, March 1843, vol. 12, p. 201.

17. *Hereford Journal*, 3 February 1790, p. 2.

18. James Boswell, *Life of Dr Johnson*, New York, Routledge, Warne and Routledge edition, 1859, vol. 4, p. 133.

19. John Walker, *The Universal Gazetteer*, London, F. and C. Rivington, 1822, p. 322.

20. James Pigot, *London And Provincial New Commercial Directory for 1828–9*, London, J. Pigot, 1828, p. 282.

21. Samuel Lewis, *A Topographical Dictionary of England*, London, S. Lewis, 1848, p. 446.

22. Pigot, *New Commercial Directory*, p. 282.

23. Revd David Davies, *The Case of Labourers in Husbandry Stated and Considered*, London, R. Cruttwell, 1795, pp. 135–6.

24. Sir Frederick Morton Eden, *The State of the Poor*, London, J. Davis, 1797, vol. 1, p. 411.

25. Ibid., vol. 3, p. 809.

26. Pigot, *New Commercial Directory*, p. 282.

27. *An Account of Several Work-houses*, Society for the Protection of Christian Knowledge, 1724, pp. 53–4.

28. *Derby Mercury*, 29 March 1798, p. 3.

29. *Hereford Journal*, 29 January 1817, p. 3.

30. *An Account of Several Work-houses*, p. 52.

31. Isaac Archer, 13 June 1672, in Matthew Storey, ed., *Two East Anglian Diaries, 1641–1729: Isaac Archer & William Coe*, Woodbridge, Boydell Press, 1994, p. 154.
32. All quotations from the order of service are from the *Book of Common Prayer*.
33. Lawley, *History of Bilston*, p. 45.
34. Staffordshire Record Office, D 5254/3/1/3, the Revd Edward Best's sermons.
35. Ibid.
36. Libraries of Tasmania, CON 18/1/4, p. 177.
37. Libraries of Tasmania, CON 31/1/3, p. 85. The handwritten record reads, 'widower 1 child' and 'widower 4 children' on the same page.
38. Essex Record Office, D D/P 139/12/7.
39. Essex Record Office, D D/P A72.
40. Daniel Lysons, *The Environs of London: Volume 4, Counties of Herts, Essex and Kent*, London, T. Cadell and W. Davies, 1796, p. 203.

CHAPTER TWO

1. Charles Knight, ed., *London*, London, Charles Knight, 1841, vol. 1, p. 138.
2. George Augustus Sala, *Life and Adventures*, London, Cassell & Co., 1895, pp. 86–8.
3. The Reverend Henry Kett, essay from *Olla Podrida* dated 29 December 1787, in Robert Lynam, ed., *The British Essayists*, London, J. F. Dove, 1827, vol. 28, p. 408.
4. *Morning Post*, 2 April 1824, p. 1.
5. Ibid., 12 January 1824, p. 1.
6. Ibid., 21 November 1821, p. 4.
7. Ibid., 2 August 1821, p. 4.
8. Ibid., 27 June 1822, p. 4.
9. Ibid., 2 June 1825, p. 4.
10. Ibid., 7 January 1822, p. 1.
11. Ibid., 15 July 1830, p. 4.
12. *Saint James's Chronicle*, 3 October 1833, p. 1.
13. *Morning Post*, 8 September 1824, p. 1.
14. *The Times*, 4 March 1824, p. 1.
15. *Morning Post*, 28 January 1824, p. 1.

16. *Saunders's News-Letter*, 10 February 1836, p. 4.

17. *Morning Chronicle*, 29 August 1835, p. 1.

18. Richard King, *New Cheats of London Exposed*, London, A. Swindells, 1795, p. 29.

19. *Morning Post*, 28 January 1824, p. 1.

20. TNA PROB 10/7444/7.

21. Edward Walford, *Old and New London: Volume 6, The Southern Suburbs*, London, Cassell, Petter & Galpin, 1893, p. 285.

22. *Morning Post*, 13 January 1818, p. 4.

23. Jeremiah Weal, *The Young Groom's Guide*, London, Sampson Low, 1833, p. 1.

24. Ibid., p. 51.

25. William Beckford to Gregorio Franchi, 22 Sept. 1816. Printed in Boyd Alexander, ed., *Life at Fonthill*, London, R. Hart-Davis, 1957, p. 194. It is unclear how old the groom was.

26. *Saint James's Chronicle*, 16 July 1816, p. 3.

27. Reverend George Brown, *The New English Letter-writer*, London, Alexander Hogg, 1770, pp. 170–1.

28. Charles Johnson, *The Complete Art of Writing Letters*, London, Thomas Lowndes, 1779, p. 40.

29. Boleyne Reeves, ed., *Colburn's Kalendar of Amusements in Town and Country*, London, H. Colburn, 1840, p. 237.

30. *Observer*, 19 August 1832, p. 4.

31. Boleyne Reeves, ed., *Kalendar of Amusements*, p. 239.

32. *British Neptune*, 24 August 1818, p. 6.

33. *Bristol Mirror*, 31 July 1819, p. 2.

34. LMA, A/FH/A/03, Foundling Hospital Building Cttee Minutes.

35. Guy Williams, *Augustus Pugin Versus Decimus Burton: A Victorian Architectural Duel*, London, Cassell, 1990, p. 20.

36. 'The Foundling Hospital and Doughty Estates', in *Survey of London: Volume 24, the Parish of St Pancras Part 4: King's Cross Neighbourhood*, ed. Walter H. Godfrey and W. McB. Marcham (London, 1952), pp. 25–55, *British History Online*, http://www.british-history.ac.uk/survey-london/vol24/pt4/pp25-55, accessed 31 December 2020.

37. Walter H. Godfrey and W McB. Marcham, eds., *Survey of London: Volume 24, the Parish of St Pancras Part 4: King's Cross Neighbourhood*, London, London County Council, 1952, p. 50

38. Williams, *Pugin Versus Burton*, p. 19.

CHAPTER THREE

1. So named after the shipbuilders Dudman & Company.
2. *Observer*, 13 April 1835, p. 2.
3. Samuel Lewis, *A Topographical Dictionary of England*, London, S. Lewis, 1835, vol. 2, 'Deptford' entry.
4. John Bew, *The Ambulator*, London, 1820, p. 84.
5. *Kentish Weekly Post*, 9 August 1811, p. 4.
6. Thomas Cosnett, *The Footman's Directory*, London, printed for the author, 1825, pp. 165, 167, 175, 12.
7. Reverend George Brown, *The New Young Man's Companion*, London, Alexander Hogg, 1779, p. 14.
8. Charles Johnson, *The Complete Art of Writing Letters*, London, Thomas Lowndes, 1779, p. 39.
9. A Pedestrian, *Rambles and Remarks on the Borders of Surrey and Kent*, Deptford, Agnes Brown, 1833, p. 31.
10. HMSO, *Second Report of the Commissioners of State of Large Towns and Populous Districts*, London, W. Clowes, 1845, appendix, part 2, p. 38.
11. HMSO, *First Report of the Commissioners of State of Large Towns and Populous Districts*, London, W. Clowes, 1844, p. 112.
12. *Report of the Medical Officer of Health for Greenwich District*, 1855, p. 12.
13. Nathan Dews, *The History of Deptford*, London, Simpkin, Marshall & Co., 1884, p. 311.
14. *Standard*, 28 September 1835, p. 4.
15. James Pigot, *Pigot and Co.'s London and Provincial New Commercial Directory*, London, J. Pigot, 1823, p. 26.
16. A Pedestrian, *Rambles and Remarks*, pp. 15–16.
17. Lewisham Archives, St Paul's Deptford, Vestry Order Books, MFM SPD 3, September 1824.
18. See John Rule, 'The Labouring Classes in Early Industrial England, 1750–1850', in Dr J. Stevenson, ed., *Themes in British Social History*, London, Longman,1986, p. 286
19. *Trades Newspaper*, 31 July 1825.
20. TNA ADM 359/44B/89 and 90.
21. *Morning Chronicle*, 1 February 1825, p. 3.
22. Ibid.
23. HC, 21 February 1825, vol. 12, col. 597.

24. *First Report of the Commissioners of State of Large Towns and Populous Districts*, 1844, p. 115.

25. LMA, *An Account of the Kent Dispensary*, 1799, p. 5.

26. Ibid., p. 29.

27. Ibid., p. 10.

28. Alexander Gordon, *Treatise on the Epidemic of Puerperal Fever in Aberdeen*, London, G. G. and J. Robinson, 1795, p. 64.

29. James Pigot, *Pigot and Co.'s Pocket Atlas, Topography and Gazetteer of England*, London, J. Pigot, 1838, p. 260.

30. Some claimed that this was by Charles Muss, enamel painter to the king, but William Collins exhibited his design at the Royal Academy in 1816.

31. Bridget Cherry and Nikolaus Pevsner, *London 2: South*, Penguin, 1994, p. 403.

CHAPTER FOUR

1. Francis Grose, *A Classical Dictionary of the Vulgar Tongue*, London, S. Hooper, 1785, p. 29.

2. *Yokel's Preceptor, or More Sprees in London!*, London, Henry Smith, 1855, p. 6.

3. Joseph Aston, *A Picture of Manchester*, Manchester, W. P. Aston, 1826, p. 204.

4. BL Add. Mss.75899, Althorp Papers, vol. DC, *Voluntary Examination of Thomas Rix, Late of Manchester*.

5. Edward Walford, *Old and New London: Volume 6, The Southern Suburbs*, London, Cassell, Petter & Galpin, 1893, p. 500.

6. Ned Ward, *The London Spy Compleat*, London, R. Baldwin, 1753, part III, p. 62.

7. Henry Playford and Thomas D'Urfey, eds, *Wit and Mirth or Pills to Purge Melancholy*, London, W. Pearson, 1707, vol. 4, p. 67.

8. *London Journal*, May 1726.

9. *London Evening Post*, 11 August 1772, p. 3.

10. PP, 1828, vol. VI, paper 533, *Report from the Select Committee on Cause of Increase in Number of Commitments and Convictions in London and Middlesex, and State of Police of Metropolis*, p. 73.

11. TNA HO 44/18/426.

12. *Yokel's Preceptor*, p. 6.

13. George Parker, *A view of Society and Manners in High and Low Life*, London, 1781, vol. 2, p. 85.

14. *The Ordinary of Newgate's Account of the Behaviour, Confession, and Dying Words, Of the Four Malefactors, who were executed at Tyburn, On Wednesday the 12th of November, 1755*, reproduced at the Old Bailey Proceedings Online, www.oldbaileyonline.org, oa17551112, accessed 1 July 2004. Hanson was hanged for stealing a watch.

15. John Brown, *The Historical Gallery of Criminal Portraitures, Foreign and Domestic*, Manchester, J. Gleave and Sons, 1823, vol. 1, p. 612.

16. *The Examiner*, 14 September 1823.

17. *The Proceedings at the Sessions of Peace ... on Wednesday the 22d, Thursday the 23d, Friday the 24th, and Saturday the 25th of February, Number III*, London: Printed for J. Roberts, at the Oxford-Arms in Warwick-Lane, 1738, p. 46.

18. *Yokel's Preceptor*, p. 6.

19. Robert Holloway, *Phoenix of Sodom; or The Vere Street Coterie*, London, Holloway, 1813, pp. 13–14.

20. Johann Wilhelm von Archenholz, *A Picture of England: Containing a Description of the Laws, Customs, and Manners of England. Interspersed with Curious and Interesting Anecdotes*, Dublin, P. Byrne, 1791, p. 197.

21. Cited in translation in Rictor Norton, *Mother Clap's Molly House*, 1992, p. 128.

22. *Morning Chronicle*, 27 August 1825, p. 3.

23. Edward Gibbon, *The History of the Decline and Fall of the Roman Empire* [1782], ed. David Widger, 1996 Project Gutenberg Edition, vol. 4, 2008.

24. Minister of the Church of England, *The Sodomites Shame and Doom, Laid before Them with Great Grief and Compassion*, London, J. Downing, 1702, p. 1.

25. William Wilberforce, *A Practical View of the Prevailing Religious System of Professed Christians, in the Higher and Middle Classes in this Country*, London, T. Cadell & W. Davies, 1797, p. 372.

26. Society for the Suppression of Vice, *Objects etc*, London, S. Gosnell, 1825.

27. *Morning Chronicle*, 28 September 1810, p. 3.

28. Holloway, *Phoenix of Sodom*, p. 16.

29. HC, 5 May 1828, vol. 19, col. 354.
30. *Morning Post*, 6 May 1828, p. 2.
31. 9 George IV, ch. 31, s. 18.
32. Sir William Oldnall Russell, *A Treatise on Crimes and Misdemeanours*, London, Saunders and Benning, 1843, vol. 1, p. 699.
33. TNA CRIM 4/124.
34. TNA CRIM 4/175.
35. Cited in Harry Cocks, *Nameless Offences, Homosexual Desire in the 19th Century*, H. G. Cox, I. B. Tauris, London, 2003, p. 52.
36. Anon., *A Letter to a Member of the Society for the Suppression of Vice*, London, J. Cawthorn, 1804, p. 7.
37. *Northampton Mercury*, 9 January 1810, p. 3.
38. Wakefield Local Studies, 920:TOM, Journals of Matthew Tomlinson of Doghouse Farm, Lupset, vol. 5, 1806–12, pp. 1,049–50.
39. I am grateful to the work of Eamon O'Keeffe and Claire Pickering for unearthing Williamson's views, The 200-year-old diary that's rewriting gay history, https://www.bbc.co.uk/news/education-51385884
40. Bentham, Jeremy and Crompton, Louis, 'Offences Against One's Self: Paederasty Part 1', *Journal of Homosexuality*, vol. 3(4), Summer 1978, Haworth Press, p. 389.
41. Ibid., p. 390.
42. Ibid., p. 402.
43. Lord Byron, *The Complete Works of Lord Byron Including His Suppressed Poems and Others Never Before Published*, Paris, J. Smith, 1833, vol. 2, p. 622.
44. *Leeds Mercury*, 14 July 1810, p. 2.
45. *Morning Post*, 10 July 1810, p. 3.
46. *Morning Advertiser*, 12 July 1810.
47. *Star*, 28 September 1810, p. 3.
48. *Morning Chronicle*, 28 September 1810, p. 3.
49. *The Times*, 28 September 1810, p. 3.
50. *Observer*, 26 September 1825, p. 4.
51. *Weekly Dispatch*, 28 August 1825, p. 2.
52. *Observer*, 26 September 1825, p. 4.
53. *Globe*, 27 August 1825, p. 3.
54. *Weekly Dispatch*, 15 July 1827, p. 3.
55. W. H. D. Winder, 'The Development of Blackmail', *Modern Law Review*, 5 July 1941, p. 26.

56. Clause 9: 'And, for defining what shall be an infamous Crime, within the Meaning of this Act, be it enacted, That the abominable Crime of Buggery, committed either with mankind or with beast, and every Assault with Intent to commit the said abominable Crime, and every attempt or Endeavour to commit the said abominable Crime, and every Solicitation, Persuasion, Promise, or Threat offered or made to any Person, whereby to move or induce such Person to commit or Permit the said abominable Crime, shall be deemed to be an infamous Crime within the Meaning of this Act.'

CHAPTER FIVE

1. *London Evening Standard*, 1 March 1830, p. 3.
2. *Morning Advertiser*, 10 April 1830, p. 3.
3. James Greenwood, *A Night in the Workhouse*, London, Pall Mall Gazette, 1866, p. 12.
4. PP, 1834, vol. XXVII, paper 44, *Royal Commission of Enquiry into Administration and Practical Operation of Poor Laws*, 1905, p. 52.
5. Ibid., p. 88.
6. Ibid., p. 89.
7. Ibid., p. 53.
8. LMA, Greenwich, 8 December 1836.
9. HC, 14 February 1832, vol. 10, col. 348.
10. John Snow, *On the Communication of Cholera*, London, John Churchill, 1855, p. 55.
11. John Poland, *Records of the Miller Hospital and Royal Kent Dispensary*, Greenwich, H. Richardson, 1893, p. 47.
12. Deptford was also proud of its ancients. Everyone knew the tale of Deborah Wybrow, who was 'about 103' when she came to an untimely end by falling downstairs and dislocating her neck in April 1835. She was living at Crossfield Lane near St Paul's church at the time – and had been lined up to be the very first passenger on the new Greenwich Railway. It was said that 'she was an excellent knitter and up to the day of her death partly gained her livelihood by her needle'.
13. *Globe*, 2 December 1830, p. 2.
14. *The Times*, 30 March 1830, p. 3.
15. *Morning Advertiser*, 6 April 1830, p. 4.

16. *Morning Advertiser*, 13 April 1830, p. 4.

17. *The Times*, 26 April 1830, p. 3.

18. *The Times*, 21 May 1830, p. 4.

19. HC, vol. 8, col. 803.

20. Namely the landlord Robert Eagle, John Renard, Charles Williams, William Trimmer, Joseph Barnard and William Franklin.

21. *The Times*, 19 April 1830, p. 3.

22. *Evening Mail*, 19 April 1830, p. 4.

23. *Suffolk Chronicle*, 31 July 1830, p. 3.

24. *Morning Post*, 29 August 1832, p. 4.

25. *Morning Post*, 19 September 1832, p. 4.

26. *Manchester Times*, 17 August 1833, p. 2.

27. Keele University Library, Ralph Sneyd MSS SC17/39.

28. Violet Dickinson, ed., *Miss Eden's Letters*, London, Macmillan, 1919, p. 152.

29. He became a judge in 1834 and was ennobled as Baron Abinger when he left the Commons in 1835. The following year he claimed £626 2s 2d in compensation for thirty slaves on his Spring Grove estate in Manchester, Jamaica.

30. *Morning Chronicle*, 3 December 1833, p. 3.

31. *Public Ledger*, 28 December 1833.

32. British Museum, Banks Collection, D.2.4118, business card.

33. Sir John Simon, *Report on the Sanitary Condition of the City of London*, London, Brewster & West, 1848, p. 19.

34. *London Evening Standard*, 25 February 1834, p. 3.

35. *Morning Advertiser*, 18 September 1835, p. 3.

36. In 1841 they let rooms to a stonemason called William Moffett with his wife and daughter; a widowed forty-year-old furrier called Mary Upton with her sons John, a copper plate printer, and Joseph, a twelve-year-old errand boy; and another stonemason called Richard Williams.

37. Humphrey Cole died as a major in the British Army in Jamaica in 1796; Frank captained several Royal Navy frigates under Sir Edward Pellew. Christopher also served with distinction in the Royal Navy for thirty-four years before retiring as a Knight Commander of the Bath in 1815, marrying the daughter of the earl of Ilchester and being elected as a Member of Parliament for Glamorganshire; and John entered the Church, became vice-chancellor of the University

of Oxford, rector of Exeter College and domestic chaplain to the duke of Clarence before he became William IV.

38. *Morning Post*, 2 July 1827, p. 3.
39. Edward Hawker, *Statement Concerning Certain Immoral Practices Prevailing in His Majesty's Navy*, London, J. Hatchard, 1821, p. 25.
40. Ibid., pp. 1–2.
41. Bentham, Jeremy and Crompton, Louis, 'Offences Against One's Self: Paederasty Part 2', *Journal of Homosexuality*, vol. 4(1), November 1978, Haworth Press, p. 105.
42. See N.A.M. Rodger, *The Wooden World: An Anatomy of the Georgian Navy*, New York, W.W. Norton, 1996, p. 80; and David Cordingly, *Women Sailors & Sailor's Women: An Untold Maritime History*, New York, Random House, 2001, p. 145
43. *Gentleman's Magazine*, vol. 31, 1761, p. 532.

CHAPTER SIX

1. *Morning Post*, 29 August 1835, p. 1.
2. Ibid., p. 3.
3. *West Kent Guardian*, 5 September 1835, p. 1.
4. *West Kent Guardian*, 29 August 1835, p. 4.
5. *Standard*, 25 July 1835, p. 3.
6. *Observer*, 3 August 1835, p. 3.
7. *Morning Chronicle*, 22 August 1835, p. 3.
8. *Essex County Standard*, 14 August 1835, p. 4.
9. *Bell's Weekly Messenger*, 30 August 1835, p. 4.
10. *Rambles and Remarks on the Borders of Surrey and Kent*, Deptford, Agnes Brown, 1833, p. 5.
11. Ibid., p. 12.
12. Charles Dickens, *Oliver Twist or The Parish Boy's Progress*, London, Richard Bentley, 1838, vol. 3, p. 241.
13. *Evening Mail*, 3 August 1831, p. 2.
14. Ibid.
15. *Morning Chronicle*, 17 January 1835, p. 1.
16. *Morning Post*, 6 January 1835, p. 1.
17. *Morning Chronicle*, 7 January 1835, p. 1.
18. *Hampshire Telegraph and Naval Chronicle*, 23 February 1835, p. 1.
19. *Observer*, 6 November 1825, p. 3.

20. John Fisher Murray, *The World of London*, 1843, vol. 2, p. 72.

21. William Rendle, *Report of the Medical Officer of Health for Surrey, The vestry of the parish of Saint George the Martyr*, London, W. Barnes, 1856, p. 9.

22. *First Report of the State Commissioners on Large Towns and Populous Districts*, London, HMSO, 1844, p. 112.

23. Rendle, *Report*, p. 3.

24. Samuel Leigh, *Leigh's New London*, London, Samuel Leigh, 1830, p. 216.

25. HL, 28 August 1835, vol. 30, col. 1067.

26. *Leicester Journal*, 13 June 1834, p. 1.

27. *Weekly True Sun*, 24 April 1836, p. 1.

28. *Weekly Dispatch*, 3 May 1835, p. 9.

29. *Weekly True Sun*, 20 April 1836, p. 8.

30. *Morning Chronicle*, 24 March 1835, p. 1.

31. Augustus Hare, *Walks in London*, London, Smith, Elder & Co., 1878, vol. 1, pp. 102–3.

32. Dickens, *Oliver Twist*, vol. 1, p. 129.

33. *Yokel's Preceptor, or More Sprees in London!*, London, Henry Smith, 1855, p. 5.

34. See John Taylor, *The Carriers Cosmographie*, Ann Griffin, London, 1637, from which this information is gathered.

35. TNA PROB 11/2070..

36. *Public Ledger and Daily Advertiser*, 10 December 1827, p. 4.

37. *Morning Advertiser*, 14 October 1830, p. 1.

38. *Bell's New Weekly Messenger*, 22 April 1838, p. 4.

39. For instance, *Morning Post*, 21 April 1838, p. 4.

40. *Morning Advertiser*, 28 April 1832, p. 4.

41. Dickens described a turn-up bedstead as 'a blunt, honest piece of furniture; it may be slightly disguised with a sham drawer; and sometimes a mad attempt is even made to pass it off for a book-case; ornament it as you will, however, the turn-up bedstead seems to defy disguise, and to insist on having it distinctly understood that he is a turn-up bedstead, and nothing else – that he is indispensably necessary, and that being so useful, he disdains to be ornamental.'

42. Leigh, *Leigh's New London*, p. 64.

43. Lewisham Archives, St Paul's Deptford, Vestry Order Books, MFM SPD 3, September 1830.

44. *Weekly Dispatch*, 27 September 1829, p. 1.

45. *London Evening Standard*, 24 September 1830, p. 4.
46. PP, 1830, vol. XXIII, paper 505, *Return of Number of Metropolitan Police; General Orders issued by Secretary of State*, p. 11.
47. Ibid., p. 10.
48. PP, 1837, vol. XXXIV, paper 259, *Report from the Select Committee of the House of Commons on Metropolis Police Offices*, p. 10.
49. PP, *Number of Metropolitan Police*, p. 12.
50. Ibid.

CHAPTER SEVEN

1. The others were at Queen's Square, Great Marlborough Street, Worship Street, Lambeth Street, Shadwell, Hatton Garden and Wapping (covering the Thames).
2. PP, 1837, XXXIV, paper 259, *Report from the Select Committee of the House of Commons on Metropolis Police Offices*, p. 28.
3. John Fisher Murray, *The World of London*, Edinburgh, no publisher identified, 1843, vol. 2, p. 226.
4. PP, *Metropolis Police Offices*, p. 18.
5. Samuel Leigh, *Leigh's New London*, London, Samuel Leigh, 1830, p. 65.
6. PP, 1834, vol. XVI, paper 600, *Report from the Select Committee on the Police of the Metropolis*, p. 189.
7. Ibid.
8. *Sun*, 31 January 1835, p. 1.
9. *Cork Constitution*, 22 January 1835, p. 4.
10. *Dublin Morning Register*, 24 February 1835, p. 2.
11. *London Courier and Evening Gazette*, 31 March 1835, p. 4.
12. *Saint James's Chronicle*, 11 April 1835, p. 3.
13. *Bucks Gazette*, 1 August 1835, p. 3.
14. H. E. Litchfield, ed., *Emma Darwin, A Century of Family Letters, 1792–1896*, London, John Murray, 1915, vol. 1, p. 59.
15. Nora Barlow, ed., *Erasmus Darwin, The Works of Charles Darwin*, vol. 29, New York, NYU Press, 1989, pp. 98–9.
16. Henriette Litchfield, *Emma Darwin: A Century of Family Letters*, London, John Murray, 1915, vol. 1, pp. 242–3.
17. *Standard*, 6 April 1833, p. 4.
18. PP, *Metropolis Police Offices*, p. 106.

19. Fisher Murray, *The World of London*, vol. 2, p. 227.

20. Joseph Fletcher, 'Statistical Account of the Constitution and Operation of the Criminal Courts of the Metropolis', *Journal of the Statistical Society of London*, Dec. 1846, vol. 9, no. 4, p. 298.

21. *Morning Post*, 9 August 1841.

22. TNA MEPO/2/24/2.

23. *News*, 4 September 1825, p. 7.

24. Leigh, *Leigh's New London*, p. 75.

25. Henry Mayhew and John Binny, *The Criminal Prisons of London*, London, Griffin, Bohn and Company, 1862, p. 623.

26. *London Evening Standard*, 29 November 1832, p. 1.

27. *Bucks Herald*, 30 March 1833, p. 4.

28. *Cambridge Chronicle and Journal*, 16 August 1833, p. 2.

29. *Morning Post*, 2 December 1834, p. 4.

30. Cyrus Redding, *Fifty Years' Recollections, Literary and Personal*, London, 1858, vol. 1, pp. 274–5.

31. William Hepworth Dixon, *The London Prisons*, London, Jackson & Walford, 1850, p. 286.

32. PP, 1833, vol. XXVIII, paper 12, *Reports and Schedules Pursuant to Gaol Acts*, p. 238.

33. PP, 1837, vol. XXXII, paper 89, *Second Report of the Inspectors of Prisons of Great Britain, I, Home District*, p. 155.

34. PP, 1835, vol. XLIV, paper 33, *Reports and Schedules Pursuant to Gaol Acts*, p. 215.

35. PP, 1836, vol. XLII, paper 31, *Reports and Schedules Pursuant to Gaol Acts*, p. 144.

36. Ibid.

37. *Yorkshire Herald*, 6 December 1834, p. 2.

38. *Stamford Mercury*, 19 June 1812, p. 1.

39. John Church to Mr. K--g, Aug. 10, 1818, in John Church, *The Voice of Faith in the Valley of Achor*, Southwark, R. Thomas, 1820, vol. 1, p. 5.

CHAPTER EIGHT

1. TNA HO 77/42/323.

2. *London Encyclopaedia*, London, Thomas Tegg, 1829, vol. XIII, p. 229.

3. Augustus Hare, *Walks in London*, London, George Allen, 1894, vol. 1, p. 132.
4. Charles Dickens, *Sketches by Boz*, London, Chapman & Hall, 1839, p. 208.
5. Ibid., p. 209.
6. Ibid., p. 213.
7. Henry Mayhew and John Binny, *The Criminal Prisons of London*, London, Griffin, Bohn and Company, 1862, p. 592.
8. PP, 1836, vol. XXXV, paper 117, *First Report of the Inspectors of Prisons of Great Britain*, p. 17.
9. Ibid., p. 44.
10. John Campbell, *Lives of the Chief Justices*, London, J. Cockcroft, 1874, vol. III, p. 75. Apparently, this tradition continued into the 1960s.
11. Arthur Griffiths, *The Chronicles of Newgate*, London, Chapman & Hall, 1884, vol. 1, p. 7.
12. Charles Dickens, *Sketches by Boz*, London, Chapman & Hall, 1839, p. 215.
13. After whom the Howard League for Penal Reform is named.
14. Dickens, *Sketches by Boz*, p. 220.
15. HL, 24 March 1835, vol. 27, col. 156.
16. Griffiths, *The Chronicles of Newgate*, vol. 1, p. 8.
17. *The Pamphleteer*, vol. XI, London, A. J. Valpy, 1818, p. 280.
18. Ibid., p. 279.
19. Prisons Act, 5 & 6 Will. IV, cap. 38.
20. PP, *First Report of the Inspectors of Prisons*, p. 75.
21. *Morning Advertiser*, 28 October 1835, p. 2.
22. *Public Ledger and Daily Advertiser*, 14 October 1835, p. 3.
23. *London Evening Standard*, 2 November 1835, p. 4.
24. Victor Plarr, *Lives of the Fellows*, online edition at livesonline. rcseng.ac.uk.
25. PP, *First Report of the Inspectors of Prisons*, p. 34.
26. Ibid.
27. Ibid., p. 10.
28. Ibid., p. 5.
29. John Wade, *A treatise on the Police and Crimes of the Metropolis*, 1829, p. 244.
30. PP, *First Report of the Inspectors of Prisons*, p. 153.
31. Ibid., p. 33.

32. *Morning Advertiser*, 19 June 1835, p. 1.
33. *Morning Advertiser*, 17 December 1834, p. 3.
34. *Sun*, 19 December 1834, p. 2.
35. PP, *First Report of the Inspectors of Prisons*, p. 7.
36. Ibid., p. 8.

CHAPTER NINE

1. A satire, *Memorandums of my Mayoralty, by Lord Winchester* was published soon after he left office in 1835.
2. *Bell's New Weekly Messenger*, 18 March 1838, p. 1.
3. *Cassell's Family Magazine*, vol. 4, 1878, p. 345.
4. Charles Dickens, *Sketches by Boz*, London, Chapman & Hall, 1839, p. 210.
5. See *Ceremonials to be Observed by the Lord Mayor, Aldermen, Sheriffs, and Officers of The City of London*, London, Arthur Taylor, 1850.
6. *The New Monthly*, London, H. Colburn, 1836, p. 186.
7. 4 & 5 Will. IV, chapter 36.
8. *Surrey & Middlesex Standard*, 15 July 1837, p. 3.
9. *Morning Advertiser*, 22 September 1835, p. 3.
10. *Sun*, 21 September 1835, p. 2.
11. *West Kent Guardian*, 26 September, p. 3.
12. *Morning Advertiser*, 22 September 1835, p. 3.
13. The last grand jury sat in 1933, but the last legal vestiges of it were abolished by the Criminal Justice Act 1948.
14. *Morning Advertiser*, 30 October 1835, p. 4.
15. HL, 6 September 1831, vol. 6, col. 1,172.
16. *Morning Post*, 26 September 1835, p. 4.
17. *Westminster Review*, XXXIX, January 1834, p. 147.
18. Thomas Wontner, *Old Bailey Experience*, London, James Fraser, 1833, pp. 59–60.
19. William Ballantine, *Some Experiences of a Barrister's Life*, New York, Henry Holt and Company, 1882, p. 67.
20. Dickens, *Sketches by Boz*, p. 210.
21. Charles Dickens, *Great Expectations*, London, Chapman & Hall, Household edition, 1871, p. 213.

22. Thomas Wontner, *Old Bailey Experience*, London, James Fraser, 1833, p. 188.
23. Henry Blencowe Churchill, ed., *Arabiana*, London, private distribution, 1843, p. 3.
24. PP, 1836, vol. XXXV, paper 117, *First Report of the Inspectors of Prisons of Great Britain*, p. 17.
25. Buckler recorded that the case was heard by the 'third jury', led by John Peter McNeill Wiley, but the recorder's list in TNA CRIM 6/1 has nine identical names with three others who sat on different cases during the week: Edward Ingram, William Marriott and John Bull.
26. Its rate assessment rose in 1841 from £120 to £165; *Morning Herald*, 18 February 1841, p. 4. The Hobhouse meeting was reported in the *Morning Advertiser*, 24 February 1834, p. 1.
27. The recorder's diary of events in TNA CRIM 6/1 has Alderman Thos. Wood.
28. Or the Society for the Recovery of Persons Apparently Drowned, as it was originally named.
29. Ballantine, *Barrister's Life*, p. 219.
30. Ibid.
31. *Jackson's Oxford Chronicle*, 29 September 1810, p. 4.
32. *Morning Chronicle*, 18 August 1817, p. 3.
33. *Baldwin's London Weekly Journal*, 12 January 1835, p. 3.
34. *Morning Advertiser*, 29 July 1835, p. 3.

CHAPTER TEN

1. *Proceedings of the Old Bailey*, 15th October 1777, p. 374. He was charged with rape – and acquitted.
2. HC, 6 April 1824, vol. 11, col. 191.
3. All reports from the trial are from Buckler's Appendix.
4. *Morning Post*, 28 March 1874, p. 6.
5. *A Report of the Trial of the Reverend Thomas Jephson, for a Misdemeanor, at the Cambridge Summer Assizes, 1823, on Wednesday, July 23, Before Mr. Serjeant Bosanquet, and a Common Jury*, London, no publisher, 1823.
6. The regiment has had several names through the centuries, including Scottish Regiment of Foot Guards and Third Regiment of

Foot Guards, but William IV renamed it the Scots Fusilier Guards in 1830.

7. TNA HO 17/16/41.

8. *London Evening Standard*, 29 September 1835, p. 4.

9. Caleb Brown, ed., *The Gretna Green Memoirs by Robert Elliott*, London, The Gretna Green Parson, 1842, p. 40.

10. *Law Magazine*, xliv, p. 291.

11. William Ballantine, *Some Experiences of a Barrister's Life*, New York, Henry Holt and Company, 1882, p. 68.

12. Ibid., p. 10.

13. *Morning Advertiser*, 29 September 1835, p. 1.

14. Twenty-nine more convicts were transported for seven years, one woman was transported for ten years and forty-eight others were sent to prison.

15. HC, 9 February 1810, vol. 15, col. 366.

16. HC, 21 May 1823, vol. 9, col. 397.

17. Judgment of Death Act, 4 George IV, cap. 48.

18. *Suffolk Chronicle*, 31 July 1830, p. 3.

19. Coinage Offences Act, 2 & 3 Will. IV cap. 34.

20. Punishment of Death etc. Act, 2 & 3 Will. IV cap. 62.

21. Forgery, Abolition of Punishment of Death Act, 2 & 3 Will. IV, cap. 123. Also in that session the Anatomy Act ended the practice of handing the corpses of murderers to medical authorities to be anatomised. Murderers hanged at Newgate had been dissected at the next-door Surgeons' Hall.

22. PP, 1836, vol. XXXV, paper 117, *First Report of the Inspectors of Prisons of Great Britain*, p. 183.

23. *Morning Advertiser*, 29 September 1835, p. 1.

24. PP, *First Report of the Inspectors of Prisons*, p. 12.

25. *Morning Advertiser*, 29 September 1835, p. 1.

26. *London Evening Standard*, 29 September 1835, p. 4.

27. *Evening Chronicle*, 29 September 1835, p. 4.

28. *Morning Advertiser*, 29 September 1835, p. 1.

29. *Evening Chronicle*, 29 September 1835, p. 4.

30. *Morning Advertiser*, 29 September 1835, p. 1.

31. Several variations on the theme were used, but this version is cited by Peter Linebaugh in *Albion's Fatal Tree*, New York, 1975, p. 65. In William Guthrie's account the words are almost identical: *A*

Geographical, Historical and Commercial Grammar; Examining the Present State of the World, London, Rivington, 1819, p. 162.

32. *London Evening Standard*, 29 September 1835, p. 4.

33. Martin Madan, *Thoughts on Executive Justice*, London, J. Dodsley, 1785, p. 26.

34. PP, *First Report of the Inspectors of Prisons*, p. 139.

35. *Evening Chronicle*, 29 September 1835, p. 4.

CHAPTER ELEVEN

1. Henry Mayhew, *The Criminal Prisons of London*, London, no publisher identified, 1862, p. 200.

2. Charles Dickens, *Great Expectations*, London, Chapman & Hall, Household edition, 1871, p. 18.

3. Criminal Law Act 1779, Geo. 3, c. 74, section 27.

4. PP, *Third Report from the Select Committee of the House of Lords appointed to enquire into the present state of the several Gaols and Houses of Correction*, 1835, p. v.

5. Lazarus Levy, Robert George, Jacob Levyson, Samuel Pratt, John Welch, Michael Hayes, John Short, Thomas Harries, John Marr, Henry Wells, George Miller, James Andrews, William Smith, William Meaes, James Shrimpton and Thomas D. Feeley.

6. TNA HO 13/067/00422.

7. *West Kent Guardian*, 14 March 1835, p. 8.

8. TNA HO 9/2, *Convict hulks moored at Chatham: Fortitude, Euryalus: Register of prisoners.*

9. *Kentish Mercury*, 27 June 1835, p. 4.

10. PP, 1835, vol. XLIV, paper 33, *Reports and Schedules Pursuant to Gaol Acts*, p. 267.

11. Ibid., p. 269.

12. TNA ADM 105/36, Colin Browning to John Montague regarding sickness on board *Lord Lyndoch*, 21 September 1836 (emphasis in original).

13. Charles Cozens, *Adventures of a Guardsman*, London, Richard Bentley, 1848, p. 92.

14. Ibid., p. 78.

15. Libraries of Tasmania, CON 18/1/4, p. 177.

16. Libraries of Tasmania, CON 13/1/8 Assignment Lists.

17. Leonard, Peter, *The Western Coast of Africa*, Philadelphia, Edward Mielke, 1833, p. 5.
18. TNA ADM 101/5/7/1 fol. 17.
19. *Bell's Life in London*, 8 November 1835, p. 1.
20. TNA ADM 101/5/7/1 fol. 17.
21. *Bent's News and Tasmanian Three-penny Register*, 27 February 1836, p. 4.
22. Libraries of Tasmania, CON 18/1/4, p. 177.
23. James Ross, *Statistical View of Van Diemen's Land*, Hobart, no publisher, 1832, p. 116.
24. James Bischoff, *A Sketch of the History of Van Diemen's Land*, London, John Richardson, 1832, p. 69.
25. *Sydney Morning Herald*, 16 January 1839, p. 4.
26. Sir George Arthur, *Observations Upon Secondary Punishment*, Hobart Town, James Ross, 1833, p. 26.
27. John Frost, *The Horrors of Convict Life*, London, Holyoake, 1856, p. 11.
28. *Hobart Town Magazine*, Hobart, April 1833, vol. 1, no. 2, p. 67.
29. TNA ADM 101/5/7/1 fol. 17.
30. *Bent's News and Tasmanian Three-penny Register*, 5 March 1836, p. 4.
31. *Sydney Herald*, 14 March 1836, p. 2.
32. Libraries of Tasmania, CON 27/1/2 p. 71, appropriation list of convicts.
33. Libraries of Tasmania, CON 31/1/3 p. 85, Conduct Record.
34. TNA CO 37/130.
35. Libraries of Tasmania, CON 31/1/3 p. 85, Conduct Record.
36. *The True Colonist Van Diemen's Land Political Despatch*, 17 July 1840, p. 6.

CHAPTER TWELVE

1. Anon., *The History of the Press-Yard*, London, T. Moor, 1717, p. 2.
2. Charles Dickens, *Sketches by Boz*, London, Chapman & Hall, 1839, p. 224.
3. John Howard, *The State of the Prisons in England and Wales*, London, William Eyres, 1777, p. 152.

4. William Dillon Sheppard, *Some Particulars Relating to the Life of William Dillon Sheppard, Who Was Executed at St. Michael's Hill Gallows, for Sodomy, on Monday the 1st of June, 1761*, Published at His Own Request, and by the Authority of the Sherriff, Bristol, E. Ward, 1761, p. 10.

5. *London Evening Post*, 28 July 1761.

6. Dickens, *Sketches by Boz*, p. 222.

7. PP, 1836, vol. XXXV, paper 117, *First Report of the Inspectors of Prisons of Great Britain*, p. 12.

8. Ibid., p. 13.

9. Dickens, *Sketches by Boz*, p. 223.

10. PP, *First Report of the Inspectors of Prisons*, p. 13.

11. Arthur Griffiths, *The Chronicles of Newgate*, London, Chapman & Hall, 1884, vol. 2, p. 102.

12. PP, *First Report of the Inspectors of Prisons*, p. 13.

13. PP, 1815, IV, *Report from the Committee on King's Bench, Fleet and Marshalsea Prisons*, p. 226.

14. PP, *First Report of the Inspectors of Prisons*, p. 139.

15. Edward Gibbon Wakefield, *Facts Relating to the Punishment of Death in the Metropolis*, London, James Ridgway, 1831, p. 169.

16. Pierce Egan, *Tom and Jerry: Life in London*, London, John Camden Hotten, 1869, pp. 315–16.

17. *The Newgate Monthly Magazines, or Calendar of Men, Things and Opinions*, vol. 1 (September 1824–August 1825), London, R. Carlile, p. 409.

18. William Ballantine, *Some Experiences of a Barrister's Life*, New York, Henry Holt and Company, 1882, p. 68.

19. Thomas Wontner, *Old Bailey Experience*, London, James Fraser, 1833, p. 162.

20. *The Newgate Monthly Magazines*, vol. 1, p. 226.

21. Ibid., p. 227.

22. *The Times*, 25 May 1836, p. 4.

23. Ballantine, *Barrister's Life*, p. 68.

24. PP, *First Report of the Inspectors of Prisons*, p. 140.

25. *Public Ledger and Daily Advertiser*, 22 July 1835, p. 3.

26. HC, 17 December 1847, vol. 95, col. 1,357.

27. *Morning Chronicle*, 29 September 1835, p. 2.

28. Dickens, *Sketches by Boz*, p. 223.

29. Walter Besant, *London in the Eighteenth Century*, London, A. & C. Black, 1902, p. 541

30. Ibid.

31. PP, *First Report of the Inspectors of Prisons*, p. 49.

32. TNA HO 17 120/00435.

33. Griffiths, *The Chronicles of Newgate*, vol. 2, p. 215.

34. PP, *First Report of the Inspectors of Prisons*, p. 36.

35. Dickens, *Sketches by Boz*, p. 223.

CHAPTER THIRTEEN

1. John Henry Barrow, ed., *The Mirror of Parliament*, London, Longman, Orme, Brown, Green & Longmans, 1834, vol. 4, p. 2,869.

2. Horace Twiss, *The Life of Lord Eldon*, London, John Murray, 1846, p. 272.

3. Henry Reeve, ed., *The Greville Memoirs*, London, Longmans, Green and Co., 1888, vol. 2, p. 87.

4. Twiss, *Lord Eldon*, p. 272.

5. Edward Gibbon Wakefield, *Facts Relating to the Punishment of Death in the Metropolis*, London, James Ridgway, 1831, p. 121.

6. Ibid.

7. HC, 18 March 1816, vol. 33, col. 418.

8. Ibid., col. 419.

9. HC, 20 March 1816, vol. 33, col. 497.

10. Lord Colchester, ed., *A Political Diary, 1828–1830, by Edward Law, Lord Ellenborough*, London, Richard Bentley, 1881, vol. 1, p. 47.

11. BL Add. Mss. 51754, Holland to Henry Fox, 3 March 1835.

12. The only remaining hurdle was the legal requirement that new ministers face a by-election. Sixteen of Melbourne's appointees were re-elected unopposed, but the Tories particularly disliked Russell and stood against him in his South Devon seat. When polling day came, Tories appeared 'in regular cavalcades, well mounted, attended by bands of music playing the "Bonnets o' Blue" and presenting altogether the most imposing spectacle.' The same could not be said for Russell's supporters, who arrived 'in straggling bodies "few and far between" and hanging their rueful heads like men, to say the least of it, far from possessing the inspiring enthusiasm of anticipated success.' He lost, but persuaded another Whig, General Richard

Fox, to step down in Stroud, where Russell was duly elected on 19 May, just in time to take his place at the head of the government in the Commons.

13. *Poor Man's Guardian*, 18 July 1835, p. 3.
14. TNA PRO 30/22/1E.
15. *West Kent Guardian*, 10 January 1835, p. 8.
16. He signed his own name as J. M. Phillipps.
17. TNA HO 17 120/60/00426.
18. TNA HO 17 120/60/00437.
19. TNA HO 17 120/60/00434.
20. TNA HO 17 120/60/00431–2.
21. TNA HO 17 120/60/00442.
22. TNA HO 17 120/60/00441.
23. TNA HO 17 120/60/00445.
24. TNA HO 17 120/60/00423.
25. TNA HO 17/88/66.
26. BL Add. Mss. 56541, 29 December 1819.
27. BL Add. Mss. 56541, 4 January 1820.
28. *Morning Post*, 30 December 1819, p. 2.
29. BL Add. Mss. 56541, 29 December 1819.
30. William Beckford to Gregorio Franchi, 22 September 1816. Printed in Boyd Alexander, ed., *Life at Fonthill*, London, R. Hart-Davis, 1957, p. 194.
31. Humphry Woolrych, *The History and Results of the Present Capital Punishments in England*, London, Saunders and Benning, 1832, p. 143.
32. Ibid., p. 144. Woolrych's great-grandson Stewart Perowne would be a married but predominantly gay archaeologist and explorer in the twentieth century.
33. TNA HO 13/67, p. 372

CHAPTER FOURTEEN

1. Jane Austen, *Pride and Prejudice*, London, Richard Bentley & Son, 1882 edn., p 198.
2. G. D. H. and M. Cole, eds, *William Cobbett's Rural Rides*, London, Peter Davis, 1930, vol. 2, p. 690.

3. John Bruce, *The History of Brighton with the Latest Improvements*, London, John Bruce, 1831, p. 4.

4. Ibid., p. 1.

5. Ibid., p. 100.

6. Ibid., p. 6.

7. *Brighton Gazette*, 5 November 1835, p. 2.

8. *Morning Post*, 4 November 1835, p. 3.

9. Bruce, *History of Brighton*, pp. 37–8.

10. TNA PC 2/216, Privy Council Registers.

11. TNA HO 6/20, Law to Lord John Russell, 26 October 1835.

12. TNA HO 6/20, Report of Capital Convicts, September Sessions 1835.

13. Edward Gibbon Wakefield, *Facts Relating to the Punishment of Death in the Metropolis*, London, James Ridgway, 1831, p. 121.

14. Thomas Wontner, *Old Bailey Experience*, London, James Fraser, 1833, pp. 152, 153.

15. Sir Joseph Arnould, *Memoir of Thomas, First Lord Denman*, London, Longmans, Green, 1873, vol. 1, p. 381.

16. *The Times*, 21 May 1830, p. 4.

17. *Manchester Times*, 17 August 1833, p. 2.

18. *Standard*, 19 July 1833, p. 4.

19. *The Times*, 24 June 1833, p. 7.

20. *Standard*, 19 July 1833, p. 4.

21. *The Times*, 26 June 1833, p. 4.

22. *Yorkshire Herald*, 29 June 1833, p. 4.

23. *The Times*, 14 March 1836, p. 5.

24. *Morning Post*, 5 February 1838, p. 2.

25. *Morning Post*, 31 May 1836, p. 3. It also proposed a combination of 'Lord Melbourne's Head' with 'Scene from my Neighbour's Wife'.

26. George Otto Trevelyan, ed., *The Life and Letters of Thomas Babington Macaulay*, Leipzig, Bernhard Tauchnitz, vol. 2, p. 118.

27. Ibid., p. 9.

28. James Grant, *Random Recollections of the House of Commons*, London, Smith, Elder & Co., 1836, pp. 201–2.

29. *Morning Post*, 23 October 1850, p. 3.

30. Buckinghamshire Archives, Fremantle mss 139/20/22–27.

31. *Morning Post*, 11 March 1843, p. 5.

32. Durham University Library, Grey MSS, Melbourne to Grey, 5 January 1834.

33. Windsor Castle, Grey to Melbourne, 6 January 1834, RA MP 5/118.
34. David Cecil, *Melbourne*, London, Constable & Co., 1965, p. 305.
35. Lord Colchester, ed., *A Political Diary, 1828–1830, by Edward Law, Lord Ellenborough*, London, Richard Bentley, 1881, vol. 1, p. 101.
36. Francis Bamford, ed., *The Journal of Mrs Arbuthnot, 1820–1832*, London Macmillan, 1950, vol. 2, p. 59.
37. Lord Colchester, ed., *A Political Diary*, pp. 154–5.
38. Henry Reeve, ed., *The Greville Memoirs*, London, Longmans, Green and Co., 1875, vol. 3, p. 265.
39. Maurice Brett, ed., *The Journals and Letters of Reginald, Viscount Esher*, London, I. Nicholson & Watson, 1934, vol. 1, pp. 281–2.
40. *Morning Post*, 23 November 1835, p. 3.
41. *London Courier and Evening Gazette*, 23 November 1835, p. 3.

CHAPTER FIFTEEN

1. *Weekly Dispatch*, 22 November 1835, p. 4.
2. *Oxford Journal*, 28 November 1835, p. 4.
3. *The Chronicles of Newgate*, vol. 2, pp. 251–3.
4. PP, 1836, vol. XXXV, paper 117, *First Report of the Inspectors of Prisons of Great Britain*, p. 50.
5. *The Chronicles of Newgate*, vol. 2, p. 252.
6. *The Month*, vol. 46, 1884, p. 490.
7. Henry Angelo, *Reminiscences*, London, Henry Colburn and Richard Bentley, 1830, vol. 1, p. 472.
8. Charles Dickens, *Sketches by Boz*, London, Chapman & Hall, 1839, p. 221.
9. *The Newgate Monthly Magazines, or Calendar of Men, Things and Opinions*, vol. 1 (September 1824–August 1825), London, R. Carlile, pp. 27–8.
10. Gal. 6:7.
11. 1 Cor. 10:12.
12. Edward Gibbon Wakefield, *Facts Relating to the Punishment of Death in the Metropolis*, London, James Ridgway, 1831, p. 164.
13. *Newgate Monthly Magazines*, vol. 1, pp. 27–8. He was imprisoned for three years for publishing the atheist tract *The Age of Reason* in 1824.

14. William Linwood, *The Nottingham Execution*, London, Simpkin, Marshall & Co., 1844, p. 22.

15. HL, 28 April 1845, vol. 79, col. 1363.

16. Ibid., col. 1366.

17. Ibid., col. 1361.

18. *Morning Herald*, 24 November 1835, p. 2.

19. *London Courier*, 24 November 1835, p. 2.

20. *Morning Herald*, 26 November 1835, p. 2.

21. Ibid., p. 2.

22. *London Courier*, 26 November 1835, p. 3. Italics in the original. In fact the last person whose execution was ordered by the privy council at Newgate for sodomy was William North, who was hanged on 24 February 1823.

23. TNA PRO 30/22/1E ff. 247–8.

24. TNA HO 16/6.

25. *Morning Advertiser*, 27 November 1835, p. 3.

26. PP, *First Report of the Inspectors of Prisons*, pp. 136, 139.

27. Thomas Wontner, *Old Bailey Experience*, London, James Fraser, 1833, p. 164.

28. PP, *First Report of the Inspectors of Prisons*, p. 141.

29. *Morning Chronicle*, Saturday 28 November 1835, p. 4.

30. PP, *First Report of the Inspectors of Prisons*, p. 141.

31. *Bell's New Weekly Messenger*, 29 November 1835, p. 12.

32. Ibid.

33. Ibid.

34. *Morning Advertiser*, 30 September 1837, p. 3.

35. Henry Mayhew and John Binny, *The Criminal Prisons of London and Scenes of Prison Life*, London, Griffin, Bohn and Company, 1862, p. 590.

36. Edward Bickersteth, *A Treatise on Prayer*, London, L. B. Seeley & Sons, 1822, p. 70.

37. Henry Angelo, *Reminiscences*, London, Henry Colburn and Richard Bentley, 1830, vol. 1, p. 472.

38. *The Chronicles of Newgate*, vol. 2, p. 267.

39. Ibid., p. 244.

40. *National Register*, 1 December 1822, p. 8.

41. *Morning Chronicle*, 25 February 1823, p. 4.

42. *Hull Advertiser*, 4 April 1834.

43. *Hull Packet*, 2 May 1834, p. 3.

44. *Sussex Advertiser*, 24 August 1835, p. 3.
45. *Brighton Gazette*, 27 August 1835, p. 2.
46. Wakefield, *Facts Relating to the Punishment of Death*, p. 121.
47. Henry Reeve, ed., *The Greville Memoirs, A Journal of the Reign of Queen Victoria*, London, Longmans, Green and Co., 1885, vol. 1, p. 284, 15 May 1840.
48. William Makepeace Thackeray, *The Book of Snobs and Sketches and Travels in London*, London, Smith, Elder & Co., 1869, p. 386.
49. *London Daily News*, 28 February 1846, p. 6.
50. Arthur Griffiths, *The Chronicles of Newgate*, London, Chapman and Hall, 1884, vol. 1, p. 270.
51. *Morning Chronicle*, 14 April 1829, p. 2.
52. Griffiths, *The Chronicles of Newgate*, p. 441.
53. E. Hancock, *The Groans of the Gallows; or; The Past and Present Life of William Calcraft, the Living Hangman of Newgate*, London, 1846, p. 9.
54. W. K. Wimsatt and F. A. Pottle, eds, *Boswell for the Defence, 1769–1774*, London, Heinemann, 1960, p. 304.
55. Anon., *The Trials of Arthur Thistlewood etc.*, London, John Fairburn inter alia, 1820, p. 136.
56. *Coventry Herald*, 27 March 1829, p. 2. It was the same with the three men hanged in Nottingham for rioting following the House of Lords rejection of the Reform Bill in 1832. One of them, George Hearson, expressly begged the hangman 'Give me rope enough, that I may the sooner be out of misery.' Yet all three men struggled for five minutes.
57. *Morning Post*, 28 November 1835, p. 4.
58. *Bell's Life in London and Sporting Chronicle*, 28 June 1835, p. 1.
59. *Morning Advertiser*, 9 November 1835, p. 3.
60. *Morning Advertiser*, 25 November 1835, p. 2.
61. *Poor Man's Guardian*, 12 December 1835, p. 3.
62. *Morning Post*, 23 August 1824, p. 3.
63. *Morning Chronicle*, 25 February 1823, p. 4.
64. PP, *First Report of the Inspectors of Prisons*, p. 59.
65. *Globe*, 15 May 1828, p. 4.
66. TNA RG 8/35.
67. Robert Southey, ed., *The Pilgrim's Progress, with a Life of John Bunyan*, London, John Murray and John Major, 1830, p. lxxxi.

EPILOGUE

1. *Morning Post*, 23 August 1824, p. 3.
2. *Morning Chronicle*, 25 February 1823, p. 4.
3. *Liverpool Standard*, 6 September 1833, p. 4.
4. *Public Ledger*, 28 December 1833.
5. *Hull Packet*, 2 May 1834, p. 3.
6. *Morning Chronicle*, 12 January 1830, p. 3.
7. *Yorkshire Gazette*, 27 April 1833, p. 2.
8. *Newcastle Courant*, 17 April 1819.
9. *National Register*, 1 December 1822, p. 8.
10. *Warwick and Warwickshire Advertiser*, 4 February 1832, p. 3.
11. *Morning Chronicle*, Saturday 28 November 1835, p. 4.
12. *The Times*, 28 November 1835, p. 3.
13. John Birt, *Particulars of the Execution of James Pratt & John Smith*, London, J. Birt, 1835, p. 1.
14. *Bell's New Weekly Messenger*, 29 November 1835, p. 12.
15. One other man was convicted of buggery in 1860: the Catholic priest John Spencer, but since his offence was committed against one of his young pupils, I have made a distinction the Victorians would not have made, between homosexual acts and paedophilia and abuse of power.
16. *London Evening Standard*, 21 April 1838, p. 4.
17. *Bell's New Weekly Messenger*, 22 April 1838, p. 4.
18. *Morning Chronicle*, 28 December 1835, p. 4.
19. *Morning Chronicle*, 29 July 1837, p. 4.
20. *Cumberland Pacquet*, 11 March 1845, p. 4.
21. *Sussex Advertiser*, 20 August 1850, p. 3.
22. HC, 17 December 1847, vol. 95, col. 1,357.
23. *Sussex Advertiser*, 20 August 1850, p. 3.
24. Advertisements for future sales in Sotheby's *Catalogue of a Valuable Collection of Books* (1837).
25. Cited in Barbara Wedgwood, *The Wedgwood Circle, 1730–1897: Four Generations of a Family*, Eastwood Editions, 1980, p. 230.

Bibliography

PRIMARY SOURCES

British Library
– Add.Mss.75899, Althorp Papers
– Lansdowne MSS
– Add.Mss.51754, Holland to Henry Fox, 3 March 1835
– Add.Mss.56541, 29 December 1819, 4 January 1820

Buckinghamshire Archives, Freemantle Manuscripts
Caird Library and Archive, National Maritime Museum
– ADM 73/450
– ADM 73/78
– ADM 359/49B/171 Apprentices and shipwrights in each yard
– ADM 359/44B/89 John Wilson Crocker, sending a petition
  from the shipwrights at Deptford 10 December 1824
– ADM 359/44B/89 and 90 a petition from shipwrights with
  cover letter

Essex Record Office
– D/P 139/1/13 Great Burstead, certificates of baptisms, burials
  and banns 1803–31
– D/P 139/11/1-4 Great Burstead, Poor Rates, 1783–1813
– D/P 139/13/2 Great Burstead Removal orders, 1733–1855
– D D/P A72 Great Burstead, tithe accounts, 1804–21

- D/P 139/1/4 Great Burstead, register of baptisms and burials 1768–1808
- D/P 139/16/1 Great Burstead, Rogues and vagabonds orders 1795–1815
- D/P 139/18/1 Great Burstead, Poor Law weekly relief, 1815–16
- D/P 139/18/1-4 Great Burstead, Poor Rates, 1783–1813

Keele University Library, Ralph Sneyd MSS SC17/39
Lewisham Archives
- MFM SPD 3, St Paul's, Deptford, vestry books
- SPD/2/28 St Paul's, Deptford, Vestry account books 1833–66
- SPD/4/9 Churchwardens and overseers' committee minutes book 1829–36
- SPD/F/1/A St Paul's, Deptford, Overseer rate books 1730–1835

Libraries of Tasmania
- CON 18/1/4
- CON 13/1/8 Assignment Lists
- CON 27/1/2 appropriation list of convicts
- CON 31/1/3 Conduct Record

London Metropolitan Archives
- H05/M/A/01/001 Minute Book of the Governors of the Kent Dispensary
- H05/M/D/02/001 Cash Book of the Kent Dispensary, 1822–1832
- *An Account of the Kent Dispensary*, 1799
- City of London Miscellaneous Papers, COL/CA/MIN/01/010, 398, February 178
- MJ/SB/C/002
- SKCS/614 Christ Church, Surrey, Rate Book 1833
- SKCS/770-5 St Paul's Deptford, Rate Books 1827–34
- C 108/337 Cotton v Cotton: catalogues of books and furniture of the Reverend H C Cotton

Southwark Archives
- 1821 Christ Church, Southwark census index
- 1831 Christ Church, Southwark census index
- 1821 Christ Church, Southwark rate book
- 1831 Christ Church, Southwark rate book
- St Giles, Camberwell, poor rates
- Christ Church, Surrey, poor rates
- Christ Church, Surrey, sewer rates

Staffordshire Record Office
- D5254/3/1-14, Reverend Edward Best's sermons
- Z193 copy of a map of Bilston by James Sheriff c. 1799
- CD031/3/1 St Leonard's Bilston, Overseers of the poor 1761–1850
- CD031/2/2 St Leonard's Bilston, vestry minutes 1736–66,
- AA01/6/1/2/35 (Q/SB 1776 T/105)

The National Archives

ADM
    73/78 Establishment Book of Royal Greenwich Hospital 1830–43
    73/450 Salary Book 1821-9 of Royal Greenwich Hospital

CRIM
    4/7 Central Criminal Court Felonies
    5/1 Calendar of Indictments 1833–39
    6/1 Old Court Book 1834-7
    10/1 Printed Minutes of Evidence

HO
    6/20 Judges' and Recorders' returns
    13/68 Pardon sheet for Robert Lavender et al. from Russell
    44/18/101, fols. 426–7, letter from 'an advocate of Police Reform'
    16/6 Lists of criminal court return of those committed for trial

17/16/41 John Morton appeal bundle
17/42 Newgate prisoners calendar
17/54/182 Joseph Calkett appeal bundle
17/84/3 George Cropper appeal bundle from Maidstone Gaol
17/88/66 Martin Mellett and James Farthing
17/103/119 John Strickling and James Parker appeal bundle
17/120 Pratt and Smith appeal bundle
27/50 List of Surrey criminals charged with indictable
    offences
47/75 Judges' records on Criminals
65/26 Details of approximately the first 12,300 Metropolitan
    recruits

MEPO
    4/1 weekly state of the Metropolitan Police
    4/24 daily police reports July to December 1835

PC
    2/216 Privy Council at the Court at Brighton, the 20th of
        November 1835

PCOM
    1/32 Central Criminal Court Minutes of Evidence
    2/190 Newgate Prison, London: prisoners under sentence
        of death

PROB
    11/1263/17 Will of Reverend Edward Best

RG
    8/35 Bunhill Burial Ground

Wakefield Libraries
Worcestershire Record Office
– 1671 Worcester, St John in Bedwardine, Parish Registers
– 8165/3/1 Worcester City Directors and Wardens of the Poor
– BA 4451 James Sherriff map of Worcestershire 1796

PARLIAMENTARY PAPERS

1804, vol. XIII, paper 175, *Abstract of Returns relative to the Expense and Maintenance of the Poor*

1815, vol. IV, paper 152, *Report from the Committee on King's Bench, Fleet and Marshalsea Prisons*

1818, vol. XIX, paper 82, *Abstract of Returns to the House of Commons relative to Assessments for the Relief of the Poor*

1819, vol. IX, paper 224, *Digest of Parochial Returns, Select Committee on Education of the Poor*

1828, vol. VI, paper 533, *Report from the Select Committee on Cause of Increase in Number of Commitments and Convictions in London and Middlesex, and State of Police of Metropolis*

1830, vol. XXIII, paper 505, *Return of Number of Metropolitan Police; General Orders issued by Secretary of State*

1833, vol. XXVIII, paper 12, *Reports and Schedules Pursuant to Gaol Acts*

1834, vol. XVI, paper 600, *Report from the Select Committee on the Police of the Metropolis*

1834, vol. XXVII, paper 44, *Royal Commission of Enquiry into Administration and Practical Operation of Poor Laws*

1835, vol. XXVIII, paper 42, *Third Report from the Select Committee of the House of Lords appointed to enquire into the present state of the several Gaols and Houses of Correction*

1835, vol. XLIV, paper 33, *Reports and Schedules Pursuant to Gaol Acts*

1836, vol. XLII, paper 31, *Reports and Schedules Pursuant to Gaol Acts*

1836, vol. XXXV, paper 117, *First Report of the Inspectors of Prisons of Great Britain*

1837, vol. XXXII, paper 89, *Second Report of the Inspectors of Prisons of Great Britain, I, Home District*

1837, vol. XXXIV, paper 259, *Report from the Select Committee of the House of Commons on Metropolis Police Offices*

1844, vol. XXIV, *First Report of the Commissioners of State of Large Towns and Populous Districts,*

1845, vol. XXVI, *Second Report of the Commissioners of State of Large Towns and Populous Districts*

PRIMARY AND CONTEMPORARY SOURCES

Report of the Medical Officer of Health for Greenwich District, 1855

The Proceedings at the Sessions of Peace ... on Wednesday the 22d, Thursday the 23d, Friday the 24th, and Saturday the 25th of February, Number III, London: Printed for J. Roberts, at the Oxford-Arms in Warwick-Lane, 1738

A Report of the Trial of the Reverend Thomas Jephson, for a Misdemeanor, at the Cambridge Summer Assizes, 1823, on Wednesday, July 23, Before Mr. Serjeant Bosanquet, and a Common Jury, 1823

The Trials of Arthur Thistlewood etc., London, John Fairburn inter alia, 1820

John Birt, *Particulars of the Execution of James Pratt & John Smith*, London, J. Birt, 1835

Society for the Protection of Christian Knowledge, *An Account of Several Work-houses*, 1724

Society for the Suppression of Vice, *Objects etc*, London, S. Gosnell, 1825

Minister of the Church of England, *The Sodomites Shame and Doom, Laid before Them with Great Grief and Compassion*, London, J. Downing, 1702

ACTS OF PARLIAMENT

Criminal Law Act, Geo. 3, cap. 74
Judgment of Death Act, 4 George IV, cap. 48
Offences against the Person, 9 George IV, cap. 31
Forgery, Abolition of Punishment of Death Act, 2 & 3 Will. IV, cap. 123
Prisons Act, 5 & 6 Will. IV, cap. 38
Coinage Offences Act, 2 & 3 Will. IV cap. 34
Punishment of Death etc. Act, 2 & 3 Will. IV cap. 62

NEWSPAPERS AND JOURNALS

Baldwin's London Weekly Journal
Bell's Life in London and Sporting Chronicle
Bell's New Weekly Messenger
Bell's Weekly Messenger

Bent's News and Tasmanian Three-penny Register
Brighton Gazette
Bristol Mercury
Bristol Mirror
British Neptune
Bucks Gazette
Bucks Herald
Cassell's Family Magazine
Cork Constitution
Coventry Herald
Cumberland Pacquet
Dublin Morning Register
Essex County Standard
Evening Mail
Examiner
Exeter Flying Post
Fraser's Magazine
Globe
Hampshire Telegraph and Naval Chronicle
Hobart Town Almanack
Hull Advertiser
Hull Packet
Irish Independent
Jackson's Oxford Chronicle
Kentish Mercury
Kentish Weekly Post
Lancaster Gazette
Law Magazine
Leamington Spa Courier
Leeds Intelligencer
Leeds Mercury
Leicester Journal
Liverpool Standard
London Courier
London Courier and Evening Gazette
London Daily News
London Evening Standard
London Journal

Morning Advertiser
Morning Chronicle
Morning Herald
Morning Post
National Register
Newcastle Courant
Norfolk Chronicle
Observer
Oxford Journal
Poor Man's Guardian
Public Ledger and Daily Advertiser
Saint James's Chronicle
Salisbury and Winchester Journal
Saunders's News-Letter
Star
Suffolk Chronicle
Sun
Sussex Advertiser
Sydney Morning Herald
The Age
The Month
The New Monthly
The Times
Trades Newspaper
Warwick and Warwickshire Advertiser
Weekly Dispatch
Weekly True Sun
West Kent Guardian
Western Times
Westminster Review
Yorkshire Herald

BOOKS AND ARTICLES

A Pedestrian, *Rambles and Remarks on the Borders of Surrey and Kent*, Deptford, Agnes Brown, 1833

Angelo, Henry, *Reminiscences*, London, Henry Colburn and Richard Bentley, 1830

Anon., *Ceremonials to be Observed by the Lord Mayor, Aldermen, Sheriffs, and Officers of The City of London*, London, Arthur Taylor, 1850

Anon., *The History of the Press-Yard*, London, T. Moor, 1717

Arnould, Sir Joseph, *Memoir of Thomas, First Lord Denman, formerly Lord Chief Justice of England*, 1873, 2 vols

Arthur, Sir George, *Observations Upon Secondary Punishment*, Hobart Town, James Ross, 1833

Aspinall, A., 'The Grand Cabinet, 1800–1837', *Politica*, December 1838, vol. III, no. 14

Aston, Joseph, *A Picture of Manchester*, Manchester, W. P. Aston, 1826

Ballantine, William, *Some of the Barrister's Life Experiences*, New York, Henry Holt and Company, 1882

Bamford, Francis, ed., *The Journal of Mrs Arbuthnot, 1820–1832*, London Macmillan, 1950, vol. 2

Barlow, Nora, ed., *Erasmus Darwin, The Works of Charles Darwin*, vol. 29, New York, NYU Press, 1989

Barrow, John Henry, ed., *The Mirror of Parliament*, London, Longman, Orme, Brown, Green & Longmans, 1834

Bateson, Charles, *The Convict Ships*, Glasgow, Brown, Son & Ferguson, 1969

Bentley, David, *English Criminal Justice in the Nineteenth Century*, London, Hambledon Press, 1998

Bew, John, *The Ambulator*, London, 1820

Bickersteth, Edward, *A Treatise on Prayer*, London, L. B. Seeley & sons, 1822

Boswell, James, *Life of Dr Johnson*, New York, Routledge, Warne and Routledge edition, 1859

Boyce, James, *Van Diemen's Land*, Melbourne, Black Inc., 2008

Brown, Caleb, ed., *The Gretna Green Memoirs by Robert Elliott*, London, The Gretna Green Parson, 1842

Brown, Reverend George, *The New English Letter-writer*, London, Alexander Hogg, 1770

— *The New Young Man's Companion*, London, Alexander Hogg, 1779

Bruce, John, *The History of Brighton with the Latest Improvements*, London, John Bruce, 1831

Burnett, John, *Useful Toil: Autobiographies of Working People from the 1820s to the 1920s*, London, Routledge, 1994

Campbell, John, *Lives of the Chief Justices*, London, J. Cockcroft, 1874

Cecil, David, *Melbourne*, London, Constable & Co., 1965

Cockburn, J.S., 'Punishment and the Brutalisation in the English Enlightenment', *Law and History Review*, 12, Spring 1994

Cocks, H. G., 'Safeguarding Civility: Sodomy, Class and Moral Reform in Early Nineteenth-Century England', *Past & Present*, 190, February 2006

— *Nameless Offences, Homosexual Desire in the 19th Century*, Bloomsbury Academic, 2010

— *Visions of Sodom: Religion, Homoerotic Desire, and the End of the World in England, C. 1550–1850*, University of Chicago Press, 2017

Coke, Sir Edward, *Institutes of the Laws of England*, London, 1649

Colchester, Lord, ed., *A Political Diary, 1828–1830, by Edward Law, Lord Ellenborough*, London, Richard Bentley, 1881

Cosnett, Thomas, *The Footman's Directory*, London, printed for the author, 1825

Cozens, Charles, *Adventures of a Guardsman*, London, Richard Bentley, 1848

Crompton, Louis, *Byron and Greek Love: Homophobia in Nineteenth Century England*, Berkeley, 1985

Culpeper, Nicholas, *Culpeper's Directory for Midwives: or, A guide for women*, London, 1662

David Douglas, ed., *Familiar Letters of Sir Walter Scott*, Boston, Houghton Mifflin, 1883, 2 vols.

Davies, Revd David, *The Case of Labourers in Husbandry Stated and Considered*, London, R. Cruttwell, 1795

Devereaux, Simon, 'Imposing the Royal Pardon: Execution, Transportation, and Convict Resistance in London, 1789', Law and History Review, Spring, 2007, vol. 25, no. 1 (Spring, 2007)

Dews, Nathan, *The History of Deptford*, London, Simpkin, Marshall & Co., 1884

Dickens, Charles, *Great Expectations*, London, Chapman & Hall, Household edition, 1871

— *Oliver Twist or The Parish Boy's Progress*, London, Richard Bentley, 1838

— *Sketches by Boz*, London, Chapman & Hall, 1839

Dickinson, Violet, ed., *Miss Eden's Letters*, London, Macmillan, 1919

Dixon, William Hepworth, *The London Prisons*, London, Jackson & Walford, 1850

Eaton, T., *A Concise History of Worcester*, Worcester, T. Holl, 1808

Eden, Sir Frederick Morton, *The State of the Poor*, London, J. Davis, 1797, 3 vols.

Egan, Pierce, *Tom and Jerry: Life in London*, London, John Camden Hotten, 1869

Emsley, C., *Crime and Society in England, 1750–1900*, Harlow, 3rd edn., 2005

Entick, John, *A New and Accurate History and Survey of London, Westminster, Southwark and Places Adjacent*, London, Edward and Charles Dilly, 1766

Fletcher, Joseph, 'Statistical Account of the Constitution and Operation of the Criminal Courts of the Metropolis', *Journal of the Statistical Society of London*, Dec. 1846, vol. 9, no. 4

Gatrell, V. A. C., *The Hanging Tree: Execution and the English People, 1770–1868*, Oxford, 1994

Gilbert, Arthur, 'Sodomy and the Law in Eighteenth- and Early Nineteenth-Century Britain', *Societas* 8 (1978)

Goldsmith, Netta Murray, *The Worst of Crimes; Homosexuality and the Law in Eighteenth-Century London*, Routledge, 1998

Gordon, Alexander, *Treatise on the Epidemic of Puerperal Fever in Aberdeen*, London, G. G. and J. Robinson, 1795

Greene, Jody, 'Public Secrets: Sodomy and the Pillory in the Eighteenth Century and Beyond', *The Eighteenth Century*, vol. 44, no. 2/3, Summer-Fall 2003, pp. 203–232

Greenwood, James, *A Night in the Workhouse*, London, Pall Mall Gazette, 1866

Griffiths, Arthur, *The Chronicles of Newgate*, London, Chapman & Hall, 1884, 2 vols.

Halliday, S., *Newgate: London's prototype of hell*, Stroud, 2006

Hancock, E., *The Groans of the Gallows; or; The Past and Present Life of William Calcraft, the Living Hangman of Newgate*, London, 1846

Hare, Augustus, *Walks in London*, London, Smith, Elder & Co., 1878

Hawker, Edward, *Statement Concerning Certain Immoral Practices Prevailing in His Majesty's Navy*, London, J. Hatchard, 1821

Howard, John, *The State of the Prisons in England and Wales*, London, William Eyres, 1777

James Grant, *Random Recollections of the House of Commons*, London, Smith, Elder & Co., 1836

Johnson, Charles, *The Complete Art of Writing Letters*, London, Thomas Lowndes, 1779

Johnson, William Branch, *The English Prison Hulks*, Chichester, Phillimore, 1970

King, Richard, *New Cheats of London Exposed*, London, A. Swindells, 1795

Kriegel, Abraham D., ed., *The Holland House Diaries, 1831–1840*, London, Routledge & Kegan Paul, 1977

Lawley, George T., *History of Bilston*, Bilston, Price & Beebee, 1868

Leigh, Samuel, *Leigh's New London*, London, Samuel Leigh, 1830

Leonard, Peter, *Records of a Voyage to the Western Coast of Africa, in His Majesty's Ship Dryad, and of the Service on that Station for the Suppression of the Slave Trade, in the Years 1830, 1831, and 1832*, London, Andrew Shortrede, 1833

Leonard, Peter, *The Western Coast of Africa*, Philadelphia, Edward Mielke, 1833

Lethbridge, Lucy, *Servants: A Downstairs History of Britain from the 19th Century to Modern Times*, New York, W. W. Norton & Company, 2013

Lewis, Samuel, *A Topographical Dictionary of England*, London, S. Lewis, 1848

Linwood, William, *The Nottingham Execution*, London, Simpkin, Marshall & Co., 1844

Litchfield, H. E., ed., *Emma Darwin, A Century of Family Letters, 1792–1896*, London, John Murray, 1915

Lupton, Donald, *London and the Countrey Carbonadoed and Quartred into Seuerall Characters*, London, Nicholas Okes, 1632

Lynam, Robert, ed., *The British Essayists*, London, J. F. Dove, 1827

Lysons, Daniel, *The Environs of London: Volume 4, Counties of Herts, Essex and Kent*, London, T Cadell and W Davies, 1796

Madan, Martin, *Thoughts on Executive Justice*, London, J. Dodsley, 1785

May, Allyson Nancy, *The Bar and the Old Bailey, 1750–1850*

Mayhew, Henry and Binny, John, *The Criminal Prisons of London and Scenes of Prison Life*, London, Griffin, Bohn and Company, 1862

McConville, Sean, *A History of English Prison Administration*, London, Routledge & Kegan Paul, 1981

McCormick, Ian, ed., *Sexual Outcasts, 1750–1850: Sodomy*, London, Routledge, 2000, vol. 2

Murray, John Fisher, *The World of London*, Edinburgh, no publisher identified, 1843

Norton, Rictor, *Mother Clap's Molly House*, 1992

Paley, R., 'An Imperfect, Inadequate and Wretched System? Policing London before Peel', *Criminal Justice History*, 10, 1989

Parker, George, *A view of Society and Manners in High and Low Life*, London, 1781

Parsons, Harold, *Portrait of the Black Country*, London, Robert Hale, 1986

Petrow, S., 'The Rise of the Detectives in London, 1869–1914', *Criminal Justice History*, 14, 1993

Philips, D., 'A New Engine of Power and Authority: The Institutionalization of Law Enforcement in England, 1780–1830', in V. A. C. Gatrell et al. (eds), *Crime and the Law: The Social History of Crime in Western Europe*, London, 1980

Pigot, James, *London and Provincial New Commercial Directory*, London, J. Pigot, 1823

Pink, Henry, *Report of the Medical Officer of Health for Greenwich District*, Greenwich, W. Flashman, 1855

Playford, Henry and D'Urfey, Thomas, eds., *Wit and Mirth or Pills to Purge Melancholy*, London, W. Pearson, 1707

Poland, John, *Records of the Miller Hospital and Royal Kent Dispensary*, Greenwich, H. Richardson, 1893

Poole, Charles Henry, *The Customs Superstitions and Legends of the County of Stafford*, London, Rowney, 1875

Price, Joseph, *An Historical Account of Bilston, from Alfred the Great to 1831*, Bilston, Joseph Price, 1835

Protheroe, Iorwerth, *Artisans and Politics in Early Nineteenth Century London*, Abingdon, Routledge, 2013

Radzinowicz, L., 'The Waltham Black Act: A Study of the Legislative Attitude towards Crime in the Eighteenth Century', *Cambridge Law Journal*, 1945, vol. 9, no. 1

Redding, Cyrus, *Fifty Years, Recollections, Literary and Personal*, London, 1858

Reeve, Henry, ed., *The Greville Memoirs, A Journal of the Reign of Queen Victoria*, London, Longmans, Green and Co., 1885, vol. 1

Reeves, Boleyne, ed., *Colburn's Kalendar of Amusements in Town and Country*, London, H. Colburn, 1840

Rendle, W. and Norman, P., *Inns of Old Southwark*, London, 1888

Rendle, William, *Report of the Medical Officer of Health for Surrey, The vestry of the parish of Saint George the Martyr*, London, W. Barnes, 1856

Reynolds, E. A., *Before the Bobbies: The Night Watch and Police Reform in Metropolitan London, 1720–1830*, Basingstoke, 1998

Richmond, Lesley and Turton, Alison, *The Brewing Industry: A Guide to Historical Records*, MUP, 1990

Robert Holloway, *Phoenix of Sodom; or The Vere Street Coterie*, London, Holloway, 1813

Rumbelow, D., *The Triple Tree: Newgate, Tyburn and the Old Bailey*, London, 1982

Rush, Richard, *Memoranda of a Residence at the Court of London*, Philadelphia, Carey, Lea & Blanchard, 1833

Russell, Sir William Oldnall, *A Treatise on Crimes and Misdemeanours*, London, Saunders and Benning, 1843

Simon Devereaux, Simon and Griffiths, Paul, eds., *Penal Practice and Culture, 1500–1900*, Palgrave, 2004

Snow, John, *On the Communication of Cholera*, London, John Churchill, 1855

Southey, Robert, ed., *The Pilgrim's Progress, with a Life of John Bunyan*, London, John Murray and John Major, 1830

Stanley, John, *Stanley's Worcester and Malvern Guide Book*, Worcester, John Stanley, 1852

Stone, Sarah, *A Complete Practice of Midwifery*, London, Thomas Cooper, 1737

Storey, Matthew, ed., *Two East Anglian Diaries, 1641–1729: Isaac Archer & William Coe*, Woodbridge, Boydell Press, 1994

Strange, Carolyn, ed., *Qualities of Mercy: Justice, Punishment and Discretion*, Vancouver, University of British Columbia Press, 1996

Taylor, D. Crime, *Police and Punishment in England, 1750–1914*, Basingstoke, 1998

Taylor, John, *The Carriers Cosmographie*, Ann Griffin, London, 1637

Ted Ruddock, *Arch Bridges and their Builders, 1735–85*, Cambridge University Press, 1979 (reprinted 2009)

Thomas, Deborah A., 'Thackeray, Capital Punishment, and the Demise of Jos Sedley', *Victorian Literature and Culture*, vol. 33, no. 1 (2005)

Trevelyan, George Otto, ed., *The Life and Letters of Thomas Babington Macaulay*, Leipzig, Bernhard Tauchnitz, vol. 2

Upchurch, Charles, *Before Wilde: Sex Between Men in Britain's Age of Reform*, University of California Press, 2009

von Archenholz, Johann Wilhelm, *A Picture of England: Containing a Description of the Laws, Customs, and Manners of England. Interspersed with Curious and Interesting Anecdotes*, Dublin, P. Byrne, 1791

Wade, John, *A Treatise on the Police and Crimes of the Metropolis*, London, Longman, Rees, Orme, Brown and Green, 1829

Wakefield, Edward Gibbon, *Facts Relating to the Punishment of Death in the Metropolis*, London, James Ridgway, 1831

Walford, Edward, *Old and New London: Volume 6, The Southern Suburbs*, London, Cassell, Petter & Galpin, 1893

Ward, Ned, *The London Spy Compleat*, London, R. Baldwin, 1753

Ward, Robert, *The Man Who Buried Nelson, The Surprising Life of Robert Mylne*, 2007

Wardroper, John, *The World of William Hone*, London, Shelfmark, 1997

Weal, Jeremiah, *The Young Groom's Guide*, London, Sampson Low, 1833

Wedgwood, Barbara, *The Wedgwood Circle, 1730–1897: Four Generations of a Family*, Eastwood Editions, 1980

White, J., *London in the 19th Century: A Human Awful Wonder of God* London, Vintage, 2008

White, William, *History, Gazetteer, and Directory of Staffordshire*, Sheffield, Robert Leader, 1834

Wilberforce, William, *A Practical View of the Prevailing Religious System of Professed Christians, in the Higher and Middle Classes in this Country*, London, T. Cadell & W. Davies, 1797

Williams, Guy, *Augustus Pugin Versus Decimus Burton: A Victorian Architectural Duel*, London, Cassell, 1990

Wimsatt, W. K. and Pottle, F. A., eds., *Boswell for the Defence, 1769–1774*, London, Heinemann, 1960

Winder, W. H. D., 'The Development of Blackmail', *Modern Law Review*, 5, July 1941

Wise, Dorothy (ed.), *Diary of William Tayler, Footman, 1837*, London, St Marylebone Society, 1987

Wontner, Thomas, *Old Bailey Experience: Criminal jurisprudence and the actual working of our penal code of laws*, London, James Fraser, 1833

Woolrych, Humphry, *The History and Results of the Present Capital Punishments in England*, London, Saunders and Benning, 1832

Acknowledgements

I am indebted to the work of several published authors, who have written about homosexuality in and around this period. Rictor Norton, the author of *Mother Clap's Molly House*, hosts a website (http://rictornorton.co.uk/eighteen/), which is an invaluable resource on homosexuality in the eighteenth and nineteenth centuries. Charles Upchurch's work, *Before Wilde: Sex Between Men in Britain's Age of Reform* (University of California Press, 2009) and Harry Cocks's, *Nameless Offences, Homosexual Desire in the 19th Century* (I. B. Tauris & Co, 2010) are both important works, although neither goes into any detail about James and John and both struggle to fill the lacuna in gay history between the eighteenth century and the trial of Oscar Wilde. Father Frank Ryan has also produced a very useful self-printed manuscript work, *The law to take its course – Redeeming the past, securing our future*, which looks at some of the archival material relating to James and John. He also unsuccessfully petitioned the then Justice Secretary, Chris Grayling MP, for a posthumous pardon for James and John in 2014. I have parted company with Father Ryan on many of the key facts of the case, but I agree with his passionate opposition to the death penalty.

Even more important has been the assistance of a large number of archivists and librarians who went out of their way to point me in the right direction online during the Covid lockdowns and in person afterwards. In particular I was helped by Elizabeth Lee at Lambeth Archives, Lisa Soverall at Southwark Archives, Amanda Bevan at the National Archives at Kew, Sally Eaton at Lewisham

Archives, and the staff at the British Library, Worcestershire Record Office, the London Metropolitan Archives, Essex Record Office, the Caird Library and Archive at the National Maritime Museum and Staffordshire Record Office. In addition, I have used extensively the online archives of the Libraries of Tasmania (https://www.libraries.tas.gov.au/), the Convict Records of Australia (https://convictrecords.com.au/) and the Proceedings of the Old Bailey Online (https://www.oldbaileyonline.org/).

The team at United Agents – especially my agent James Gill – have provided insight, advice and corrective common sense at every stage of developing the book, for which I am grateful. Many thanks to Jasmine Horsey and Alexis Kirschbaum at Bloomsbury, who believed that this story was worth telling – and to Bill Swainson, who helped bash it into better shape.

Above all I am grateful to the people of the Rhondda who have shown such generosity to me over the years, to my family and friends who have put up with me recounting my every archival discovery and to everyone who has campaigned against the death penalty and for equality for all under the law across the world.

Index

Image Credits

Press Ltd/Alamy Stock Photo; William IV and his Ministers in Council: © The Trustees of the British Museum; Levee day: © The Trustees of the British Museum; James Pratt's letter: The National Archives, Kew; Dr Cotton, Ordinary of Newgate, Announcing the Death Warrant, W. Thompson, date unknown. Purchased as part of the OppÚ Collection with assistance from the National Lottery through the Heritage Lottery Fund 1996. Photo: Tate; The gallows: Guildhall Library & Art Gallery/Heritage Images/Getty Images; The day of the execution: © Heritage Image Partnership Ltd/ Alamy Stock Photo; Crowd for an execution: Museum of London/ Heritage Images/Getty Images; Bunhill Fields: Guildhall Library & Art Gallery/Heritage Images/Getty Images; St Paul's Church, Deptford: Look and Learn/Peter Jackson Collection/Bridgeman Images.

Images integrated in the text
p.xi: Scene at the Central Criminal Court at the Old Bailey showing the trial of Daniel McNaughten © Illustrated London News Ltd/Mary Evans; p. 21: Universal History Archive/ UIG/Bridgeman Images; p. 35: taken from The Young Groom's Guide and Valet's Directory, made available by the University of California; p. 56: London Metropolitan Archives/Main Print Collection; p. 62: 'The Trials and Behaviour of George Cropper and William Allen, who were Executed', taken from Dying Speeches, made available by Harvard Law School Library, Harvard University; p. 71: © National Portrait Gallery, London; p. 82: British Library; p. 98: London Metropolitan Archives/ Crosby Collection; p. 116: anonymous illustration, out of copyright; p. 121: Illustration for Dickens' "Sketches by Boz": A Visit to Newgate, by (W.E. Marshall, after Felix Octavious Carr Darley), Princeton University Art Museums collections online; p. 133: RIBA Collections; p. 156: London Metropolitan Archives/LCC Photograph Library; p. 170: SSPL/Getty Images; p. 178: Tasmanian Archives, "William Bonill", Description Lists of Male Convicts (1835–1838), CON18/1/4; p. 184: © National Portrait Gallery, London; p. 189: © Chronicle/Alamy Stock

Author's Note

Chris Bryant is an acclaimed historian of Parliament and a *Sunday Times* bestselling author. He has been the MP for the Rhondda since 2001 and is now Shadow Minister for Creative Industries and Digital. Between 2020 and 2023, he chaired the Committees on Standards and Privileges, which have guardianship of the Code of Conduct and adjudicate on individual cases. Bryant was the first gay MP to celebrate his civil partnership in the Palace of Westminster. *Code of Conduct* was an instant number two *Sunday Times* bestseller and *The Glamour Boys* won the 2020 Parliamentary Book Award for Best Non-Fiction.

A Note on the Type

The text of this book is set in Linotype Stempel Garamond, a version of Garamond adapted and first used by the Stempel foundry in 1924. It is one of several versions of Garamond based on the designs of Claude Garamond. It is thought that Garamond based his font on Bembo, cut in 1495 by Francesco Griffo in collaboration with the Italian printer Aldus Manutius. Garamond types were first used in books printed in Paris around 1532. Many of the present-day versions of this type are based on the *Typi Academiae* of Jean Jannon cut in Sedan in 1615

Claude Garamond was born in Paris in 1480. He learned how to cut type from his father and by the age of fifteen he was able to fashion steel punches the size of a pica with great precision. At the age of sixty he was commissioned by King Francis I to design a Greek alphabet, and for this he was given the honourable title of royal type founder. He died in 1561